Lying

Lying

Man's Second Nature

GEORGE SERBAN

PRAEGER

Westport, Connecticut
London

Library of Congress Cataloging-in-Publication Data

Serban, George, 1926–
    Lying : man's second nature / George Serban.
      p. cm.
    Includes bibliographical references and index.
    ISBN 0–275–97226–7 (alk. paper)
    1. Truthfulness and falsehood.   I. Title.
  BJ1421.S47   2001
  177′.3—dc21   00–049189

British Library Cataloguing in Publication Data is available.

Library of Congress Catalog Card Number: 00–049189
ISBN: 0–275–97226–7

First published in 2001

Praeger Publishers, 88 Post Road West, Westport, CT 06881
An imprint of Greenwood Publishing Group, Inc.
www.praeger.com

Printed in the United States of America

∞™

The paper used in this book complies with the
Permanent Paper Standard issued by the National
Information Standards Organization (Z39.48–1984).

10 9 8 7 6 5 4 3 2 1

Disclaimer

The case studies presented in this book do not refer to any specific individual. While the
psychodynamic of each case is real, the persons with whom it is associated are fictional.

Contents

Introduction: The New Social and Moral Paradigm

It seems that a combination of at least three social conditions (part of the new social paradigm), working together or separately, have contributed to our new interpretation of what may be construed as truth and falsehood or, from the moral point of view, right and wrong. The outcome has been the emergence of a new ambiguous moral relativism.

The first societal factor to consider is related to the social-political changes undergone by our country in the last three decades. As we know, one of the initial outcomes of the civil rights movement and the feminist revolution of the 1960s was the implementation of equal work and pay opportunities for minorities. At the same time, these disadvantaged citizens, by the nature of their demands, questioned the fairness of the societal view of right and wrong. If the principles of the Constitution were not respected by the governing bodies of society while they were claiming to be guided by them in ruling the country, then their honesty and adherence to truth were a sham. Since that social order did not quite reflect the position and spirit of the Constitution, the leaders of the underprivileged together with social activists fought and won to a large extent the argument for a new, more equitable social system. A new political outlook emerged that automatically distanced itself from the old social values and ethics while groping to establish novel ones that would better represent the view of the current social reality. It was only normal that a new concept of social truth be promoted based on an all-encompassing interpretation of equality. Human rights and justice started to be viewed by the new "liberated" individual whose experience of his social condition, in turn, influenced or determined his view of right and wrong. The Pandora's box for reinterpretation of the old moral values, virtues, and justice became wide open. Previous social truths and old social values have been ridiculed or discarded by the social activists who introduced political yardsticks for assessing the recast standards of morality in conformity with the new concept of "political correctness."

The emerging social values, in essence politically inspired, tend to reflect the new social realities as brought about by the civil rights changes such as affirmative action or the ambiguous concept of sexual harassment. They have become the guiding principles for the evaluation of right and wrong in morality and justice. In a roundabout argument the legitimization of these pseudotruths has become itself an instrument for the sanction of the social changes.

The evolved code of morals minimized the previous distinction between right and wrong, creating confusion for their social and legal interpretation. Socially, the notion of right has gradually taken a utilitarian connotation to imply behaviors in conformity with the interest of the new societal paradigm while wrong has been surreptitiously equated with inappropriateness. The validity of most work and family values became questionable or irrelevant for the new pluralistic, culturally diverse society. The awareness of racial and gender rights added an arbitrary dimension for the interpretation of conflicting social situations, including penalties for antisocial behavior. This has further slanted the truth of facts toward subjectivity and relativism. Concomitantly, it has been an additional decline of religious morality among believers because organized religion was seen as unresponsive to the emancipation of women and as neutral toward the causes of the civil rights movement. Ultimately, truth became officially manipulated to fit the demands of the new, unfolding, pluralistic, multiracial social system where multiple truths about the same reality can coexist side by side.

Interestingly, the new moral paradigm got a boost from certain neosocial thinkers and philosophers who questioned the concept of truth as reflecting a universal reality. Leaving aside the ancient sophists who played with the notion of truth as disclosed by logical methods, more recently the Marxists attacked the capitalist formulation of social truths as being instruments of oppression of the underprivileged while the existential philosophers elaborated on the meaning of the subjective truth for the individual's view of reality. Promoted by these views, the neosocial reformists's concept that any truth is a matter of personal perspective gained momentum to the point of becoming incorporated into political correctness. The neoreformists as part of the postmodernist current espouse a pluralistic view of the world based on diverse versions of reality, experienced by people in a variety of ways and resulting in multiple truths. According to them, an alternate reality is very genuine for the people who experience it as part of their belief system. In this context, one may reasonably argue that the experience of social reality of a white man is different from that of an Afro-American, which makes either one respond in a dissimilar manner to the same events. Practically, both may believe that their reaction has been correct, based on their interpretation of the matter under consideration. However, this interpretation ignores the fact that beyond personal interpretations, people share a common-sense perspective of what is right and what is wrong, of what is permissible and what is not. Certainly, there is a subjective truth, but this truth represents either a projection of individual/group experiences and needs or an attempt to justify one's actions, which more often is at variance with general notion of truth. Personal truth leads to a distorted, fragmented, and reconstructed view of facts used to support a self-serving version of reality. At best, it attempts to deny the existence of an independent truth of one's perception, at worst it is a gross manipulation of factual truth. Biased reformists consider this fact as irrelevant. However, this idea has received the enthusiastic support of opportunistic politicians and litigation lawyers who have became the exponents of the validity of subjective, relative, and interpretative truths as parts of simultaneous multiple truths.

This approach to social reality has been expanded into the art of twisting and recasting of the facts by "spin doctor" specialists who reconstruct versions of the truth to fit a desired new reality, most likely, a virtual reality created to justify one's unacceptable behavior. Yet, this ability to create a semblance of truth, a secondhand truth, out of elusive, evasive, and interpretable evidence is considered a highly appreciated skill by the public. People who possess this facility to fabricate illusions of truth based on hazy, ambiguous, misleading data are social winners in the field of their choice, from politics, public relations, advertising, media, and law to other associated areas lending to espousing pseudotruths. In general, lying and deception have become extremely useful tools to cope with unfavorable situations or to get an edge in any social competition.

This combination of factors has contributed to the public's wavering in opinion about the wrongs of lying, particularly when related to what is considered the sacred right for self-protection. The concept of self-defense has been further broadened by people to incorporate a variety of personal actions claimed to be essential for one's social survival. As a result, this undeniable right has been perverted and liberally used in defending one's action unrelated to any remote vital threat to himself. In fact, people expect that any socially smart person should have or develop creative skills for manipulating the truth in support of his claims for self-protection regardless of the facts pointing against him. There is a normal tendency for people to employ whatever means available to them in order to protect their interests when perceived to be threatened by others. However, people doubting the strength of their rightful arguments feel compelled to fabricate evidence to increase their chances of winning. The expanded idea of self-protection, reinforced by the work of spin doctors, may partially explain the tolerance and empathy of the public with Clinton's devious defense in the Monica Lewinsky sex scandal case, for example.

In court, not only do lawyers for plaintiffs magnify their claims and the defense lawyers use various degrees of distortions and lies in support of their plea for the client's exoneration of the committed crime, but the activist judges also contribute to the perversion of justice. The jury itself may have its own biases or incompetence which could vitiate the process of justice. The establishing of truth has become a hazardous experience for anyone relying on a court decision.

The arbitrariness of the concept of acceptable versus nonacceptable lying is reflected in the government's approach to its self-protection and to national security. The government is always exonerated for lying during war in defense of the country. By extension, no one would question the moral integrity of a partisan, who under torture deliberately lies about the hiding place of his comrades to the enemies. One may argue that during war, the rules of morality are changed and the protection of national interests takes priority. But any attempt for defining precisely which actions during peace time can be construed against national interest may be controversial. Did the government make an error of judgment by permitting a manufacturing company to sell satellites and high technology to China, a potential enemy? Whose interests were really protected? Should the government extend financial credits to nondemocratic regimes under the claims of influencing their civil rights policies? To justify these ambiguous decisions the government is compelled to distort records, twist facts, and make favorable assumptions.

More often the government lies to protect its own political agenda and maintain power. In this respect, should the Labor Department collecting data for the consumer report tell the truth to the public that the data are misleading about gauging inflation since they represent either the lowest price for that month or are selected on the basis of "geometric weighting" (only those products with the lowest price)? Certainly, if they want to lose the elections. Examples are countless when truth is ignored, discarded, or at least softened, since it would be harmful to them.

Truth is brutal. It is final. It does not permit any debate. It does not leave any room for hope, while lies offer new expectations. Societies, like individuals, try to strike a balance between the acceptance of truth and falsehood, since both of them play an equal role in the adaptation to the environment. This may explain the fact that from the dawn of history, truth and falsehood have been intertwined, attempting to alleviate human life confronted with its tragic sense of existence. People who know when to lie and when to tell the truth are considered true survivors, able to beat the odds under adverse human circumstances. From the adaptational point of view, they are positively successful. At the same time, people who have been repeatedly cheated are viewed as losers. This attitude is rooted in the concept that self-protection is related to survival of the fittest (cleverest). Is there an evolutionary assumption behind this?

In nature, throughout the insect, avian, or animal world the ability to fake, change appearance in order to frighten, or let the enemy believe it has seen something other than themselves represents a question of survival. Some time ago, an avian researcher made a fascinating discovery by identifying a fraudulent sentinel bird named shrike tanager, which gives false warning signals about nonexistent predators in order to be the first to catch a tasty meal of a bug. The signal sends other birds racing to cover and gives the sentinel the opportunity to reach the bug first.[1]

Deceptive behavior among chimpanzees is well known. In this context, if anthropoid behavior has any relevance to the human, then some parallels may be drawn. The observation of Jane Goodall of a male chimp that after driving away other males from a pile of bananas, creeps back to eat them, is classic.[2] More recently, researchers noticed that male chimps use unusual devious means while fighting for alpha status to the point of undertaking clever conspiratorial strategies carried out with partners. Their devious behavior to win status is pursued, until they either succeed or circumstances have changed by death or injury of one of the conspirators.[3]

Since lies and deceit, together with other physical qualities, have played a significant evolutionary role in the adaptation of the species, one can safely assume that this also applies to humans. From time immemorial smart people who knew when to lie and deceive had a better chance of survival than those who had been bad liars or by default honest to the point of incriminating themselves. Because basic survival consists of access to food and reproduction, it means that those who knew how to take advantage of others in conditions where these commodities were scarce, whether by physical force or by cleverness, had a better chance to transmit their genes to the next generation. Does this mean that men have always had to lie? Not necessarily so, because it would have been counterproductive in relating to other members of the community whose support they needed in case of crisis, attack of enemies, and so on. Smart people's lying has always been selective in order not to affect their credibility, which is necessary for acceptance by the community. From the pool of people, clever and flexible in their approach toward truth, those imaginative in finding solutions to problems have been chosen the leaders. They knew how to impose their thinking and social beliefs on others. An example, among many, is Moses.

Imagine the plight of Moses, the zealot leader, who felt commissioned by God to take his Israelites out of Egyptian slavery and bring them back to the land of Canaan, the Promised Land. Moses, the diplomat, after years of struggle, succeeded in persuading the Pharaoh to let the Israelites return to their land. When he realized that his people were falling into a state of self-indulgence, which would have made it impossible for them to sustain a long journey full of dangers and hardship, Moses, the prophet, gave them the determination to pursue the journey by invoking God's protection. After deliverance from slavery, when they reached the Sinai mountains, Moses, the visionary lawmaker, created and brought them the Ten Commandments as a gift from God to save them from the moral turpitude into which they had fallen. Moses's strategy was indeed brilliant. It worked, even though it took his people about 40 years of wandering through the desert until they reached home. Yet, it is highly debatable to what extent he believed he had communicated with God or felt inspired by Him. Practically speaking, his stratagems increased his authority and people believed and followed him. Certainly, other religious visionaries had changed the course of the history of nations, if not of mankind, by their beliefs, which they claimed to have been communicated by God in order for the masses to accept them. While Jesus Christ acted as God's son, Mohamed, who came later, thought himself to be God's prophet.

Throughout history respectable leaders of nations who have appeared responsible and upright have not always been fully truthful to their citizens in moments of making important political decisions, under the firm belief that they were serving their nation. President Franklin D. Roosevelt, allegedly "unaware" of the imminent Pearl Harbor attack by Japan, justified it as the reason for our entry into World War II. President Lyndon B. Johnson's alleged "incident of North Vietnamese aggression" in the Gulf of Tonkin led to our official entry into the Vietnam War. Yet, in the historical context of the time, these decisions, based on half-truths, were considered to be important for our global policies in the context of the political or ideological balance of power of the time, regardless of the unforeseen consequences.

Is there any purpose in this digression about our evolutionary and historical heritage related to lying? Can this evolutionary-historical perspective help an individual to become aware of the extent to which lying has been practiced? Can an individual learn lessons from the deviousness of human behavior and the unpredictable morality about protecting himself or attaining his goals?

Man has learned to cope with a variety of situations confronting his uncertain existence, while knowing that favorable solutions may require the manipulations of the factual truth. Out of self-defense, he may be forced, even reluctantly, to lie, distort, or twist the facts in order to overcome adverse social events. He has also to realize that it is his job to know how to separate the truth from lying, facts from fiction, in order to avoid being victimized. But this presupposes awareness of the whole gamut of all available options. However this does not mean that someone should necessarily lie as an easy way out of an unfavorable situation. Yet, if he feels compelled to do so, as a last resort against ruthless forces opposing him, then he should think twice about the unforeseeable consequences of his lying. As strange as this may sound, a good, credible lie made to pass for truth is not easily devised. It presupposes imagination, pseudological consistency, and the calculation of odds against possible discovery of its falsehood. Unfortunately, many people with these qualities use lying and deception as a means of taking advantage of others in order to enrich themselves or to gain power and control over others. Many of them are politicians, lawyers, journalists, businessmen, and outright con artists. Other people with noticeable personality defects lie to give a sense of consistency to an otherwise inordinate life. Some habitual liars try to compensate for a marginally functional life. Most of them are bad liars. This may be one reason why society treats them with contempt.

Presently, our new social paradigm relentlessly implemented by its politicians requires an alert discriminating judgment to separate facts from fiction, political spinning from valid social issues. The more someone denies the power of these elaborated distortions acting as a social force that influences, directs, and changes human relationships, the less he shows an understanding of the society's dynamics and the less he will be able to compete socially. The government reserves the right to intervene, not always successfully, when the balance is excessively tilted by abusive individuals toward malicious lying and deception, beyond the perimeter of legal ambiguity. It exercises this right, however, in a biased manner to reinforce the new social activism with its political correctness. This biased approach has made many individuals more vulnerable to social multiple truths, spinning, and legal manipulations. Many people feel left to a great extent to their own devices to protect themselves from the ambiguities of the new social order and justice.

Ultimately, from the societal perspective, being deceived and victimized by others reduces one's degree of adaptability and maneuverability and hence social functioning. It makes him a candidate for being categorized as socially "unfit."

NOTES

1. E. Eckholm, "Deceit Found Pervasive in the Natural World," *New York Times*, January 14, 1986, sec. C1.

2. J. Goodall, *The Chimpanzee of Gombo: Patterns of Behavior* (Cambridge, MA: Harvard University Press, 1986).

3. R. Wright, *The Moral Animal* (New York: Vintage Press, 1994), 250–262.

Chapter 1

The Manipulation of Truth by Society

Lord, Lord how this world is given to lying!
Shakespeare, *Henry IV*, Pt.I, 5.4

THE ROOT OF THE CONFLICT BETWEEN SOCIETY AND PEOPLE

A Historical Perspective

Throughout human history the common people have accused their rulers of controlling their destiny either by brute force or a variety of deceptive manipulations. In turn, the rulers of society, for self-serving reasons, have entertained the belief that their subjects tend to shy away from meeting their responsibilities toward community or state by lying, cheating, or misleading. Their mutual suspicion of other's intentions and actions has been fostered by their limited common interests. Their relationships have, at best, fluctuated around an uneasy truce. In the not too distant past, at extreme points of tension, one or the other side attempted to get the upper hand; the citizens hoping for a change for the better by popular uprising and the ruling elite, when not wiped out of power, by imposing various styles of state oppression.

Complex and conflicting societal and psychological dynamics have conspired to push man into this insoluble dilemma. Apparently, the whole mess began tens of thousands of years ago, when small bands of nomads faced with the relentless and exhausting hardship of pure survival in a hostile environment either by chance or design felt compelled to join other groups for self-protection. In the process, they were slowly forced to give up some of their individual freedom by placing themselves under the new authority of the leadership of the newly formed group. Gradually, these loose associations, pressed by the same inimical surrounding forces, became organized as tribes that further improved the individuals' chances for survival in extremely hostile conditions, but for a price. The tribe protected its members against enemies or starvation by sharing their food, in exchange for submission to the rules and decisions of its leaders. In this context, one may argue that this represents the first step toward the development of society gradually built upon the regulation and control of people's behavior and of their instinctual needs. This trade-off worked relatively well at the tribal level because of the coercing power of taboos and mainly because of the homogeneity of those communal societies, which were strongly interrelated by kinships. However, when the tribes grew historically into heterogeneous hordes or nations, the relationships between leaders and subjects progressively became more impersonal and distant, hence less interested in responding to the needs of ordinary citizens. The formation of social classes stratified society by the degree of economic, social, and political power held by each class. It led to the emergence of a morality regulated by the strict and elaborate rules imposed by the ruling class. In this gradually evolved pyramidal social system, the exploitation of the lower classes by the upper class was part of the society's dynamics of functioning. The outcome was simple: people at the bottom of society were exploited by all the others higher up in this new social pecking order. In a sweeping statement one may say that throughout history the balance of political power was unremittingly challenged, if not changed, in all societies either through internal fights between various aristocratic factions or through military conquests by another nation. After either an internal "change of guard" or a foreign military victory, the conquerors imposed their ideas of social order and morality on the controlled majority. The important fact to note is that the victors created a morality basically to protect their own interests. To put it bluntly, the force of the sword crushed the previous social order and introduced a new one, perpetuating the previous distinction between the oppressors and the oppressed, but reinforced by different masters. For the oppressed the struggle for survival became the foremost preoccupation, fought with all available means. The conflict brought out in ordinary people the instinctual drive for self-preservation, which employed lying, deception, and betrayal in addition to other social survival behavior. Even in their routine interaction, when necessary, ordinary people were as treacherous, deceptive, and rapacious as their masters with the main preoccupation of surviving in an uncertain tomorrow. In brutal conditions, religion acted as a pacifier, offering man comfort for accepting existing injustices and the promise of retribution in the next life.

It can be metaphorically argued that the entire history of mankind has been punctuated by a continuous replay of the biblical story of Cain and Abel, taking place in a variety of scenarios and orchestrated circumstances. It is a history full of wars, genocide, fratricide, slavery, torture, rape, flagrant injustice, deception, and betrayal, to mention only a few expressions of the outcome of the rapacious human need for power, greed, and exploitation, unwittingly following a Darwinian script.

Basically, throughout history, a perverse and hypocritical morality of submission of the weaker to the stronger prevailed as a guide for human relationships. Under this morality, people survived periods of savage oppression by feigning submission and servitude in order to slowly swing open the door to revolt whenever conditions were favorable. With the French revolution, ordinary people started to fight back against the tyranny of the autocratic state. Since then, periodic cataclysmic revolutions in the Western societies liquidated the despotic classes in power in favor of more liberal ones, which fought for democratic principles. Nevertheless, the same basic human instincts for acquiring status and power triumphed in the end with the new leaders, the former champions of civil liberties who gradually became themselves exploiters of citizens' social rights. But at least the conflict between classes became somewhat more evenly fought, relying more often on cunning and deception to outsmart opponents than on brute force. All in all, considering the past tyrannical control of the states, common people in the Western societies have gained impressive civil and political liberties.

What did not change much is the inner moral attitude of the leaders and their subjects. If in the past, kings abused their subjects in the name of their divine rights, if the aristocracy exploited the common people on the basis of their inherited rights, if the military conquerors subjugated them by sheer brute force, the newly democratically elected political representatives of the people attempted quite often to take advantage of them by deception and deviousness. Knowingly or not, the leaders have always tried to apply, to a large extent, the political principles for governing of Niccolo Machiavelli, the 16th-century Italian historian and political thinker. In his books *The Prince* and *The Discourses*,[1] Machiavelli outlined how necessary it is for rulers or leaders to lie and use deception in order to control their subjects and defend their position of power. While these books are treatises on the psychosocial dynamics of politics, they also reveal the political realities of his time, with their intrigues, deceptions, and lies. Nevertheless, these books are valuable lessons in the methods of successfully achieving or maintaining political or social power, since the struggle for power still goes on. Even today in the most advanced democratic states with the most liberal guarantees of citizens' rights, there is a tug of war between individuals and authorities because of people's frustration with the government's abuse of power and encroachment on their rights. This conflict can be reduced to two issues, namely, overtaxation and the overregulation of people's civil liberties, old issues that have been intermittently responsible for popular discontent, the fall of governments, and/or street riots.

The unsolved issue of governments tampering with individual's rights is today mainly fought by democratic rules, within the boundary of the legal system either by parliamentary debates or in a court of the higher law. However, not all conflicts between the government and segments of the population can rally public support or find legislative solutions. The other way to challenge a governmental deed or law is for citizens to take legal action, which is a very costly and risky proposition and as such not available to all. For many, an expedient solution for attempting to avoid any dispute, as learned from their collective past experience in dealing with the authorities, seems to be that of resorting either to outright bribery or distortions and manipulations of facts. It is a quid pro quo solution: The government protects its interests by discriminatory laws and deceptive practices to maintain itself in power, while the citizens lie and cheat to defend themselves from what they perceive as excessive use of authority against them.

In general, the methods of fighting conflicts have been refined by opposing parties almost to an art by emphasizing attributes such as cunning, deception, lying, and betrayal, in addition to the subtle economic exploitation. Ironically, all these traits are regarded by the moralists as negative behaviors, although they are part of man's animal heritage, inborn and adaptive safeguards used whenever needed to either overcome antagonistic conditions to man's well-being or to help him gratify his needs. In evolutionary terms, all these traits have apparently played a vital role in the survival of the fittest or the cleverest.

THE MACHIAVELLISM OF THE GOVERNMENT

Unfortunately, lies and manipulations of the truth by the government is not a rare occurrence. On the contrary, it is often a part of the philosophy of governing. In order to win in a general election, any political party has to promise better solutions to existing local or national problems than the party in power. This may create problems after winning an election, because of the inherent conflict between the sponsored party program and the other social and political national issues important to other segments of the population that do not embrace the ideological framework of the government. In its attempts to reconcile this diversity of needs, a governing party has a very difficult task; on the one hand, it must try to please its own party's constituency, and on the other hand, it still must be able to meet some of the needs of the remainder of the population.

Elected officials quite often solve problems of national interest by simply lying and manipulating the truth according to the political circumstances. This is exactly what was masterfully done by Johnson during the Vietnam War or less successfully by Eisenhower's testy U2 incident with the Soviet Union, Kennedy's awkward denial of government knowledge of the Bay of Pigs invasion, Nixon's puzzling expansion of war in Cambodia, Reagan's confusing Iran Contra Affair, and Clinton's embarrassing reversal policy toward China's civil rights abuses. Certainly these manipulations of truth were dictated by national reasons, but the same can not be said about Nixon's Watergate or Clinton's Monica Lewinsky scandal.

There is no consolation that the abuse of the public is far from being specific only to our government; it rages in most foreign governments, which either are blatantly corrupt or manipulate the political platform on which they were elected in favor of vested interests.

However, quite often, our government put its credibility at stake by going beyond the limits of fair play. For instance, to allegedly implement the quota system of hiring, the Justice Department sued public and private institutions for noncompliance. The established pattern has been a financial settlement with hefty monetary compensation for the alleged "victims" of discrimination. At first glance this sounds right. A recent suit against the North Carolina Department of Correction, however, broke the lucky spell of these deceitful settlements when a federal judge carefully scrutinized them. The political scam perpetrated by the Justice Department misrepresented crucial statistical data and lied about the existence of the alleged victims. In the North Carolina case, the Department of Correction had been asked by the Justice Department, as part of the settlement, to set aside $5.5 million, for eight years' payback to compensate any woman selected by the Justice Department "who applied or would have applied" for a job with the Correction Department. This highly discriminatory and fraudulent act was carried out at the expense of the taxpayers.[2]

However, sometimes agents of other federal law enforcement agencies such as the Bureau of Alcohol, Tobacco, and Firearms (BATF) or the FBI have committed worse acts of abuse of power, entrapment, false arrests, lying, or killing innocent people. A case in point is the Waco disaster. This is considered the deadliest law enforcement operation in American history. Finally, after six years of denying the use of pyrotechnic tear gas canisters against the Davidian compound at Waco, Texas, the FBI admitted using it in the day the fire erupted.[3] Though a new investigation of the role of the federal government in the siege absolved them of any wrongdoing, doubts still linger.

The bad faith of the government is also shown in other more subtle ways. Statistics have been used by the government in an attempt to reinterpret data unfavorable to its policies. For instance, components of the statistical index of inflation are manipulated to reflect a desirable lower inflation.

The controversy about the calculation of the CPI (consumer price index), which reveals the cost of living, is still raging. Meanwhile, the Labor Department already made some significant changes in the calculation of the CPI by using dubious formulae from "geometric weighting" to that of including "quality adjustments" of the prices, which allegedly reflect more realistically the level of inflation. The falling price of technological items, like computers, fax machines, and so on are calculated as part of the inflation index, as if they were staple items for people on social security. This has helped to drive the CPI down, which is beneficial for the government in calculating the social security raises and income tax brackets indexed to it.[4]

But, what about the integrity of our congresspersons? Can people trust any of their congresspeople, particularly after the recent exposures of certain members cashing uncovered checks and committing postal fraud? Do people realize the extent to which they are manipulated by these politicians? Should one forget the self-serving role played by the five senators in what is known as the Keating affair? This has been described by newspapers as "the biggest campaign finance scandal" of the 1980s.[5] The senators who received over $1.4 million in political contributions from Charles Keating intervened with the federal regulators on his behalf and for his Lincoln Savings and Loan Bank to save it from going into federal receivership. Mr. Keating was accused of fraud and racketeering and later convicted. The senators were reprimanded by the Ethics Committee of the Senate. But his financial manipulations cost the taxpayers $3.4 billion. But what about the reaction of the voters? The senators who decided to run for reelection won without difficulty. No wonder so many people are already politically jaded, impassive to the political process, and interested only in reducing their obligations toward the government. The political opportunism has been exacerbated by the relatively recent social upheaval, which has triggered political changes affecting the functioning of the entire society and resulting in ambiguous moral standards. This is reflected in all aspects of human interaction, from business to intimate relationships.

THE NEW SOCIAL PARADIGM AND THE MORAL RELATIVISM

This moral relativism has been inadvertently fostered to a large extent by the quasi-silent but unswerving civil rights demands of ethnic minorities and women. What started as a legitimate protest developed during the social movement of the 1960s and 1970s and less militantly in the 1980s, has resulted into an impressive display of civil rights and economic gains that has twisted our work and family values. For instance, the social revolt that encouraged housewives to leave their household duties in favor of gainful employment has been that of significantly changing marital relationships and the dynamics of family life. As a consequence, it has had dramatic repercussions on child rearing and marital relationships.The bottom line is that in the process, family values have inadvertently collapsed.The unforeseen effect was the erosion of this social capital, the powerhouse of community stability.

Another side result was the departure from the initial demands for equal rights and equal employment opportunities (for all people regardless of gender or race) to that of affirmative action, a concept devised for the elimination of racial and gender discrimination by the creation of employment quotas giving priority in hiring to minorities. This has meant new rules for work hiring, which required overlooking any inadequate experience and disregarding to a great extent merit in favor of the new credentials based on gender or race. Affirmative action has created a fierce and passionate national debate with arguments in favor supported by liberal-progressists and against it conservative-traditionalists. The basic argument surrounding affirmative action has been whether the implementation of the demand for social justice, which is fundamentally sound, based on Constitutional principle of equal rights, has not militated against this very basic precept. Both arguing sides, the traditionalists versus progressists, agree that nobody should deny the right of any citizen, regardless of race, color, or sex, to equal opportunities for employment. They also acknowledge that it was pushed from the beginning as a matter of political necessity and in the name of immediate compensatory justice for the previously disadvantaged people. However, they drastically differ about the methods of its implementation.

Leaving aside the controversy, the problem is that many common people believe that this arbitrary method of creating equal opportunities clashes with and seriously undermines the American ethic of hard work, perseverence, ingenuity, fair competition, and reward based on merit. They also think that this approach does not conform to the American spirit of free choice and entrepreneurship. Anyway, this issue has become a bone of contention for college entrance or postgraduate training and it has particularly upset people who claim to have experienced "discrimination in reverse." It also has increased the frustration of some members of ethnic minorities who feel that affirmative action perpetuates against them a stereotype of racial inferiority and low competence. For all these reasons, this controversial issue is still fought in the higher courts, either by those who feel wronged by affirmative action or by others who would like to take advantage of it at work and met the alleged resistence of the corporate culture. For instance, the Supreme Court decision in the Adarand case in 1995 has attempted to regulate racial preference in the awarding of federal contracts.[6] In some universities affirmative action has been under attack since the Supreme Court decision in the case of *California v. Bakke* in 1978[7] (by now, California and Texas have almost ended its implementation), while in the area of employment affirmative action has made significant gains after class action suits against corporations that were found to practice discrimination (Texaco, Mitsubishi, etc.).

THE POLITICIZATION OF JUSTICE

This reformist ideology has extended to the politicization of justice. Most illegal and criminal acts have come to be interpreted through a gender or racial perspective. This has seriously affected the judicial process. Justice has become less impartial, less directed toward establishing the truth, and more politically sensitive to government policies. Quite often judges have become socially militant, introducing their own brand of social justice in order to be popular with the politicians. While it is true that the U.S. concept of law is based upon the doctrine of natural law, the role of judges is only to apply the law. By introducing their concept of natural law in the court, they violate their sworn duty. When they replace the law with their own interpretations, they depart from the court's traditional task of objective inquiry into available evidence in order to determine the truth about disputed facts. In this case, facts become politically and socially interpreted to justify committed acts. This has been possible because the judicial system has functioned for a long time with a few simplistic concepts and plenty of organizational deficiencies. For example, one problem has been and still is the selection by a defendant's lawyer of a potentially politically or socially biased jury, sympathetic to his client. In other cases the selection of the jury is perversely based on their limited intellectual ability to understand sophisticated technical issues under litigation. This makes a fair evaluation of the facts by them almost impossible in order to ascertain the degree of culpability of the defendant. In addition, in other cases, the jurors' social frustrations due to their unemployment or poverty make them incapable of a realistic appraisal of economic crimes under consideration and of the reasonable or necessary punishment and award to the injured party. It is well known that exorbitant awards are dispensed by juries in product liability, negligence or malpractice cases, under the simplistic assumption that insurances are "loaded." In 1995, when a jury awarded millions of dollars to an elderly lady for the alleged sustained damages after she spilled a cup of hot coffee on herself at a McDonald's restaurant, one might rightly wonder about the seriousness of justice based on the jury system.

Lately, the same degree of irresponsibility of juries has been extended to criminal cases[8] where the decision of guilt or innocence was reached politically, with a total disregard for evidence to the contrary. The verdict of acquittal reached by the jury in 1993 in the famous case of Lorena Bobbit, who cut off her husband's penis after he allegedly repeatedly abused her and ultimately attempted to rape her, was influenced by feminist press rhetoric. The irony of this one-sided justice is that three years later, she, the allegedly abused wife, ended up again in court—this time arraigned for beating her mother.[9] The other sensational acquittal, that of O.J. Simpson in 1995, who was accused of killing both his ex-wife and her male friend, is generally acknowledged to have been politically motivated. Currently, justice seems to be increasingly politically motivated and tends to ignore the evidence, regardless of its weight against the accused, in order to favor one constituency group or another. The new politically biased justice promoted by many activist judges no longer attempts to establish the truth, but rather aims to justify the actions of the criminal according to his social credentials of privileged minority. Recently, the nation was astonished when a federal judge in New York refused to indict a gang of minority cocaine dealers caught red-handed by the police while transporting cargo valued at $4 million. The reason given by this judge was that the police acted illegally by searching the truck without any motive for suspicion. In the judge's eminent opinion, the cocaine dealers who ran at the approach of the police were exhibiting a normal behavioral reaction in response to potential police brutality, which allegedly is often assumed by minorities.[10]

The accumulation of these types of slanted judicial decisions has seriously shaken our faith in our justice system. Our doubt has been reinforced by lawyers, who have discovered ways to make big money by reinterpreting and defending the "constitutional rights" of anyone who, regardless of his wrongdoing, can claim to be socially deprived because of race or sex. The argument can be valid so long as judge and/or jury are persuaded to see the case from the perspective of a social activism.

The judicial process gets even trickier when it comes to elusive claims of sexual harassment. A woman working for a Cincinnati developer received $250,000 in punitive damages in 1995, because her coworkers joked about her by suggesting to name the next plot as "Twin Peaks."[11] But the most astonishing award ever handed by a jury for alleged sexual harassment was in 1998 to a woman, who while working at UPS, was jabbed in the breast by a male driver during a verbal argument. The driver was fired but he allegedly started to stalk her. Meanwhile, she was moved to other jobs, where she claimed she was not being equally treated by the male employees and was excluded from some meetings. As a result, she claimed to have developed anxiety and sued the company. A jury awarded her $80.7 million for her suffering![12] While some cases of sexual harassment are valid and properly documented, in other cases, women without direct proof can accuse a company and/or its supervisors of allegedly creating a "hostile environment" in which the women are at the receiving end of comments they deem inappropriate. In many cases there is no further need for hard proof of personal harassment by the company; and there is no room left for any assumption of ulterior motives on the part of the plaintiff(s) such as a personal work conflict (e.g., the UPS case) or an unshared expression of emotional interest by the male.[13]

In general, 24 percent of the claims of sexual harassment, as reported by companies, are associated with office romance and 17 percent are complaints of retaliations after the affair has ended. The average amount awarded in sexual harassment cases, in which complaints run from making a tasteless remark to posting a sexy pin-up on the wall, has been estimated to be about $250,000 and higher. The cost of these suits to business, including payments for sexual harassment seminars and insurances, is huge.[14] All of these expenses are part of the new political correctness, abused by some plaintiffs who start dubious suits with the support of lawyers for financial gain. Ultimately, these political and financial games are costing consumers dearly in the jacked-up price of goods.

Striking back, in an unprecedented move against these suits of alleged sexual harassment, some American companies recently started to introduce the so called "office love contracts," which are supposed to be signed by both parties emotionally interested in each other before any further involvement. The companies hope to protect themselves from any liability in case the office romance turns sour, and the rejected lover, usually a subordinate, wants to sue under the claims of sexual harassment. So much for office romance![15]

LAWYERS AS DEFENDERS OF THE NEW MORAL RELATIVISM

Is it an exaggeration to say that lawyers run our country? And if so, is there anything wrong with it? Our legislating bodies of Congress and of the state assemblies are more or less run by lawyers. They regulate almost all facets of human interaction, allegedly to protect the citizens' rights. Big business, small business, and private affairs all are also regulated by federal and state governments with the help of lawyers. Laws, rules, and regulations are organizing, directing, and controlling all aspects of our life. As a result they create all types of conflicts between individuals or between the public and private sectors. Aside from this telling us about the "honesty"of people, these conflicts are mediated or fought with the help of lawyers. Certainly, most of these laws have been enacted for a good cause, but the immediate beneficiaries are definitely the lawyers. The net outcome has been that the number of lawyers as well as their income has more than doubled in the past decades. There are now over 800,000 lawyers and they will do anything to make people more litigious. One can no longer function in this society without a lawyer. As prophetically said long ago by Fred Dutton, a Kennedy administration aide, "lawyers have become secular priests." They are indispensable, since they decode for laymen the mumbo-jumbo jargon of laws, which they have themselves written in an undecipherable language. Unfortunately, the problem with lawyers does not end here. In fact, it becomes more serious from this point on.

Their code of ethics and their manipulation of truth help the miscarriage of justice. The bad lawyers mess up the clients while the good lawyers manipulate the system, complicating matters by endlessly delaying trials on technical grounds at the expense of both the plaintiff and the defendant. Furthermore, the adversarial system, a concept of establishing the truth and rendering justice as a result of the clashes between two opposing positions, has led to the misrepresentation and obfuscation of truth, since each side emphasizes the beneficial facts and dismisses those that don't. This method creates confusion and distortion, favoring the most clever and most dishonest of the lawyers to win. As a New York public interest lawyer, Eric Schnapper once quipped: "Lawyering is within the narrow category of occupations where borderline dishonesty is fairly lucrative." The reality is that lawyers trained and oriented toward sophistry and duplicity in arguing their cases have greatly contributed to the dissolution of the social morality. They have politicized trials with total disregard for the criminal evidence; they have manipulated cases, playing the racial card before either biased or ignorant juries selected specifically to win. Mark Perlmutter, the author of the book *Why Lawyers Lie* and a lawyer, justifies their lying on many reasons ranging from seeking the truth through artful deception to fear of emotional humiliation and loss of income in case of the loss of a case. Ultimately, he concludes in a roundabout argument that in our judicial adversary system lawyers have to lie since their opponents lie too. Perlmutter concludes that by not lying any lawyer is placed at a great disadvantage in court of possibly losing the case.[16]

But the bad faith of most criminal lawyers does not stop here; they have another method of making fast money by entering in a "plea bargain" agreement with prosecutors, most often at the expense of the client. The defendant most often is unaware or too frightened to realize that accepting a plea bargain deal could be to his disadvantage since the prosecution may not have enough evidence against him to secure a conviction. For the prosecutor, the deal is favorable by closing a case with a sentence, which makes him look good to his superiors, while for the defense lawyer it is beneficial by getting his fees as agreed upon with the client but without the necessary work for a trial. As a trial judge commented on this matter "most criminal defense lawyers cannot make a living without pleading their clients guilty."[17]

Worse, in their dual role as politicians and lawyers they have made a mockery of the constitutional principle of the separation of power among the executive, legislative, and judicial branches of government. Most of the time, lawyers are in control of the executive branch even when the president is not a lawyer. The American Bar Association recommends lawyers for judgeships from their ranks after they are politically selected, but by doing so, it has vitiated the justice process. At the same time, let us not forget that about one third of Congress are lawyers and other members of the

Congress have lawyers on their staff. This means that lawyers also control the executive and legislative structure of the nation. This separation of branches of power is a perverse interpretation by lawyers of their constitutional intent. In addition, their unethical tendencies and behavior have, by and large, a negative influence on our social code of ethics. While posturing as defenders of the truth and of justice, lawyers have made most laws confusing, conflicting, and cumbersome enough to create problems of interpretation in all aspects of human affairs. As a result, their "salutary intervention" is required in almost all business or social contracts, but it is provided only for a hefty fee.

Lawyers have invaded Washington, D.C., the place of high political and legislative action. There are tens of thousands of lawyers in the capital. Roughly, half of them work for the government and the other half are in the private sector as general practitioners or specialists in governmental relations. And here starts the revolving door strategy of trial lawyers, which is another way to control the legislative system. The ones working for the government make inside political contacts and at the same time become part of the legislating process and the others in private practice most often come from previously held governmental jobs. They moved into private practice for sheer enrichment after "the financial sacrifice" they claimed to have made in performing a service to the public by working for the government. Certainly, this system works well for the corporate lawyers. They reverse roles from legislators or prosecutors to that of defenders by joining private law firms for the highest pay. Their job is simple: either help clients by using personal governmental contacts to solve the issues under dispute or defend the clients in court. In court, lawyers attempt to use the loopholes of the very laws created for protecting the interests of some special lobby groups. It also helps if the litigated case is against the governmental agency where the lawyer had previously worked. This tight recycling system assures the former governmental litigators of a very good living played at the expense of the public. No wonder corporations and people are cynical about the integrity and morality of lawyers for whom, to put it mildly, the truth is flexible or at worst expendable.

PRODUCT LIABILITY: PROTECTION FOR CONSUMERS OR WINDFALL FOR LAWYERS?

There is no question that corporations in promoting their business image or some of their dubious products have attempted to twist the truth using the same methods of sophistry as advertisers. Quite often corporations either make false claims about the quality and safety of their products or worse they hide negative data that may affect marketability. Take, for example, the recent press report about a company called Presstek that was fined $2.7 million by the Securities and Exchange Commission for publishing false and misleading information about its sales and business projections. Its executives edited and distributed a research analyst's report and also a promotional newsletter that exaggerated the projected earning of the company and overstated its outlook, while failing to disclose to the SEC in their periodic filings the adverse developments in its business.[18] It is only normal that the public should be protected from the companies that misrepresent themselves. On the other hand, the thorny question is whether the complaints against the products of some companies or the behavior of professionals are always legitimate or are sometimes invented by unscrupulous people and lawyers. Existing documentation suggests that product liability laws like those concerning professional malpractice or certain products have been abused by the public in association with lawyers for pure financial gains. To win these litigations many people lie, fabricate evidence, and misrepresent facts with the support of the lawyers.

No wonder that the trial lawyers were against the law of liability passed by Congress and vetoed by President Bill Clinton in 1995 because it would have affected their main source of fast enrichment, as clearly shown by their recent fight with states' prosecutors and judges for securing billions of dollars in exorbitant fees from tobacco settlements.[19] Obviously, the trial lawyers are pursuing these suits for personal gain and less for the public good. They are the ones who, like their low-class confederates, the ambulance-chaser lawyers, seek out the product liable for potential litigation and advertise for client-plaintiffs to sign for class-action suits, as it has been pursued against the drug companies that make fen-phen (Pomidin-Redux), a combination of drugs used for weight reduction. The drugs have been shown to induce a high risk of pulmonary hypertension and possibly heart valve disease—two serious, sometimes fatal conditions. The announced settlement with American Home Product, the drug manufacturing company, is $3.8 billion, from which over $1 billion goes to the class-action lawyers! The cost of the product litigations for the year 1995 alone reached the staggering amount of $152 billion and is rapidly growing.[20] Less than half of this money might have reached the consumers. The bulk of it has also been cashed by lawyers. Worse than the suits themselves, instead of investing the capital to expand or hire new workers, the firms have had to fight predatory lawyers in court. Any attempt even at a state level to reform the liability law is met with a fierce opposition from lawyers. In support they use fraudulent tactics, as came to light in relation to a California ballot that contained three reform initiatives they wanted to defeat. The political action committee of these trial lawyers spent about $15 million to defeat these tort propositions, which basically sought to reduce the huge profits the lawyers were raking in at the expense of companies and consumers. To attempt to sway the public in their favor was not a crime, but to use the money for false advertising was unethical to say the least. In their ads, the lawyers falsely and misleadingly attacked a CEO of a high-tech company who was a supporter of these reforms. As a result of a libel suit, the lawyers were forced to withdraw the ads. In other false ads, they baselessly tried to induce in the public fears of financial disasters, regarding the effects that these reforms could have if they were passed.[21] While companies do not always manufacture safe products and in some cases their malfunctioning can produce serious accidents, if not death, such as defective cars, electronics, and so on, in other cases the relationship between cause and effect of product and injury cannot be factually established. Consider silicone breasts implanted for cosmetic purposes. Lawyers argued in court that they induced collagen diseases and possibly activated cancer. Financial settlements with Dow Corning, the primary manufacturing companies, have reached about $3.2 billion, although the alleged cause–effect relationship has not been scientifically proven.[22,23] In the case of tobacco smoking and its relationship to lung disease, emphysema, and cancer, the facts are well established. The issue here is not whether or not heavy smoking contributes to lung cancer in genetically prone individuals but whether smokers know these facts. This issue is still debatable. To start with, we know that it takes between 20–30 years for a heavy smoker to develop cancer, if he is going to develop it at all. This means that most individuals who started smoking in the 1970s have had plenty of chances to read the warning labels on cigarette packages, which had been introduced at that time. We also know that nicotine is very addictive for many people, particularly those presenting a high degree of neuroticism. The fact that tobacco companies knowingly did not inform the public about the addictive effect of smoking is a strong argument against them. Moreover, for the tobacco industry to withhold information about the addictive effect of nicotine found by their research, and in addition, to increase the nicotine content of cigarettes, thereby raising the possibility for addiction, is truly unconscionable. The tampering with the content of nicotine in cigarettes is indeed criminal. Unfortunately, the fact of knowing the potential addictive effect of smoking still does not act as a deterrent since some people continue to smoke anyway, basically because of nicotine's relaxing properties. In fact, its palliative effects on depression, anxiety, and other psychiatric conditions have been recently documented by research indicating that it is acting on certain receptors of the frontal brain.

While part of the claims of the class action suit against the tobacco industry are, in principle, legitimate, they do not solve the problem of people smoking. Yet, the hundreds of billions ($206 billion) obtained at this time from the settlements of 46 states will fill the coffers of the states and lawyers, without any real benefits to the already addicted smokers. In the Florida settlement alone, the local firms want a $2.5 billion booty. Do the addicted people get free anti-smoking medications or enrollment in behavioral programs and financial incentives to lick the addiction? Not meaningfully, since only 8 cents of every tobacco dollar will go toward anti-smoking programs. It means that the addicts will continue to smoke and later, when ill, become a financial burden for the health care system. Then, what are these settlements all about, if not a way to help the states to implement their politically rewarding programs and enrich the lawyers? Certainly, the problem of smoking cannot be solved as long as people continue to exercise their prerogative to smoke while not accepting the responsibilities associated with it.

But by the same token, why does the government not go after other, similarly addictive products, ranging from coffee to alcohol, that are known to be as unhealthy for the individual? Alcohol seems to be the worst of all. It is well known to lead to dependency and contribute to the development of cancer of the esophagus, pancreas, and other organs. In addition, it produces cirrhosis of the liver and many neurological and mental diseases, to mention just a few of its deleterious effects. Alcohol truly devastates the human organism and at the same time, brings financial ruin to the alcoholic and his family. As a "bonus," it genetically affects the alcoholic's offspring. Yet, no class-action suits against this plague have been filed in any court. Since the repeal of prohibition, the government stays clear of any alcohol consumption control. But what about gambling, recognized as highly detrimental to the individual and society but highly profitable for the gaming companies and government, bringing in a revenue of about $29 billion? In any case, hypocrisy on the part of the government is feeding the insatiable greed of lawyers.

It is also interesting to note how these class-action suits are won. For instance, in Texas, a litigation lawyer obtained inside information from the Texas Department of Insurance that auto insurance companies were "double rounding" the premiums for the and yearly six-month calculations of their fees, resulting in an extra 1.00 payment for the insurer. This was done with the written consent of the Department of Insurance. However, it seemed that the approval was incorrect, though the general counsel of the Department of Insurance knew about it. While still in office the general counsel did nothing about it, but after leaving office, he masterminded a class-action suit together with a well known class-action lawyer from Texas. They started the suit by asking for damages from two insurance companies at a value of $109 million, from which they would have collected $30–40 million if they won. To ensure victory, they filed the suit through a local lawyer in a remote area of Texas. This was done because this lawyer was highly connected with that court, and would almost guarantee the suit's success. The same country lawyer recently won another high-profile case against an insurance company. It should come as no surprise that under such conditions the insurance companies involved in the suit would consider settling. Most of the loot is shared by the predators-lawyers. The final losers are the taxpayers.[24]

In this respect, the political hypocrisy and cynicism of the government and lawyers has reached the ultimate level of deception in its approach to AIDS. While it is universally admitted that AIDS is a transmissible sexual disease like syphilis, individuals are not routinely tested for it and they are not required to report it. The authorities have put the whole population of the country at risk in order to please a minority political lobby that fears mandatory testing for HIV will lead to possible job and/or social discrimination. Meanwhile, people who are HIV positive have been infecting innocent heterosexual women and homosexual men. It is estimated that there are over 1 million people in this country infected with HIV, of which only about 20 percent have been tested. Without testing, imagine how many millions more will be infected by those with HIV but will not know that they are infected. The billions of dollars spent in treating AIDS, the hours of lost labor, and the loss of human lives do not count in the political judgment of the politicians. But why are lawyers not starting a class-action suit against the government to protect the interest of the public? Because it would be politically incorrect.

A NEW CONCEPT OF PUNISHMENT FOR CRIME

What happens if a defendant is not fortunate enough to have a "dream team" of lawyers like O.J. Simpson and/or a favorably biased jury and ends up convicted? Being right does not necessarily mean winning and finding justice in court. The danger of an unfair trial looms from many directions. It may come from partial judges, or an incompetent or biased jury that may be easily manipulated by smart lawyers. Technicalities such as the exclusionary rule may help criminals avoid conviction, if the defense can prove that the evidence has been tainted by the arresting party. No wonder more people have begun to believe that crime pays in the end. But one may argue that crime is not profitable because of the possible harsh life in prison. Far from it, thanks to the government's cavalier attitude toward the implementation of the punishment. In fact the problems with the system of dispensing justice are compounded by the lax implementation of punishment. One duty of governmental law enforcement agencies, among others, is to carry out the court sentence of imprisonment as a punishment for an unlawful activity. The assumption is that the guilty party, in addition to losing his freedom, is deprived physically and emotionally of the benefits of a free individual. Is this truly the case?

With the new concept of rehabilitating criminals, the punishment has basically been reduced to denial of freedom while reeducating the offender. The concept of retribution for misdeeds that until recently meant bare conditions of living has been recast into a parody of the classic notion of punishment. To illustrate this point, a videotape recently taken in a prison and shown on the Discovery Channel, in the context of a program related to our justice system, featured a well known convicted murderer of eight young Chicago nurses, snorting cocaine, flashing $100 bills, and having sex with another male. As if this were not enough, he boasts about the fun that he is having while living in prison.[25] Another case shows the lax attitude of the prison administration, as illustrated by an ex-convict who sued the Illinois State Prison in 1999, accusing a guard and other employees for neglecting to help him when he was raped and treated as a "sex slave" by a gang member while in prison.[26]

On the other hand, other inmates have sued prisons for alleged "cruel and unusual punishment" related to trivial charges, like serving soggy sandwiches or broken cookies for lunch. A Florida murderer sued the officials of his prison between 1992–1995 over 200 times for different reasons, from being served food on paper plates to not receiving enough juice with breakfast.[27] It is estimated that the cost of these suits to the government reaches over $83 million annually. The idea behind them is to protect the right of the convict and to teach him a sense of justice in order for him to become a law-abiding citizen. Certainly, there is no need to further comment on the alleged sound program for the rehabilitation of criminals, most of whom remain recidivists. And who has been responsible for this loose implementation of justice?

The legislators and lawyers are guilty for the permissive atmosphere in prisons by gradually liberalizing the laws to the point of almost invalidating the meaning of punishment for crime. Why? For quite a while there has been a tendency among legislators to interpret the committed crime in the context of the criminal's social environment and to hold the latter responsible for his antisocial behavior. While this is a contributing factor in many cases, it does not follow that by teaching offenders skills they automatically become socially rehabilitated. There are other personality factors contributing to their antisocial behavior. Most of the hard core criminals are recidivists.[28]

Now, after they have distorted any sense of retribution for a crime, the opportunistic legislators, afraid that the discontented voters supersaturated with crime will throw them out of the lucrative business of governing, have decided to change their tune. They want to be tough on crime. "Three strikes and you are out" is the new message against crime in our society. Will this approach change drastically the pervasive crime and corruption? Doubtful, unless it is supported by a new moral commitment of fair and equal justice to all people and also by more spartan conditions in jails. As long as punishment is only a temporary removal of the criminal from society for alleged social reeducation, prisons will continue to operate on a revolving door policy.

LYING AND DECEPTIONS PROMOTED BY THE PRIVATE SECTOR

Wall Street: A Hotbed of Financial Scams

The reinterpretation of social values and the reformulation of a liberal justice have also promoted a high class of criminals who financially mug or ruin naive people. They are bank executives, venture capitalists, investment bankers, and Wall Street brokers who deliberately take advantage of the loose legal system of regulating business in the investment area in order to defraud the public. Helped by the deregulation of financial markets, these respectable crooks, most often investment bankers, have schemed up financial operations beyond any acceptable norm of business conduct. They have pushed the notion of creative investments or business deals into a fuzzy area, fringing on deception, if not outright fraud. In due time, their financial manipulations brought their banks or investment companies to insolvency, with the result that taxpayers were forced to rescue them. Yet the abuse of the public continues; a recent report released by the Florida Official Investigation Commission has concluded that for the last decade the Prudential Insurance cheated its customers as a matter of corporate policy![29]

Wall Street has also become the hotbed of criminal conspiracies, from inside trading to rogue brokers selling worthless securities. We all know about the scandal of the inside traders who masterminded an elaborate and interconnected series of securities scams that culminated in a temporary domination of a great part of the financial markets in the late 1980s. Their cunning was matched only by their greed and yearning for power. In 1990, an inventive junk bond dealer cleverly succeeded in making $550 million in a single year, the same year that he was caught for his fraudulent manipulations of companies and securities with junk bonds. If it had not been for one gang member's extreme greediness and desire to show off, the chances of others being caught would have been slim.[30] An amusing sideline of this financial scandal was the campaign of support launched by some corporate executives, former business associates of the "junk bond king" who proclaimed in ads of major newspapers his innocence and praised his great contributions to the financial markets. This tells us a lot about the ethics of these business leaders and their respect for the truth.

Swindles, frauds, scams, and stock manipulations or investment promotions by dishonest investment salesmen and brokers are not isolated incidents, but are a part of Wall Street's less acknowledged activities. In fact, 30 brokerage houses, including the biggest ones, were accused in a class-action suit of fixing the spread between ask and bid on the sale of stocks on NASDAQ from 1989 to 1994. They settled in December 1997, agreeing to pay $910 million as damages to investors.[31] Sophisticated computer programs permit an even faster, more impersonal and less detectable deception through the use of simple electronic manipulations of financial markets or outright misappropriation of financial assets. The latest case of fraud of hundreds of millions dollars in insurance business perpetrated by Martin Frankel has shown the unforeseen level that can be reached by a devious financial creativity and skillful manipulations of electronic bank techniques for carrying out crooked schemes.[32] These are the crimes of the cyber age. They are the ultimate product of the new moral relativism. However, white collar crime is unfortunately treated with leniency by the courts.

The Manipulation of the Truth by the Media

It would be unfair to blame only the lawyers and politicians or Wall Street for this climate of general equivocation; there is another culprit: the media. Media communications, through a new loose interpretation of facts and evidence, have created a new relative concept of truth that has almost become the norm for any level of reporting or documentation. Media people have learned to master this evasive, equivocal, distorted, fragmented presentation of the truth. In the past, the only rule for journalists was that of accurately and impartially reporting news of national interest or news of importance for the people of a community and state. It was viewed as unconscionable for an editor or reporter of an independent newspaper to intentionally select or distort the news for supporting a particular political ideology or corporate interest. If they did, then their newspaper was officially labeled as biased by representing a particular ideology or interest group. Now, we are dealing with a different concept of journalism. While not admitting any ideological or emotional affiliation to any political or special interest group, newspapers conceal their convictions by subtly promoting their version of the truth about events or by inserting their opinion into factual presentations. Furthermore, to give credibility to their slanted stories, frequently they quote anonymous hence unverifiable sources, since they refuse to disclose them when questioned. A relative and subjective truth is created by omissions or fragmentation of facts to fit their political biases. Quite often, without any qualms, people in the media have replaced truth with half-truths. Repeatedly, they have totally ignored the truth when it has been in disagreement with their point of view. Many of us may remember the 1993 NBC documentary on a specific GM truck that allegedly could catch fire at the slightest impact. The documentary was in support of a verdict of over $100 million rendered by a jury in a suit claiming this fact. The presentation of NBC was spectacular and convincing, except that it was faked, created in a studio by a dishonest producer! GM sued NBC for it and they settled the suit. After being caught, they indignantly argued that their main intention as always has been to emphasize an important issue that needed to be recognized by the public, even if the facts might have been slanted.[33] A similar hoax was recently perpetrated by a British documentary broadcast by CBS's *60 Minutes* program about drug smuggling from Columbia. It featured drug couriers swallowing plastic fingers filled with heroin before boarding flights to London, interviews with drug lords in their hideouts, and so on. It turned out that the alleged couriers were performers hired to play those roles by the film-maker and the hideout was his hotel room![34] So much for a TV documentary enlightening the public.

The reality is that we are dealing with a biased media attempting to indoctrinate the public according to their ideological beliefs. To do so, most journalists, reporters, editors, or TV broadcasters selectively present information, manipulate the truth, or blatantly lie. For instance, during the Vietnam War, regardless of whether it was a justified or unjustified war, reporters decided that the American army would lose the battle against the Viet Cong before the famous Tet offensive. Newspapermen, playing military strategists, claimed to have attempted to "prepare the public for the defeat." After our army won the battle, they played down the victory, claiming it was inconsequential for the outcome of the war. It was a calculated self-fulfilling prophecy, purposefully designed to discredit the war and demoralize both the war efforts at home as well as the fighting troops.[35]

This interpretive reporting of the news gradually became an almost standard method of presenting political or social issues for the whole media industry. This is bad journalism. It attempts to create or influence public opinion in accordance with the vested interests or political aims of the publishers or the board of directors of media companies. A case in point is a 1992 article in the Sunday *New York Times* by Ann Quindlen, who after the news of presidential candidate Bill Clinton ten-year affair with Gennifer Flowers broke in the press, attempted to preempt the scandal by concluding that either the story was not true or if it was, it was a paid public revelation of a private affair from a dubious source, whose act was more reprehensible than the adultery itself. And if it did happen, it was of no significance to the present political issues. This was a biased attempt to influence public opinion. In fact, in the same evening, Clinton, on TV, after neither admitting or denying the affair with Flowers, followed the line of the *New York Times* writer, stating that "There is a recession on. Times are hard and I think you can expect more and more of these stories as long as they are down there handing out money."[36] (Later, in 1998, he admitted the affair, in a sworn deposition in the Paula Jones case.)

One of the biggest hoaxes recently perpetrated by the media was that of a CNN investigative report on Operation Tailwind,[37] the alleged use of the nerve gas sarin by the U.S. army in Vietnam, in order to kill the American soldiers who had defected to the enemy. A celebrated CNN reporter—a Pulitzer Prize winner as a war correspondent for the Associated Press during the Vietnam War—supervised, together with a senior vice-president of

CNN, a team of producers who aired this grossly distorted, and mostly fabricated story as a journalistic scoop (in reality they used tear gas) at the launching of the collaborative TV program *News Stand* of CNN-Time. *Time* magazine carried an article about this mission signed by the same reporter. Three weeks later, the story was retracted by both CNN and *Time*, after an internal investigation triggered by protests and a rebuttal by the quoted sources.[38] The net result was not only the media's loss of credibility but also a suit of $100 million for defamation by an ex-Green Beret who was repeatedly presented in the alleged documentary, even though he never had participated in that operation.[39]

The fact that the press invents or distorts facts is nothing new. In fact, recently the *Boston Globe* was forced to dismiss two reporters because they had invented people and eloquent quotes to support their arguments.[40] This brings us to another method the press uses to manipulate the truth: selectively slanting its content, in contradiction to the proclaimed article of faith on the front page that "All the news that's fit to print" is reported to the public. The content of the news, unless it is sensational or earthshaking, is selected according to the subjective judgment and political bend of the media's editorial boards, themselves following the imposed policies of the board of directors, who represent the interests of the big corporations to which they belong.

Until recently no serious attempt has been made to objectively evaluate and criticize the news reports of the media. A recent attempt has been made by a monthly magazine called *Content*. In its debut issue in June 1998 this allegedly impartial magazine of criticism of the biased reporting of the media itself fell into the same trap of subjective and interpretive journalism. It misrepresented data and reported it out of context in its lead article, according to other newspapers and the people quoted in the alleged exposé. All this was apparently done for the purpose of gaining public attention.[41,42] For the media industry, their boards of directors, and for many journalists, it seems that political power and money are decisively more important than the truth. At the same time, it is questionable whether or not the public itself is interested in knowing the truth, since people are divided and biased according to their political and social orientation. People have to understand that they are being subtly or aggressively manipulated by the media for the benefit of particular political and social interest groups. However, it is not always easy to discover the distortions and omissions of truth by the media since they are most often presented in a subtle form.

As if this were not enough, media corporations have another god to serve: advertising agencies and the companies they represent. Here we are talking about big money, providing life support for all media channels of communication. Withdrawal of the financial revenue from advertising spells disaster for media corporations. This can happen if editorials, news, or other programs offend the political opinions or policies of sponsoring companies. However, the idea of radio or TV broadcasters selling commercial time to businesses was presented to the public as a way of helping to keep the media free from political influence, and free of charging a fee. Neither statement is quite true. The advertising price is added to the price paid by the consumer. This advertising has been recently calculated to cost over $1,000 per household per year. As a "bonus," the flow and the presentation of the news is controlled by the media ownership, as dictated by its vested interests. The interests of the media have become interlocked with the interests of these corporations. Louis Brandeis, the late Supreme Court judge, eminently used to call it "an endless chain" of interlocking interests that "tends to disloyalty and violation of the fundamental law that no man can serve two masters." Unusual to say the least, this was recently recognized by the *New York Times*, when one of its reporters concluded that a WNBC station in New York went "amok" when instead of discussing in depth the significant news of the day, it used prime time to present an interview with a sports-team owner, beneficial to their conglomerate. In journalism, the use of the media to promote the business of their own companies is called "synergy." It represents a conflict of interests though it is widespread in TV broadcasting. The reporter quoted similar situations of synergy at ABC-Walt Disney and seemed concerned about the mergers in the broadcasting industry, like that of Time-Warner-CNN-Turner or the collusion of reporting between CBS and one of their sponsors, the Nike Corporation. He thought that these mega-mergers might cause potential problems for journalists and the public.[43]

Another example of dubious service to the public by the media is a story produced by the *20/20* broadcasting program in 1996. This program attempted to explain the social conflict between blacks and whites as being based on the two populations' differing perceptions of their relationships. To prove this point, the TV reporter discussed some bizarre rumors circulating in black communities about a white conspiracy against them. One rumor was that the letter *K* on the Snapple drink bottle stands for KKK (Ku Klux Klan) in some blacks' opinions. Another story was about the boat depicted on the same bottle, which allegedly represented a slave ship. In reality, *K* stands for "kosher" and the boat stands for the Boston Tea Party. The reporter went on to discuss a rumor that Liz Claiborne did not want her black clothes to be sold to blacks, as she allegedly stated at her appearance on the *Oprah Winfrey Show*. However, according to Oprah's statement, reported in the next segment of the same show, Claiborne was never interviewed by her. The *20/20* reporter proceeded in his attempt to justify these beliefs, on the basis of the allegations that in the 1960s the government assaulted peaceful demonstrators and that the FBI conspired against Martin Luther King. Leaving aside his explanations for these beliefs, the whole documentary was an insult to the black community. His conclusion that "It's hard to know what is true" was not only simplistic but ill conceived.[44]

In the same vein of manipulative reporting the *New York Times* on November 1997 presented an article about the persistence of cultural biases against the underprivileged students on the standardized SAT test scores and gave as an example the unfair use of the word "regatta" on the vocabulary test. In reality, regardless of its arguable use, the word "regatta" had been removed from the test since 1974! Furthermore, according to the College Board, the minority students did not do better or worse on the regatta question than on other similar verbal items. Interestingly, when blacks were compared in their overall scoring within the same range to those of white students, their answers were comparable.[45] In this case, the test discrimination appears to be in the mind of the reporter. However, this allegation fits with a wider conspiracy theory raised by liberal politicians and some black activists and lawyers who have total disrespect for the truth. The theory alleges a "plot" by the federal authorities to prosecute more black crack-cocaine defenders than whites. The issue became so heated due to the activist reporters and lawyers' clamoring discrimination that it was finally brought before the U.S. Supreme Court. The Supreme Court's decision rejects the theory that race statistics alone support the claims of selective racial prosecution.[46,47] The impression of unequal prosecution stems from the fact that the federal guidelines for sentencing for crack possession or use are more punitive than those for cocaine. This disparate sentencing is due to the fact that crack is considered to induce more violent behavior than cocaine. Apparently, there are more black dealers and users of crack than there are white. Most of the press glossed over this psychologically important decision.

The traditional objectivity of the media has reached a very low point. Not only is the news selected or omitted according to the political or social orientation of editorial boards or broadcasting teams, but journalists and their bosses directly and aggressively attempt to guide the political and social direction of the country. Can they impartially report political news? Historical evidence fails to support this assumption. No wonder then that 57 percent of the public surveyed in the same year thought that journalists were no more honest than the politicians they criticized and 53 percent of the same sample believed that journalists are more interested in wielding power than in what is good for the country.[48]

The Creative Truth of the Advertising Industry

The relatively subtle deception of the press is intertwined with the clever lying of advertisers who, in an attempt to sell a product, make extravagant claims to influence consumers. Advertising has gradually taken control of TV broadcasting, becoming its main source of income. Advertisers can influence the content of TV programs according to their moral beliefs and/or their assumptions about consumer reactions. Advertising relies on its formidable psychological power to influence the buying patterns of consumers. To do so, it has refined its methods of persuasion to the point of a science through extensive research in human emotional responses to visual and auditory stimuli. Though still an art form, advertising techniques combine entertainment and information with psychological methods of persuasion. The message to consumers has to convey the advantages of buying a particular product that is allegedly superior to all others of the same kind. Advertisers address their ads to human emotions. They try, directly or indirectly, to associate a product with positive emotions, hence creating a need to buy it. However, this has nothing to do with the value of the product. A recent TV ad shows an attractive woman driver tightly holding the steering wheel of a car as a powerful wave of water hits the hood. The next frame shows her in a state of ecstasy, while a background voice concludes, "Ah, sweet mystery of life." The lady wakes up in her bed moaning, "What a machine!" To make sure that the message is properly understood, the ad shows her male partner next to her commenting, "Oh, yeah but why did you keep asking me to signal?" The advertisement is for a Mercedes-Benz, obviously a comparably satisfying and powerful machine.[49]

Certainly, they are not like the old classical deceptions of selling a miraculous cure for rejuvenation or a salve promoted by a 19th-century medicine man, but rather, subtle distortions, exaggerated claims or suggestions of marvelous effects by simple associations with enchanting scenes and situations. If a man or woman uses a particular product, the unsaid but implied idea is that someone will fall in love with the buyer as suggested by the accompanying scene of flirting. The worst and most blatant deceptions take place on certain commercials run on cable TV where schemes of getting rich are expounded by entrepreneurs in persuasive infomercials supported by testimonials made by people who allegedly became rich by applying the promoter's teachings. The catch is to buy the promoter's books, at exorbitant prices, that indeed inform you about facts already well known to that type of business, particularly if it is real estate.

Another approach to pushing a product on the market is to commission some research that will put a favorable light on that merchandise. Some product research on nutrition did exactly that, identifying special qualities of a targeted merchandise that automatically made it more desirable and would therefore tend to increase its sales. The research findings are sometimes either outrageous or funny. A reported research of this type claimed that eating eight slices of white bread per day did not increase the subjects' weight over the eight weeks in which they were studied, all other things allegedly being equal. These conclusions, which go against common sense and medical knowledge, were sponsored by the makers of Wonder Bread. Another unusual research finding was based on a dental study reaching a conclusion against established facts, that chocolate has the marvelous capacity to inhibit cavities in teeth owing to a special chemical substance called tannins found in cocoa. The study failed to mention the effect of sugar on teeth. Suffice to say, it was sponsored by the makers of M&Ms. The trouble is that the press, by uncritically reporting these alleged scientific findings, indirectly advertised them.[50]

Most of the ads, in reality, are an insult to human intelligence. Some of them take advantage of people's lack of knowledge in a particular area of concern to them, like health. Various pills against colds, pains, or headaches, medications that basically have the same effects and only work symptomatically, have been advertised as "salutary." In the battle to increase their market share, each product claims superiority over the others. The reality is that the company that can afford to spend more money in advertising will increase its share of the market, at the expense of its competitors. This has been the case for Tylenol, which has surpassed various other brands of aspirin in sales, as a result of an aggressive advertising campaign. Is this good for the public, considering that the efficacy of similar products is within the same range? It seems that the only benefit is the increase in their price paid by consumers.

Advertising is a business of over $30 billion in annual revenue for the broadcasting industry. From a business perspective, it attempts to change human behavior in agreement with the commercial needs of the manufacturers of certain products. Therefore, broadcasting corporations, working together with advertisers, have attempted to develop more subtle methods to keep the viewers' attention glued to the screen while the commercials are being shown. After all, the broadcasters sell units of 30 seconds of advertising spots for tens of thousands of dollars, and in exchange, the sponsoring companies want sales results. Psychologically, they figured out that the association of an ad with an entertaining, dynamic, and arresting show may bring a strong response by increasing viewers' attention. In general, out of 1,600–2,000 messages daily bombarding the consumers, only 8–10 may succeed with the viewers. With the help of media research the broadcasters have discovered that TV shows depicting violence and sex in addition to a few classical sitcoms or sporting events are the winners. They are popular with young TV viewers and also lucrative with advertisers. While the promoting of these types of shows may seem to indignant social ethicists and outraged parents to indicate an irresponsibility on the part of the broadcasting industry, in reality it is based on a pure business decision. Certainly, this thinking shows the hypocrisy and cynicism of the sponsoring corporations and their counterpart broadcasters, who are only interested in maximizing their profits at the expense of public concern with TV's effect on social violence. In fact, advertisers have gradually departed from traditional American values and from basic decent concepts of social and family life. It has been noticed that many sitcoms, drama, and daytime soap programs are "deeply hostile to families, highly sexual and amoral at best."[51]

The music division of Time-Warner, publisher of the obscene, antisocial "gangsta" music, is an example of the thrashing of traditional values. A *Newsweek* poll taken in June 1994 tell us that 67 percent of the respondents thought that TV programs were responsible for negatively influencing social morality. Television was the third considered cause for the low morals in this country, coming after the breakdown of the family and the general problem with the individual's lack of "personal character." In fact, a recent book extensively debates the effect of media violence on children. According to its authors, the media provide a model of violence for children, influencing their acting-out behavior.[52]

The problem of misleading in advertising has gradually become of concern to many educators who have thought of teaching children about true and false advertising by introducing classes on "media literacy."[53] The weak point is that these classes are sponsored by commercial organizations that provide TV sets or computers, software, maintenance, and so on, for education, but in exchange, they run their own commercials, particularly addressed to children. The benefit is that children under the guidance of teachers may become aware of false advertising.

Politicians, media, and advertisers all have in common that peculiar, subjective tendency of twisting the presentation of facts, events, or any evidence leading to the establishment of the whole truth in favor of an adulterated or diluted version of it coinciding with their own needs or ideological orientation. This sophistic approach ultimately leads to questioning, debating, fragmenting, and distorting the facts to the point of creating doubts, if not negating the whole existence of the issue under discussion. In the process, a new vague, imprecise, ambiguous, and hazy semblance of truth emerges, which is supported and disseminated as an ultimate truth.

AN EDUCATION SYSTEM PROMOTING RELATIVE VALUES

Unfortunately, this flexible approach to the truth is not limited to the adult world of hustle and bustle, where everyone tries to outsmart the other for a better piece of the action. It is slowly instilled in the minds of children under dubious educational pretexts. The justification has been the pursuit of what is called a reparative approach to historical oppression. This has become the slogan for the excuse of reshaping our values and morality. It is implemented with the help of the government. It attempts to rewrite history in terms of an alleged organized conspiracy of oppression, which obviously took place over centuries of plotting against particular minorities, identified only by race, gender, and/or sexual orientation. History is interpreted outside the context of the thinking and beliefs prevailing during those times when the events took place.[54] Ultimately, this is a deceptive interpretation of human social interaction, which indirectly promotes hate and strife. Regrettably, these distortions and subjective interpretations of history are already reflected in the study programs of our public school system. To give credibility to these political theories and beliefs, the supporters have vaguely associated their views with a philosophy of secular humanism.

Another approach of bashing old values is the "revolutionary concept" that "learning should be fun."[55] Forget about discipline, responsibility, and commitment. The school system ingeniously found a shortcut to the hard work of serious learning. For instance, to make the learning of math fun, children have to invent their own strategies in multiplying. It is not as important to find the right answer as it is to be able to justify a wrong one. This approach is supposed to help the student understand the mistakes in his thinking, but in reality it is a mandate for fuzzy math. As a matter of fact, public school students are not taught algebra until the 9th grade, since it is considered to be too hard for them to understand abstract math,[56] although they are old enough to have sex in the school's basement or to shoot each other. Anyway, the net results for public schools have been a high rate of illiteracy at graduation and a high frequency of pregnancy among female teenagers. Sexual activity is part of the fun. But even this is not necessarily carried out in the name of love. It has become part of a casual social interaction between the sexes. Yet, all these forms of fun cost the taxpayers approximately $400 billion annually to run the public schools, averaging out to $6,000 per student ($8,300 in New York City). With the merit system and hard work out of vogue and with guaranteed graduation regardless of illiteracy, most public school children are poorly prepared for the job market or for college entrance. According to the Educational Testing Service, which administers the SAT, about 98 percent of the high school students admit to cheating.[57] The latest scandal in New York City public schools looks like the last straw for our shaky educational system. A report released by the special commissioner of investigation for the New York City School District implicates two principals and dozens of teachers and assistants in supplying students with answers during standardized reading and math tests. By improving children's scores by cheating, they were helping themselves maintain their jobs. Some teachers claim that they were asked by the principal to help children or to change the scores.[58] In fact, it is known that the first years of college have become partly directed toward remedial English and math. These students who are not used to hard work and/or lack a family tradition of regular work or instilled work discipline by their parents will be unprepared for the labor market. Unable to meet the requirements of disciplined work and now unable to take advantage of welfare like their parents, these aimless young adults, used to having a good time, have a hard time functioning socially. They already represent quite a problem for society. For instance, there is a problem creating work incentives for single teenage mothers who used to receive generous welfare benefits, thereby becoming themselves the victims of past misguided social policies. The only hope is that other teenage girls will wise up and not get pregnant.

The irony is that the failure of the schools to prepare responsible, productive citizens is still attributed to social discrimination and a lack of work opportunities, which obviously do not apply to immigrants from Asia, who do very well in schools. Clearly, the fault is not with the children; it is with the politicization of the school system and the perfunctory interest of most teachers in their students' academic performance. According to a reporter, in recent years, an idea has spread among ghetto schools around the country that doing well academically is "acting white."[59] Teachers themselves feel trapped by the new system. They have to fail as few students as possible regardless of their scholastic achievements, in order to maintain their positions and reflect a good performance level for the school, as documented by the New York Public Schools scandal. In addition, the teachers have very few means to control children, which makes harder for them to maintain any discipline in class. In some schools teachers are afraid of being beaten if not killed by students, as has actually happened on occasions.

The worst thing is that public schools neglect to teach social values. They are not inculcating children with what used to be called "civic virtues." On the contrary, children are exposed to a moral relativism that suggests to them that they can choose from a variety of behaviors, all free of constraint, in order to reach a desired goal. Without well-defined limits of morality taught by authority, children develop their own subjective concept of right and wrong based on their experience with success or nonsuccess in their limited life experiences but which has nothing to do with society's rules. Unfortunately, there are tens of thousands of teenagers all over the country who are quitting high school, totally unprepared for integration in the workforce. This questions the ability of our pedagogic methods to train children for a full productive integration into society. What, then, can be done about the children enrolled in public school who have negative behavior patterns, resulting in a high degree of illiteracy and antisocial activity within the school system and after leaving school? How can we help them change their behavior?

Since the teachers cannot enforce any effective discipline, which would not work anyway, the only possibility is to give the pupils an incentive for doing well. But this presupposes that it has some meaning for the pupil in order for him/her to respond to it. Most children would not respond to any scholarly initiative without the support of their parents. Thus the task is left to the parents to discipline, guide, and encourage them. This assumes first that parents are still living together, which quite often is not the case, and second, it presupposes that they have the time and would like to be involved in their children's education. Apparently, for whatever reasons, ranging from conflicting work schedules to an unstructured lifestyle, some parents cannot or do not help their children enough to develop positive attitudes toward work in order to achieve responsible societal integration. This situation has been worsened by the disintegration of the nuclear family.

One may be surprised to learn that there is a connection between increased teenager delinquency and the changing role of women in society from that of a housewife to that of a full-time worker. This development put in motion a chain reaction of unexpected events starting with the breakdown of a structured family life to an increase in the divorce rate, with the result of less time spent with children and reduced control over their activities. Some of these children gradually fell under the influence of street values, which often open the door to the fast lane of life with all its antisocial consequences. This is compounded by the ultra permissive social climate, where young people learn amorphous social value that is at best confusing or contradictory. However, because marital relationships between men and women cannot be dictated by law, one solution is to improve the public school system.

To save children from the inefficiency of the public school system, a few states like Arizona, Wisconsin, and more recently, Florida, have developed new approaches to education. In Arizona a new type of charter school, managed by the private sector, has been introduced, replacing the old public schools. It has already produced a mini revolution by its innovative programs, which create incentives for learning. In Milwaukee, Wisconsin, a voucher school program has been introduced, permitting low-income children to attend private schools. Though both programs are in their initial stages, they jolted the inept and lethargic public school system, forcing it at least to compete for students or lose their allocated funds.[60]

But many people believe that children in the public school can compensate for their lack of a meaningful value system and moral directions by learning about them through religious education. It is understood that this learning would respect the religious denomination of the students. However, there are strong political arguments against this policy. The reality remains that children who cannot afford private schools that may offer religious education and who therefore attend public schools are being deprived of developing solid moral concepts. But to what extent will the teaching of ethics help the students?

THE DECLINE OF RELIGION'S INFLUENCE OVER SOCIAL MORALITY

Religious influences have gradually decreased according to statistical polls. A poll taken in 1995 indicated that 58 percent of respondents felt that religion was losing its influence on people's lives. In fact, social writers have claimed that churches have not properly used their influence in communities to help in the fight against crime, violence, and drugs. To do so would require a revival of religion and introduction of socially and educationally oriented religious programs. Then the question remains as to what extent a religious moral education that teaches children moral values can influence their immediate approach to life and long-term behavior. It seems that religiously inspired morality alone has been unable to stave off rising crime, violence, family breakdown, and turpitude, which have become national problems. Apparently, a blow to religious morality was given by the immorality of significant religious leaders of various denominations who abused their sanctified social position in order to steal or abuse the public trust to the point in one case of laundering millions of dollars for Colombian drug traffickers.[61] The highly publicized sexual misconduct or embezzlement of a congregation's funds by some leading fundamentalist preachers from the South is well known to the public. The reality is that political and social factors are more vital to people than religion for determining and controlling their moral behavior.

The new social and political climate has directly and indirectly encouraged a moral relativism and basically ignored the family values preached by religion. The recent half-hearted support for the old family values has been unsuccessful, particularly because most families are already fragmented and disjointed and, in addition, people are highly hedonistically and egotistically oriented, mostly playing it by ear on any moral issue. The daily social example of disregard for the law and ethics reinforces their negative views.

Our attitude toward morality has always been ambivalent because of the conflict between puritanical religious beliefs and the ruthless pursuit of financial success. As a nation of immigrants, our people have tried hard to rise above poverty and hardship and "make it in a country of unlimited opportunity." Success has most often been equated with becoming rich. However, in the process of achieving wealth, people have been obliged to either make concessions or sometimes to sacrifice their moral beliefs and sense of integrity. In the past, if they were caught cheating others, they were either ostracized by public opinion or punished by the law. Now things have changed because, among other things, the distinction between right and wrong gradually has become less defined. An example of our current legal and political tribulations is the recent mayor of Washington, D.C., sentenced to prison for various crimes, including cocaine use. When released from jail, he sought to regain his mayoral seat and he was reelected to office by his tolerant constituency. This tells us a lot about the moral attitudes of Washington, D.C., voters.

We are living in an egotistic, narcissistic, and permissive society where for most people the gratification of one's needs overrules any assumed social sense of restraint and reticence. In fact, social values are neglected in favor of personal gains. Traditional values are considered by many as obsolete because they fit poorly into the modern, ruthlessly competitive social reality of human relationships. The new relativistic morality strives to create a society almost free from guilt. It leads to a pragmatic and egocentric morality focusing on immediate gratification. This is a morality of expediency, dictated by the survival of the cleverest, where many people act as if anything goes, and any method of coping is valid so long as it advances their goals. For them, lies and deception become prime tools in the arsenal of self-advancement.

If we accept the findings of a poll taken in the mid-1990s by *Newsweek*, our country is "in a moral and spiritual decline." It indicated that 76 percent of the respondents agreed with this statement. People blamed the deterioration of morality to family breakdown (77 percent), individuals' lack of moral fiber (76 percent), TV and other popular entertainment (67 percent), government and political leaders (55 percent), economic conditions (50 percent), school education (44 percent) and religious institutions (26 percent).[62]

While all of these factors have contributed to this unusual state of affairs, the common denominator is the prevailing new social attitude: people by and large attempt to eschew the rules of conduct still on the "society's books" and to ignore any social propriety that antagonizes the pursuit of their goals. Most people are success driven, feel superficially connected to others, and have little faith in the secular justice and no desire to rely on divine justice when they believe themselves manipulated and abused by society. Most men fancy themselves to be the sole judge for their actions. They fiercely act to protect what they think to be their best interests with no room left for feelings of remorse, shame, or concern for public opinion. To achieve one's goals, to succeed at any price, even if it requires cheating and lying, has become a highly appreciated accomplishment in a society where only the final result counts. This new standard for morality has been confirmed by a poll taken by *New York Times*/CBS News, referring to the people's attitude toward the lying and perjury of President Clinton at the time of the Monica Lewinsky scandal.[63,64] Sixty-one percent of the interviewed people thought that the president's admission and apology should absolve him. The public response was almost unchanged after Congress voted for his impeachment. It is the ultimate expression of our society's moral relativism.

NOTES

1. N. Machiavelli, *The Prince and the Discourse* (New York: The Modern Library, 1950).

2. C. Bollick, "A Judge Takes On Clinton's See-No Quota Policy," *Wall Street Journal*, April 1, 1996, p. 21.

3. D. Thibodeau, "A Place Called Waco: A Survivor Story." *Reason Express On Line*, November 4, 1999.

4. J. Crudele, "How Uncle Sam Is Shrinking Your Social Security Check," *New York Post*, February 20, 1998, p. 30.

5. 102nd Congress, 1st Sess., November 20, 1991, Temp. Record p. S-17174, Vote No. 258.

6. C. Bolick, *The Affirmative Action* (Washington, DC: Cato Institute, 1996), p. 107.

7. Ibid., p. 59.

8. N.J. Smith, "The Heat over McDonald's Coffee," *San Francisco Chronicle*, June 19, 1995, p. A19.

9. Affirmative Action. *Encarta 98 Encyclopedia* (CD). Washington, Microsoft Corporation.

10. L. Massarella, "Lorena and Mom Bury the Hatchet," *New York Post*, December 9, 1997, p. 18.

11. M. Kramer, "Cheap Shots at Judges," *Time*, April 22, 1966, p. 57.

12. C. Young, "Now Can We Rein in Sex Harassment Law?," *New York Post*, April 7, 1998, p. 28.

13. K. Bishop, "The $80.7 Million Woman," *New York Post*, February 18, 1998, p. 21.

14. "Review & Outlook." *Wall Street Journal*, June 7, 1996, p. A14.

15. E. Cohen, "Now, Office Love Contracts. What Next?," *New York Post*, February 27, 1998, p. 21.

16. M. Perlmutter, "Why Lawyers Lie." Internet. *The Institute for Central Conflict Resolution*, 1997.

17. A.R. Fine, "Letter to the Editor," *Wall Street Journal*, December 30, 1997, p. A11.

18. Presstek Inc., From 10K, Filed April 2, 1998, SEC (10-information).

19. W.H. Jenkins, Jr., "Time to Grow Up About Tobacco," *Wall Street Journal*, February 25, 1998, p. A23; Review & Outlook. "The Senate's Tobacco Wad," *Wall Street Journal*, May 20 1998, p. A14.

20. Review & Outlook. "The Lawyer's Veto," *Wall Street Journal*, May 3, 1996, p. A12.

21. Editorial, *Wall Street Journal*, March 22, 1996, p. A12.

22. M.T. Burton, "Breast Implant Study Is Fuel for Debate," *Wall Street Journal*, February 23, 1996, p. B1; M.T. Burton, "Testimony at Silicone Implant Hearing Apparently Fails to Prove Link to Illness," *Wall Street Journal*, July 25, 1997, p. B3.

23. Editorial Page. "The Truth About Breast Implants," *New York Post*, December 3, 1998, p. 42.

24. M.A. Boot, "Texas Sized Class Action Fraud," *Wall Street Journal*, May 22 1996, p. A23.

25. A&E Biographies Series. Video. Richard Speck, July 1996 (Discovery Channel).

26. T. Kuntz, "From Thief to Cellblock Sex Slave: A Convict Testimony." *New York Times*, October 19, 1997, p. 7.

27. D. Van Etta, "The Scandal of Prisoners' Lawsuits" *Reader Digest* April 1996, pp. 65–70.

28. Crimal Offenders Statistics—Recidivism (ICPSR 2039). Washington, DC: U.S. Department of Justice, Bureau of Statistics, 1999.

29. D. Lohse, & L. Scism, "Prudential Settlement Is Cleared by Court," *Wall Street Journal*, July 24, 1998, p. B7.

30. J. Stewart, *Den of Thieves* (New York: Simon & Schuster, 1991).

31. D. Stariman and P. McGeehan, "Floor Brokers on Big Board Charged in Scheme," *Wall Street Journal*, February 26, 1998, p. C1.

32. D. Lohse, & L. Scism, "How Frankel Created an Insurance Empire," *Wall Street Journal*, July 2, 1999, p. C1.

33. W. Olson, "The Most Dangerous Vehicle on Road," *Wall Street Journal*, February 3, 1993, p. A15.

34. L. Mifflin, " '60 Minutes' Producer to Offer Apology for Discredited Report," *New York Times*, December 11, 1998, p. A27.

35. B.P. Davidson, *Vietnam at War: The History 1946–1975* (New York: Oxford University Press, 1998), pp. 485–487.

36. C. Gronbeck, *Character, Celebrity and Sexual Innuendo in Media Scandals*, ed. J. Lull, & S. Hinerman (New York: Columbia University Press, 1997), pp. 21–22.

37. J. Sharkey, "Memories of Wars Never Fought," *New York Times*, June 28, 1998, p. 6; C. Burke, & M. Greppi, "Dunleavy St. Viet Nerve," *New York Post*, July 3, 1998, p. 6.

38. Editorial, "The CNN-Time Retraction," *New York Times*, July 3, 1998, p. A20.

39. L. Cauley, & M. Geylin, "Ex-Green Beret Sues CNN-Time," *New York Times*, August 7, 1988, p. B6.

40. F. Barringer, "Boston Globe Columnist Resigns over Authenticity of 1995 Story," *New York Times*, August 20, 1998, p. A1.

41. Review & Outlook. "Tabloid Criticism," *Wall Street Journal*, June 16, 1998, p. A16.

42. M. Kelly, "The Hole in Brill's Content," *New York Post*, June 17, 1998, p. 31.

43. Editorial, "Don't Call It Journalism." *New York Times*, July 14, 1998, p. A14.

44. D. Rabinnwitz, "Race and Rumor," *Wall Street Journal*, April 29, 1996, p. A20.

45. D. Seligman, "Corrections the Times Missed," *New York Post*, December 9, 1997, p. 27

46. L. Greenhouse, "Race Statistics Alone Do Not Support a Claim of Selective Prosecution, Justices Rule," *New York Times*, May 24, 1996, p. A20.

47. L. Chavez, & R. Lerner, "Is the Justice System Rigged against Blacks?" *Wall Street Journal*, December 4, 1996, p. A19.

48. L.B. Bozell, III, "Team Clinton's News—Media Wing," *New York Post*, August 13, 1996, p. 21; L.B. Bozell, III, "PBS Just Doesn't Get It," *New York Post*, October 28, 1998, p. 23.

49. S. Beatty Goll, "Critics Rail at Racy TV Programs," *Wall Street Journal*, May 28, 1996, p. A26.

50. C. Crossen, *Tainted Truth* (New York: Simon & Schuster, 1994).

51. R. Wildavsky, "Why TV Is so Trashy," *Reader's Digest*, May 1998, p. 50.

52. M. Barker, and J. Petley, eds., *Ill Effects: The Media/Violence Debate* (London: Routledge, 1997), chap. 2.

53. D. Golden, "Media Literacy," *Wall Street Journal*, December 17, 1999, p. B1.

54. V.L. Cheney, "New History Standards Still Attack Our Heritage," *Wall Street Journal*, May 2, 1966, p. A14.

55. C. Stoll, "Invest in Humanware," *New York Times*, May 19, 1996, Op-Ed.

56. J. Kronholz, "Low X-pectations," *Wall Street Journal*, June 16, 1998, p. A1.

57. P. Bedard, "Washington Whispers," *U.S. News & World Report*, June 14, 1999, p. 8.

58. K. Kelly, "A New York Shell Game: Cheating 101," *U.S. News & World Report*, December 20, 1999, p. 57.

59. T. Sowell, "Academic Lies & Self-delusions," *New York Post*, May 25, 1997, p. 19.

60. Review & Outlook. "Schools Discover Consumers," *Wall Street Journal*, December 30, 1997, p. A10.

61. D.R. MacFadden, "Rabbis Listed among Suspects in Laundering of Drug Profit," *New York Times*, June, 7, 1977, p. B1.

62. Newsweek Poll, June 2–3, 1994, *Newsweek*, June 13, 1994, p. 36.

63. N.Y. Times-CBS Poll, *New York Times*, February 24, 1998, p. A1.

64. R.L. Berke, "The Public," *New York, Times*, December 15, 1998, p. A24.

Chapter 2

Society's Pseudomyths and
Their Victims

Man . . . is born to believe.
Benjamin Disraeli, Oxford Diocesan Conference, 1864

IS PEOPLE'S GULLIBILITY SOCIALLY INCULCATED?

Someone may wonder about the amount of fraud, deception, and cheating exposed daily by the press or heard from others, which assumes that there are many dishonest people and outright crooks in our society. But at the same time it also indicates that there are enough gullible people who become their victims. Still it is hard for us to understand how it is possible for a mature person to commit him- or herself to an important financial transaction or social interaction without a thorough verification of the other party's statements and documentation. Do they check, at least, the other party's credentials and credibility? Their acceptance of others' persuasion amounts to a suspension of their own critical judgment. What is even more amazing is the credulity of the masses who quite often are financially defrauded by obvious Ponzi (pyramid investing) schemes or are politically abused by the extravagant social promises of dishonest politicians.

To understand the degree of gullibility of the masses one needs only to recall the great and fascinating mass delusions that occasionally occurred throughout history. As unbelievable as it may sound, according to recorded documents, significant segments of populations, if not whole nations, have been caught up in the feverish pursuit of an absurd, insane idea related either to a religious belief, a social utopia, or an outright scam for getting rich quick. Most people, obsessed with being part of a "great movement" that resolutely pursues that elusive goal, are totally oblivious to the disastrous emotional, financial, or social consequences of their actions. In various social or financial crazes, like the tulipomania or Mississippi scam, they lost their fortunes and incurred other unpleasant consequences.[1] Without attempting to analyze in detail any of these fantastic stories, what seems to be their common denominator is people's obsessive pursuit of enriching themselves to the point of suspending any sound judgment. Collectively they acted irrationally. It is not surprising if some people use poor judgment and act impulsively, blinded by a situation foolishly perceived as a possible source of quick enrichment, but when large segments of a population or entire nations behave in a foolish manner, then we are truly amazed. However, it is not hard to understand people's psychology when it comes to the idea of getting rich fast. Ponzi schemes appeal to man's greed. They are based on its initial handsome payout, which attracts new "suckers" who progressively pay more for the same shares but with fewer chances of recouping their principal. There are many variations in the operation of these Ponzi schemes, but ultimately they all feed on themselves until eventually they get busted due to excessive payouts not covered by the incoming revenue from other sources. Their explosive growth is supported by rumors of extravagant financial gains, new deals, or discoveries of other sources of income that will make all the participants rich beyond their dreams. When the bubble bursts, it is as though people have awakened from a bad dream. They wonder about their inner evil that drove them to act so foolishly. This was exactly what happened recently in Albania, a small, poor state in Europe, where virtually the whole nation got caught up in the fever of getting rich quickly by giving their money to a Ponzi scheme with the result of losing everything. It led to open rebellion, the fall of the government, and social anarchy. The new government started an investigation that confirmed their worst fears, disclosing deceptive practices, corruption, and ultimately massive fraud.[2]

If the foundation of financial scams is based on false promises, illusions, and fraud, the political and religious delusions of the masses are determined by more complex emotional needs. For instance, the religious beliefs and superstitions that are cleverly manipulated and exploited by authorities for their own benefit slowly can become strong delusions for the masses. In some religious quasi-delusions like the Crusades or witch mania of the Middle Ages, hundreds of thousands of people lost their lives. The epidemic of persecutions against alleged witches and worshippers of the devil had ravaged Europe for over three centuries. In the name of the Church, but pursued for political and economic reasons, entire populations like that of Stedinger in Germany or later the Templars in France were wiped out under the false pretext of abjuring the laws of God, insulting the holy sacraments and worshiping the devil. In each Western country inquisitors were appointed to find and burn those witches who confessed (under torture) their crime of working for the devil. Regardless of how preposterous the confessions might have been, the judges and the public gave the impression they believed in them. Under this religious umbrella were political manipulations for power, acts of greed related to the appropriation of someone's else properties and accusations motivated by personal revenge to eliminate enemies. Yet, the judges of the tribunals apparently were carrying out their duty of punishing witches, the infamous tools of Satan, with a deep sense of moral responsibility.

One may justify this persecution as part of the thinking of those times, when people did believe in the power of Satanism and witchcraft. In fact, people who might have questioned the methods of investigation were considered heretics. No one dared question the obvious contradiction between the indisputable supernatural power of witches, as claimed by the inquisitors, and the witches' pitifully human response to torture. In fact, these anthropomorphic or ethereal powers were attributed to them as part of the accusations lodged against them to which they were forced to confess. This leads one to believe that even within this mass hysteria induced by the Inquisition there were strong elements of lying for self-preservation on the part of the prosecutors because of fear of retaliation by the clergy. This might also explain why this mass delusion survived for so long, feeding on itself despite common-sense evidence that questioned its veracity. It is a good example of the power of manipulation of the minds of simple people by the religious authorities in cooperation with their henchmen. The same dynamic of mass psychology has been experienced in various forms of political delusions.

The most recent political myth was manufactured by the Communist ideologists, which proclaimed the hegemony of proletarian dictatorship. The new proletarian leadership was organized for one purpose only: the liquidation of the other classes declared by them as enemies of the state. The reign of terror started in the name of a new social myth: that of a classless society, which was perversely manipulated by the Communist party. The former witch mania was replaced by a well-planned hunt to kill the bourgeoisie. Millions of innocent people were arrested and killed by the same methods of forced confessions, reminding us of the great inquisitors of the Middle Ages. All alleged political enemies admitted under physical and/or psychological torture their participation in antistate conspiracies, as demanded by the investigators. A collective madness slowly gripped all nations controlled by Communists. It was reinforced by the fear that anyone could be convicted on phony charges, if in disfavor of the party. While people had to be vigilant and denounce the political enemies of Communism, they also had to protect themselves from being accused of the same crimes. The history of the Communist party of the former Soviet Union is a vivid example of the political crimes and genocide committed by its leaders under the banners of a new social justice, an elaborate lie, uncritically accepted by the masses because of fear of reprisals or fantasy of creating an egalitarianism.

The same can be said about the Fascist ideologies, which were embraced by significant segments of the populations, accepted without any critical judgment, until it was too late. Ironically, these political delusions of the masses took place in the 20th century, coexisting with the most spectacular advances in scientific knowledge, which were used by these regimes for making war and for the sophisticated mass murder of ideological opponents and scapegoat populations. This fully documents that common people are easily influenced and manipulated by social, political, or religious activists who know to raise their hope for a better life. In this country, although we are fortunate not to have had these extremist political delusions, we have developed our own share of pseudotruths and social myths, basically arising from the philosophy of a nation of immigrants committed to the principles of a free society, fueled by free enterprise. Yet, these cherished pseudomyths, the backbones of our social morality, have found themselves lately under siege as a result of the profound political, economic, and social changes undergone by our society in the last three decades. The new, all-inclusive concept of social egalitarianism, combined with a new attitude toward personal independence, expressed as a liberation from the past constraints of the society, have led to a new ambiguous morality.

THE PSEUDOMYTHS OF OUR SOCIETY

Today ordinary people still believe in a set of social-political pseudomyths, which are used as guiding principles in the organization of their lives until they may become detrimental to their well-being. These half-truths have helped them to develop a view of their surrounding world and also support a mode of relating to society. Some of these beliefs are specific to our democratic-capitalistic society with its inherent social contradictions, while others are part of the popular folklore regarding human interaction. These prevailing illusions are not imposed by any authority in particular; they have gradually emerged and are maintained by society as part of the underlying democratic concepts guiding the social functioning of the people. In a sense they symbolize an idealized view of democracy and human relationships. However, society promotes them as beneficial for the individuals' social integration and helpful in reducing the conflict generated by the cruel realities of human interaction.

The philosophy of any democratic society is to nurture an illusion of unlimited opportunities for all its members, who in order to achieve are promised equal treatment before the law. The ultimate ideal, that of the pursuit of happiness, presupposes living in a society free of any form of prejudice, in which all citizens have equal social rights and opportunities. These ideals stand at the root of the basic concept of democracy. The old myth about kings and of aristocracy's divine rights has been replaced by the half-truths of social equality and fair justice for all people. In fact, some social activists have claimed that the United States from its beginning has been a nation of unequals, hence the assumption that we are a classless society is a myth.[3] It supports John K. Galbraith's argument that "nothing denies the liberties of the individual as a total absence of money."[4] Society does attempt to offer equal opportunities, but, as we will see, under specific terms and conditions, dictated by its shifting political outlook. For instance, the changed political and social climate after World War II led to the inclusion of minorities and women in its concept of equal opportunities. While social equality has always been considered a sacred individual right, only currently has it become more inclusive and legally enforced, though it still falls short, in practice, of an ideal of equality. Despite its shortcomings, equality, particularly in the court of law, is widely touted by the press. Holding to these inculcated beliefs makes people's hard lives more bearable. In the same vein, under fortuitous circumstances, some smart, ordinary people who have learned how to play the social game of climbing the ladder of power do succeed to attain fortune and/or status.

To succeed someone has to master not only the official rules, regulations and laws that govern our lives, but also the set of beliefs and attitudes held by the public that do influence and support people's decisions. The beliefs belong to the vague consensus of community or society about what is desirable or undesirable, what is proper or improper, primarily of what is or is not expected of us. The trouble is that these general social codes of behavior and ethics, specifying concepts of right and wrong, if literally followed could induce more frustrations and disappointments than one may expect. Complying with this alleged popular wisdom is not always advisable. Why should this be so? These beliefs convey general norms of behavior that do not always reflect the current social realities and as such they far from guarantee success or happiness. At best, they may reconcile, in broad strokes, general conflicting needs among people or between them and authorities. Let us examine how they work.

ARE EQUAL OPPORTUNITIES FOR SOCIAL SUCCESS WITHIN ANYONE'S REACH?

One popular belief claims that our society is classless and that opportunities for success are available to anyone so long as the person is actively pursuing a realistic, attainable goal. The idea behind it is the assumption, as previously discussed, that our society is truly egalitarian and achieving success only requires that someone be motivated, tenacious, and goal-directed. In fact, this is the creed of the entrepreneurial man. Even so, not all entrepreneurially oriented men succeed. In fact, people who are not entrepreneurially directed can also succeed in their careers, but in that case, it is due to their distinctive intellectual or physical assets combined with so-cializing dispositions or outstanding artistic and entertaining talents that facilitate their chances for accomplishment. However, within their own working milieu there is enough political infighting in attempting to reach the top of their professions that requires the same manipulative expertise as in the corporate world.

This belief is supported by the overblown assumption that this country offers unlimited opportunities to everyone, which just need to be explored and developed. Comparable to other countries, there is no question that this statement contains a great deal of truth. Yet, there is a catch. Except for real talented people who are highly creative and entrepreneurial like the ones now involved in high technology, others who are ambitious require ei-ther the right political and social background or at least social manipulative abilities to take advantage of the existent opportunities for launching a suc-cessful career. The majority of people are products of the social public school where they graduate with a relative ability to write and read and are vaguely aware of most of these potential breaks in their lives and have lim-ited exposure to grand opportunities. In this context, is an Appalachian child exposed to the same opportunities as a suburban one? His chances of exposure improve if he attends a college or is fortunate enough to find a business or political mentor. Stories of unusual achievements by people who started from scratch and built fabulous fortunes may appear fascinat-ing but they do not have any bearing on the lives of most ordinary citizens, organized around their jobs in a nearby factory or company with the re-mainder of their free time spent between family and friends. The world of social wheeling and dealing where opportunities are created and/or seized may be part of their fantasy.

Outside of these special careers based on prominent talents, the measure of success as celebrated by the media is represented by the corporate execu-tives who from humble beginnings in a company have smartly climbed the pyramid of corporate power, reaching the ultimate social status to which most employees aspire, that of CEO or chairman. Yet, the combinations of personal qualities required for reaching the pinnacle of power are intrigu-ing if not controversial and for sure do not exist in everyone. The young as-piring corporate manager has to have not only the required managerial skills but also an understanding of the social dynamics favoring success in order to achieve the desired status. This presupposes the ability to develop and cultivate particular traits of personality that are extremely helpful for the climber's success but not always considered honest. Can anyone main-tain a cool, detached approach while supporting his superior's views even if they are contrary to one's judgment and possibly detrimental to the corporation? This requires developing special inner skills to convey an outward sense of conformity combined with unwavering respect for the convictions of the boss, regardless of how unsound they may be. The expression of personal convictions and ideas may be a liability for the corporate climber, suggesting strong uncontrollable emotions incompatible with a rational and cool executive. Worse, some of the business ideas advanced by the subordinate might be perceived by the chief as a threat to his own status, unless they are suggested as being generated by himself or shamelessly appropriated by him. The corporate climber has to cultivate an artificial, pleasant disposition combined with a faked interest in his coworkers as part of his strategy for moving up the ladder of success. Certainly the ones who ignore the rules for corporate success will not make it, though they may be hard-working people dedicated to their companies.

If the social opportunities for success depend on so many variables, then hard work, thrift, and perseverance, remnants of the Protestant ethic, may be the main road to success. This belief might have been helpful in the pioneering days when indeed without industry, diligence, and initiative, one's chances for getting somewhere were nil. However, in our modern society these ingredients, while still important, at best simply offer the basis for making a decent living. Today, man, as part of a large and complex social system, has to master intricate and subtle relationships that require careful handling of what has become known as "political correctness" in order to be able to compete against others who may have the same qualifications and can perform the same services. In addition, his success depends, in part, on whether he is perceived by others as possessing those inner qualities, vaguely described as an "easygoing and pleasant personality." This essentially suggests avoiding confrontations and accommodating others, particularly bosses. However, more important is the ability to manipulate others, which, translated in popular language, means an aptitude for hypocrisy, dissimulation, and insincerity in expressing one's true thoughts. These "social qualities" have apparently become even more valuable in competing for jobs after affirmative action became part of social competition.Without any intention of discussing the merit or lack of merit of affirmative action, the fact remains that it has twisted the meaning of the previously held norms about the value of the work ethic.

The rules of the social competition have been, to a large extent, turned upside down. The factors of race and gender as part of job competition have changed the past concept of merit based on desirable qualifications for promotions. While theoretically the presumption is that the job credentials of the candidate selected on the basis of preferential treatment are in line with the specifications of the position, most often the reality is different; the candidate's qualifications can be mediocre. This seems to have created new problems for society. Judge Jerry E. Smith, of the Fifth Circuit of Appeals, in a decision about *Hopewood v. State of Texas*, attempted to sum up the issue of affirmative action in higher education in these terms: "The use of race in admissions for diversity in higher education contradicts, rather than furthers, the aims of equal protection. Diversity fosters, rather than minimizes, the use of race. It treats minorities as a group, rather than individuals. It may further remedial purposes but, just as likely, may promote improper racial stereotypes, thus fueling racial hostility."[5] Besides, many people have become unsure whether this preferential treatment redresses past injustices toward minorities or stigmatizes them. In other areas, reports indicate that the lowering of standards for admission and training based on gender in law enforcement agencies and other public and private sectors has already created resentment in the ranks and led from time to time to legal actions against them. Critics have objected that this new approach is totally incongruous with our capitalist system of free enterprise, built on free competition, freedom of opportunity and a free labor market.[6] It seems that under these ambiguous ethics of social competition more people have started to embellish their credentials or use political power to improve their chances for work. It is an expedient way of securing a job and getting an edge over the others. A survey of 9,000 high school and college students by the Institute of Ethics indicated that one-third of them would lie on their resumé to get a job. Furthermore, 39 percent of college students admitted to having lied to their bosses, and 35 percent to a customer within the past year.[7] Regardless of the good intentions of affirmative action, its work ethics are often conveniently leading to subjectivism and political opportunism.

At the same time, it is true that for a long time the ethical guidelines for success have been gradually eroding by companies' request for applicants to possess certain traits of personality, namely, an ability to influence and handle people smoothly (which certainly represents a departure from the traditional work ethic). Corporations, while taking into consideration the basic criteria of job qualifications, used to emphasize the ultimate importance of developing personality skills to handle people if one wanted to get ahead. Certain traits of personality became such an important factor in hiring that most of the big companies gave psychological tests to job candidates in order to find out whether their personality profile fits in with their expectations. In order to succeed in passing the tests, applicants consulted psychologists to learn how to give the right answers to questions about personality. In fact, the issue became so open that a book debating among other aspects related to the corporate philosophy in hiring employees offered an appendix describing how aspirants for employment should answer the psychological tests to succeed in being hired.[8] This was an invitation to outright lying! Now, with the advent of high information technology, employees, at least in some business sectors, need to possess other, more desirable qualities, such as resourcefulness, creativity, and critical judgment. Ultimately, anyone who competes on the job market may be confused by its two operational tiers: one still adhering to the old methods of securing a job or a promotion by fine-tuning one's credentials and attempting to manipulate the interview with the company's interviewer and another one of pushing one's "birthright power" for getting preferential treatment and moving ahead of others.

Beyond this controversy, most people still feel that in order to advance themselves, they have to convey to superiors the "right personality," which tacitly presupposes a hypocritical, calculated, and tactful behavior for climbing the corporate ladder of success. Any deviation from or denial of these rules of success could put one's promising career on hold, regardless of hard work, diligence, and perseverance. There is no consolation for people who believe that only hard work could lead to success to know that business studies suggest that approximately 15 percent of top executives misstate their educational background and one-third lie in their resumés.[9] However, there is a category of people, besides the dishonest top executives, who know how to take advantage of the unlimited opportunities for social manipulation and meet all the criteria for reaching success without working too hard. These are the politicians.

People going into politics are most often disinterested in their basic careers or are independently wealthy, but either way they have great egos and ambitions. Outrightly or not they advertise themselves as saviors of society claiming to have a great vision for remaking the community into a better place to live and to bring about changes because of their alleged power to motivate people. They remind us of the powerful priest of primitive tribes who controlled the destiny of their people based on the beliefs held about their magical power and of their dire prophesies of harsh punishment in case of disobedience. While politicians would like to play the same role, the crucial difference is that in democracies, they are elected and discarded if their "vision" turns out to be a prescription for disaster.

Certainly politicians would like to think of themselves as dedicated servants for the public good and expect to be believed by citizens. Above all, they would like people to think of them as leaders who in a spirit of self-sacrifice offer their valuable talents and wisdom for shaping a better destiny for their fellow men and society. This implicitly assumes an unspoken superiority over others, which ultimately is granted by the power entrusted to them by the public. And here begins the politician's game of selling himself to the public as the best available man for the job. Smartly packaged by public relations and advertising "gurus," he hides his opportunistic schemes under a sophisticated mixture of half-truths, equivocations, and hyperbolic promises. The main goal of a politician is to clearly convey genuine interest and concern about people's needs. He has to be articulate regarding his social and economic programs, which should be delivered with self-assurance and a sense of profound expertise. Sometimes his speeches give him away and he makes embarrassing statements that make him appear foolish, like that of a senator from Connecticut who once stated: "We have got a strong candidate. I am trying to think of his name" or of another senator from Massachusetts who said "[I favor] access to discrimination on the basis of sexual orientation."[10] Instances like the ones mentioned are many, one more ridiculous than the other. Repeated thoughtless statements may affect a candidate's political career, particularly when exploited by the press, as happened to former Vice President Dan Quayle, famous for his grammatical slip. The politician in his interaction with voters has to convey an air of restraint and humility in his demeanor. Above all he must exude an air of sincerity, integrity, and honesty. He has to gain the trust of people, and at the same time offer more convincing solutions to existing problems than his opponents. Mastering all these social and psychological variables requires, indeed, special social skills, which if not innate, have to be developed slowly throughout the person's political career. The closer he moves to the pinnacle of power, the more he dispenses with any true commitment to any set of beliefs. Truth becomes expendable for the sake of political expediency. Explanations, if offered, are at best obfuscation and equivocation of previous positions. The challenge to political demagoguery is raised only by another politician who seizes the opportunity for launching himself with higher and more outlandish promises. The public, happy to get rid of the old liar, embraces the new politician, who may be another opportunist, or worse a demagogue.

One may argue that some politicians are honest and truly attempt to meet the needs of their constituents. While this may be true in some cases, the fact remains that even then, due to various outside political forces, they may not accomplish their goals and those forces may push them either to dilute their aims and stances or to quit in disgust sooner or later. Successful politicians ultimately want to be national leaders, to direct the affairs of their nations for self-aggrandizement and power. To achieve this, they must not only eliminate their competitors but also convince voters of their indisputable quality for leadership. They succeed because the common citizens believe in the myth that the leaders are protecting their interests. The leader's power depends to a great extent on this popular belief.

DO LEADERS HAVE THE PUBLIC INTEREST AT HEART?

This belief has its origin in tribal times, when indeed the elders, due to their long life experiences, naturally were the wisest counselors for tribal affairs. Their close ties to the community made them not only knowledgeable of the people's problems but also more objective about finding solutions. They knew that any arbitrary or egotistic decision could boomerang and seriously affect them in their tribal existence.

In antiquity, common folks have created their heroes, who allegedly performed great tasks of courage and endurance beyond the ability of ordinary men, feats that have normally aroused the popular imagination. People wanted to believe in their almost supernatural skills to solve problems because they represented their only link to power, their only illusion of changing the tragic reality of their hard existence. With the development of modern societies, members of the ruling class thought of themselves as being invested by God with the right to govern, which automatically made them better than others, though not necessarily wiser.

In the present democracies, the leaders are supposed to be elected more on the basis of their merits and ability to solve social and economic problems at their level of office candidacy reflecting their competency, rather than their birthrights. Furthermore, until recently politicians advanced their political careers after proving themselves to be successful at a lower level of office tenure and gradually working their way up the ladder to a higher office according to their ability and skills. In these ways they were tested for their talents to govern. However, lately the secret for political success can be reduced to the politician's ability to raise the necessary money for campaigns and to convince voters of his alleged qualifications by flooding them with a maximum of media exposure. But here is the catch. Acquiring sufficient funds for heavy campaigning means the politician has to be either rich or financed by vested interest groups who after elections may dictate their policies to the candidate. That means that in order to gain public confidence, on the one hand he has to identify with the needs of his constituents and rely on the program of the party he represents, but on the other he has to buy votes by promising favorable political concessions for specific classes of citizens outside the party's platform. Either way, he knows that, if elected, he will not be able to meet the promises made to conflicting needs of different constituents. But he also knows that by lying and equivocating, he can pursue his career. While aware of the sham, he tenaciously tries to convince the public of his honesty and integrity. However, without the underlying support of the popular belief endowing leaders with superior qualities of governing, they would have a hard time selling their deceptive promises and programs to the public. Influenced by their own herd psychology, the public would like to have faith in the truthfulness of leaders even when evidence points in the opposite direction. It is somewhat inconceivable for the public to consider that respectable, intelligent people, with relatively secure financial positions, can look straight in the people's eyes and lie, mislead, or defraud them. They just refuse to understand the opportunistic psychology of leaders. People have difficulty seeing the leaders' true hidden ambitions through their facade of faked concern for the welfare of the citizens and dedication to the administration of the public property. If one removes their pretense of social dedication, he will be confronted with a mixed picture of hypocrisy, cynicism, greed, demagoguery, self-delusions of grandiosity, and most often a disregard for the commoners.

Are all leaders that bad? From time to time, there may emerge an outstanding leader who truly has the qualities for guiding a nation out of a crisis, war, or social chaos, but most leaders, particularly in peace time, are just clever people with an excessive sense of self-importance. Ambitious and obsessed with power, they will do anything to get it. Distorting, cheating, and lying are the easiest means to convince the public, since their own calculated aggrandizement fulfills the secret need of the masses to create heroes. Some leaders succeed to become the instant heroes of the masses, embodying the unfulfilled dreams of the common people. These "men of destiny" have been elected by them and talk to them. People are ready to overlook improprieties of behavior and emotional flaws, as long as the leaders seem ready to lend a sympathetic ear to their complaints.

ARE PEOPLE BASICALLY GOOD AND SOCIETY CORRUPTS THEM?

All these distortions, deceptions, and lies would not be possible if it were not for another basic social myth heavily supported today by either naive social idealists or opportunistic social activists who want to persuade us that man is born good but society corrupts him. The underlying assumption is obvious; if we just change the inequalities and injustices of society, which happen to have been accumulated over centuries, man will go back to his natural state of goodness and happiness. In fact, this is part of the old romantic philosophical current whose main exponent was Jean J. Rousseau, a French philosopher of the 18th century. This concept, an antithesis to the religious dogma of man's original sin, is still debated. It has raised interesting social questions and continues to be debated.[11]

The most controversial issue sparked by him is that the natural law (on which the American law is based), regarded as the basis of human equal rights, was not supported by true knowledge about the natural state of man, which in fact is unknown. This argument may lead one to contend that since we do not know the true voice of nature, all natural inequalities like intelligence, health, physical power or skills, or sexual differences may have led to social inequalities, and are thereby part of the natural law. To go one step further, they have gradually become accepted by societies as norms for their social organization. This may explain why, in the course of our history, social inequality has been the norm for societal organization and not a haphazard event. Yet Rousseau, ignoring this contradiction, strongly condemned the social inequalities of rights conferred by societies to the upper class, and advocated the replacement of inequalities of classes with a morality built on ascetic virtues. His morality favors the "natural feelings," based on the alleged natural state of equality that should help man behave morally. The fact remains that the natural state of equality of men "wherein all the power and jurisdiction is reciprocal" is a hypothetical state, envisioned as a reaction to the hereditary power of the aristocracy, strongly promoted by John Locke, the English liberal philosopher of the 17th century.[12] The argument, elaborated by philosophers of those times, reflected the alleged knowledge about the natural history of man before Charles Darwin. Darwin gave us quite a different vision of human beings competing for survival, which is far from promoting any natural equality. Yet, society tries to promote the old myth of the goodness of man, since it fits people's need for faith in a better world, a world less inimical and more gentle. The reality is that people who conduct their lives guided by this social myth are the ones often taken advantage of by others.

An example chosen from numerous similar cases may show the number of problems related to liberal and unwise assumption of human goodness. Carol, a career woman in her late fifties, lived alone in a large apartment in a city and had a niece who occasionally visited her. Joan, the niece, lived in an adjoining community but worked in a clerical job in the city. Any time Joan visited Carol, she complained of the long trips from home to work or to come see her aunt. Certainly, Joan would have liked to live in the city but she did not have the money. Carol, who was financially helping Joan, suggested to her that whenever she had to stay late in town or visit Carol she could sleep over in another bedroom. Joan started to take advantage of the offer to the point of leaving more and more of her clothes and personal belongings in the aunt's apartment. Carol did not feel truly disturbed by her niece frequently staying over, except that she was concerned about her coming home late at night. She let her niece know about it, particularly since she felt responsible for her safety. The niece reassured the aunt about her style of life as being appropriate for her generation. The conflict erupted after one weekend when she came late at night with a girlfriend to sleep over. Carol became upset and forbade her niece to bring in overnight visitors and informed her that she would lock the door at 1:00 A.M. However, Joan came in at her usual early morning hours and found the front door locked. After ringing the bell and knocking on the door, she called the police under the claim that something might have happened to her aunt. Carol was forced to open the door, but she attempted to deny entry into the apartment to Joan. In front of the policeman, Joan claimed that this was her residence by arrangement and her girlfriend had been a witness to this. The police advised her to let Joan in. Carol was forced to hire a lawyer and go to court to obtain an order for her niece's eviction. Finding a solution to the whole dispute, since Joan refused to leave, took Carol over nine months.

Carol was one among many who found out at her own expense that most people ruthlessly follow their interests with total disregard for the feelings or rights of others, so long as they can avoid any legal sanctions. Socially, what really counts is the understanding that people are self-centered and potentially devious in their interaction with others. In fact, this is in line with Calvin's theological position, which perceives man as wicked and weak to temptation. Realizing this fact, the Bible recommends that "thou shalt love thy neighbor as thyself," but in the real world people are rarely able to follow this behest. As Mark Twain once quipped, "There are 869 different forms of lying, but only one of them has been squarely forbidden. Thou shalt not bear false witness against thy neighbor."[13] On the contrary, people are more ready to deny others' rights when conflicting with their own. However, people can be good when either their needs are not at stake or when they believe that their good deeds are directly or indirectly benefitting them. In other words, altruism quite often is a form of egotism. Certainly, this sweeping statement sounds somewhat cynical; nevertheless, in the final analysis, human actions are motivated by personal needs, whether or not they are coated with a veneer of pleasantry or generosity. That means any indiscriminate acceptance of the alleged innate goodness of people may show naïveté and expose someone to deception. Even assuming that people are good, this does not mean that they are good all the time, particularly when they may perceive their interests as antagonized.

As previously mentioned, this concept that society corrupts the individual has lately been the basis for social programs created by the criminal justice system to rehabilitate criminals. However, they failed. The failure of this approach has been measured by the excessive number of crimes committed by criminals on probation.[14] This concept that society corrupts people is only partially true, since the social competition for survival requires the individual to use whatever means are available to him, as long as he does not act against himself. Then, it is hard to say whether society corrupts the individual, or conversely, people's conflict with the demands of society creates the basis for their corruption. In other words, it is within human nature to corrupt social relationships. However, can the much praised love make a difference in the unpredictability of human relationships? Some people want us to believe that love governs human relationships. Then certainly wickedness, maliciousness, and sinfulness are aberrations of human behavior. The popular belief, highly promoted by society, is that love is at the root of human interaction.

DOES LOVE GOVERN HUMAN RELATIONSHIPS?

To start with, the word "love" is indiscriminately used by people in many unrelated contexts, which confuses the issue. Indeed, there are many forms of love and all of them play an undeniably different role in people's lives. Let us start with the general popular belief that love for others is at the base of human interaction. If it is viewed in its most extensive sense as an undefined feeling of likeness and support experienced by people participating in or defending a common cause or confronting a common distress, then this assumption is correct. In this case, it is part of the socially known bond of solidarity combined with a feeling of empathy. This form of social solidarity represents an extension of primitive feelings of belonging to a group, in a sense of a fusion of one's interest with the interest of the group, community, society or nation. The individual's need for belonging is an expression of his old, inborn insecurity related to survival in a hostile environment. However, is it an expression of love, as the popular notion would have us like to think? Would we call the herd bond, very common among animals, love?

When a Thomson's gazelle, grazing with its herd, suddenly risks its life by "stotting" (leaping on its four stiff limbs in order to warn the others about the intrusion of a large predator), is it out of love for the others? By doing so it attracts the attention of the predator, thereby placing itself in danger, in an attempt to save the herd. Translated in human terms, this would be considered an act of self-sacrifice or heroism, with the underlying connotation of an act of love for fellow man. The explanation for the behavior of Thomson's gazelle is found in the social group character, a set of right responses transmitted from parents to offspring for group survival, as described by Scottish ethologist V.C. Wynne-Edwards.[15] The next question is, why do all other gazelles in the herd not react in the same manner in the face of danger? This is apparently due to a natural selection within the group that endowed some animals with higher physical qualities after they repeatedly responded better to the predator's danger, enabling them to develop a kind of "alarm reaction." The assumption behind this hypothesis is that some animals, while daringly exposing themselves to the danger of predators for the benefit of others, were able to survive long enough in order to leave enough offspring who inherited these qualities and transmitted them to the next generations, thus perpetuating this behavior. While a similar behavioral development cannot truly be extrapolated to humans, examples of human help and support of others within the same community or society are found from time to time, and are apparently based on a triggering of this herd instinct. Acts of heroism and sacrifice of oneself for a "buddy" are also encountered during wars. Are these acts of love, as some people would like us to believe? Not necessarily so. The motivation for most human actions is biologically triggered but more complexly expressed than can be reduced to simple animal reflexes. In the case of "buddy response," people act on the strength of the primitive male bond (a variation of herd bond) to which is added the human element of likeness and friendship, which selectively leads to a sense of mutual support, notably in a situation of war.

On a social level, the collective thinking of society greatly influences the behavior of individuals, attempting to teach them its own moral values for the good of the community. In this context, society for its own collective protection would like to inspire and promote among its members this spirit of brotherhood fostering mutual support, care, concern, and respect for each other. It is, at best, an empathy that goes beyond a particular person and embraces the whole community and society. In a sense this brotherly love is a loose social translation of the Biblical commandment "Love thy neighbor as thyself." Brotherly love has also been espoused by utopians. The modern utopians believe more than ever in the oneness of mankind and envision a universal society that discards the differences between people and emphasizes the core of the human being as consisting of the same basic needs and desires. They think that in this way, they have found the common denominator symbolizing the ideal spirit of brotherhood. After all, are we not reacting in the same manner to joy or pain? Are we not all facing death with the same anxieties? Therefore, since all of us are part of the same human condition, it is only logical to assist and help our "brothers" in need. How beneficial is this kind of love when it is expressed without any reservation or selectivity?

There are two problems with this promoted social belief: one is exacerbated by our current multiracial, multicultural society, which has opened wide areas of conflict between races and has ignored any spirit of brotherhood in favor of pursuing their vested interest. Inadvertently, the government reinforced the racial strife by promoting the concept of "political correctness," which also supports the new moral ambiguity. Second, like in any society, not all our "brothers and sisters" are carrying their social weight by showing a sense of social responsibility or respect for the right of others. Furthermore, many of them are cheating and scheming, taking advantage of the very trust and love entrusted to them by others.

At best, this alleged brotherly love is mainly expressed in critical conditions of a perceived threat to one's survival. The indiscriminate view of the ambiguous term "love for others," extolled by religious zealots, social utopians, or demagogues, has done a lot of harm to naive people who accepted it without reservation. It has been a constant source of abuse, deception, and extortion. In an all-embracing statement, brotherly love may be viewed as an optimistic emotional outlook on human relationships. Let us examine for a moment the relationship between the act of helping someone and brotherly love. In our society, excluding outright charity, one person may help another under specific conditions decided by the benefactor. Practically, out of compassion, someone may offer to help a stranger in distress. But helping the poor and needy is not the same as love. If one makes a donation to a charitable organization like the Salvation Army, does that mean he "loves" chronic alcoholics or other social destitutes? At best, it is an act of compassion for the unfortunate, at worst a social obligation for which one may get a tax deduction.

While a nonprofit or religious organization may try to justify their activities on the basis of brotherly love, that does not stop them from either pursuing their sectarian goals or worse by using it for self-enrichment. The most flagrant acts of corruption have been conceived by those organizations that took donations from individuals and corporations for allegedly helping the poor and needy, but instead used great chunks of this money for themselves, as was done by the United Way, or, more recently, Bennett's Foundation, The New Era Philanthropy,[16] or other religious organizations. So much for the myth of brotherly love.

But what about the most extolled and promoted type of love, that between the sexes? Romantic love is thought to be a spontaneous, strong emotional state that takes over a person in an irresistible urge for closeness and sexual gratification. Love between the sexes is advanced as a panacea for all the problems that may be experienced in intimate relationships. The first false assumption is that the inherent conflict between the sexes related to their different social needs, spanning over millennia and still lingering, can be replaced by a true partnership between lovers. The second false supposition is the acceptance by partners of the alleged sameness between the sexes, which purportedly will wipe out any dispute between them. With the conflict between the sexes present on all levels of their interaction, how can it be solved at the intimate level? By love? Let us separate facts from fiction.

CAN LOVE WORK OUT THE CONFLICT BETWEEN THE SEXES?

The relationship between men and women has been truly paradoxical. While biologically they are attracted to each other, basically triggered by reproduction, socially their interaction has always been overshadowed by the differences in their needs. This has led to varying degrees of friction. This discord is either smoldering or open, depending on the prevailing social ideology governing human relationships at the moment. The more liberal the society, the more open the conflict. In a liberal society, all individuals are permitted to express their needs, assert their individuality, and act accordingly. The women's liberation ideology ignited the preexistent but latent conflict by emotionally and economically freeing women from previous moral or social constraints. Most women wanted to be free to compete socially and economically with men. But to legitimize their demands they were supposed to minimize the existing differences in personality needs and orientation between the sexes and emphasize their similarities. To justify the new social position of women, the old psychological differences between the sexes have been reinterpreted in which important differences like forms of expression of aggression, of other emotions, or of logical abstraction, and so on, were attributed to the socialization process or framed within the new perspective that the sexes are basically the same.[17] Obviously, their differences did not disappear, though they have been inconsequential for women's access to social power. Ironically, equal sharing of social opportunities for jobs would have happened anyway, regardless of the differences between the sexes, due to new technologies that blurred the previous jobs' distinctions of the sexes' social capabilities. The same technology that made the housewife's duties obsolete has opened up vast areas of employment for women.

The real problem is that the new social role of women has created confusion and conflict in their social and marital interactions. In this conflict, men and women have sent ambivalent or contradictory messages to each other about their wants and desirable roles, which has increased the tension between them. The expectations of each other have become unrealistic and dissenting. Socially, modern women put down the old macho type of man while simultaneously ridiculing men who are oversolicitous, emotionally dependent, and sexually nonassertive. In personal relationships, they want men to cater more to their emotional needs, to be more communicative, to create a deeper sense of intimacy. Yet, any display of emotions related to personal problems may be interpreted as a sign of weakness. However, any control of his emotions is considered defensive and any holding back of those feelings that reinforce the romantic image of the relationship is suggestive of detachment. Most women like to depend on men who seem strong, independent, and successful. They want their man to be ambitious and a good provider, while at the same time his job should not intrude in the time he spent with her. They want the best of all possible worlds. Of course such unrealistic expectations lead to personal conflicts.

Many men are also confused about their expected social role. Their masculine image of strength, efficiency, and drive to achieve has been attacked by "enlightened" women as a cover for an egotistical drive for power and control leading to the exploitation and oppression of the other sex. Hence, men felt pressed to reevaluate themselves. They have welcomed women's sharing the economic power since it reduced their burden of providing. However, many of them have felt somewhat uncomfortable about dealing with women's independence and demands within marital interaction, which drastically confused their roles. Here begins the difficulty in attempting to harmonize their different needs. Although most men may have sought to accommodate women's emotional needs for closer interaction and help them with household obligations, their ability to oblige them depends on the requirements of their career ambitions. At the same time, they have remained cautious and mistrustful of any excessive personal sharing. Most men tend to see women as assertive if not aggressive, critical, demanding, and socially competitive. Quite a few men are afraid that admissions of personal weakness or sharing of business "secrets" with their wives or lovers could be used against them later on, either at the termination of the relationship or, if married, in the divorce proceedings. As a result, most intimate relationships between sexes have become often superficial, guarded, and sexually oriented.

Yet, love between the sexes is steadily publicized as a cure-all for the problems between them. The more acerbic and bitter the social and marital interaction between the sexes, the more love is praised as the ultimate solution to couples' unstable, conflicted relationships.

Paradoxically, romantic love has lately tried to regain its past mystical and exulted position. After decades of battering attacks from radical feminists, it has attempted to recover its former luster with its mysterious binding power and state of rapture. The politicization of romantic love by radical feminists has started to lose its meaning. Their denunciation of the feminine mystique and demonization of men while ridiculing the meaning of love by emphasizing love's failure to dispel the alleged smoldering conflict of power between the sexes have become hollow messages. Against their preaching that love, particularly married love, represents another form of domination of women by men, which makes women automatically vulnerable, helpless and highly dependent on the wishes of their lover, most women want to be loved by men, to get married, and raise children. Certainly, they enjoy their new found social equality, economic independence, and the idea of sharing household obligations in marriage.

In fact, in marital interaction, both working partners face the same problem of balancing closeness and intimacy on the one hand with maintaining their separate identities and independent thinking on the other. It is a delicate balance to preserve when job demands clash with marital obligations almost every day in spouses' lives. Both pretend to understand and accept each other when in reality they may gradually become mutually frustrated and disappointed in each other. After a while, they reluctantly come to the realization that their needs do not quite coincide. By then, the marriage has changed into an arena of confrontations, with each of the partners attempting to win the outcome and impose his/her priorities on the other. In the process of bickering, their sexual activity has lost its novelty, passion, and binding power; it has become routine, a physical necessity or a marital obligation. The relationship tends to become unstable. If the couple has children, their problems are even more acute and complex. The wife feels overworked by her dual role, pursuit of career and care of the children, while the husband believes himself to be caught between the demands of developing his career and endless home chores. For most people the ideal marital partnership is very hard to establish, since real equality presupposes a perfect symmetry of needs. Otherwise, both partners must make too many compromises and some are too egotistic to do so. Let us take the case of Karen, a 38-year-old woman and college graduate who before marriage was successfully employed by an investment firm. Seven years ago she fell in love with Scott, a mid-level manager, and married him. They had two children. After the birth of the first child, she chose to work part-time in order to take care of her baby. Her decision affected somewhat unfavorably her standing at work, but with the birth of the second child, she gave up her job altogether. As a housewife she gradually experienced the pressures of housework duties, care of the children, financial restrictions due to a reduction in income, and higher financial dependency on her husband. For a while she accepted her role. However, Karen progressively felt over-burdened by a variety of social obligations and family responsibilities. She found her life as a housewife unrewarding and boring. But by now the children were able to attend nursery school and she was ready to go back to work. She found a job in her previous line of work and started immersing herself in the job as she had when she was single. But things were different now because of the children, who required her attention after working hours. Her problems were aggravated whenever a child got sick or the babysitter did not show up. Her husband, though sympathetic to her concerns, was of little help with the children. He viewed his obligations as paying the household expenses and playing with the children whenever he was available. She felt that Scott was pursuing his career and neglecting his family life. Arguments erupted quite often, with mutual accusations of egotism and neglect of the other. Both were upset with each other and gradually they began to withdraw from the relationship, becoming more detached and less communicative. Their sex life started to falter to the point of occasional encounters. Both ended up frustrated and resentful, wondering what had become of their marriage. For the sake of the children and to avoid the obvious outcome of divorce, they decided to get counseling. However, after one year of therapy both felt that their problems were beyond negotiating their domestic responsibilities or frequency of sexual interactions. Her discontent revolved around her lost sense of independence and identity by feeling relegated to the status of a "second-class citizen" due to her dual role of a mother and part-time housewife. She wanted to regain her lost sense of independence. Meanwhile, he was fighting to meet the demands of work, be competitive in his career, and be a successful provider. Their arguments about an elusive equal responsibility in the children's care were exacerbating their conflict.

Unable to find a satisfactory solution to their marital problems they considered legally separating and reviewing their position after one year. Deep down both of them believed their personalities were too strong, independent, and self-sufficient to accept the sacrifices and compromises that their marriage required. They might have functioned in a marriage either without children or with enough household help to free both of them from any domestic duties. Ultimately, it seemed that whatever love had brought them together dissipated to the point of dissolving their marriage.

The nascent belief of the free exchange of marital roles is unsupported by the reality of women's main responsibility in raising children. The fact remains that there is not an adequate system of care for children when mothers are at their jobs. Society is not fully emotionally and socially prepared for this task. The alternative of hiring a nanny who can meet the role of surrogate mother is not only an expensive solution, but hardly satisfactory for the many mothers who are uneasy about leaving their children improperly attended. Certainly the children will survive, but the process of their emotional growth and socialization may suffer. The reality is that the government and its agencies have failed to meet their obligations toward working women after encouraging them to seek full employment. They have not provided either adequate care facilities for each age group of children or financial compensation for similar private arrangements for working mothers. Now, they try unsuccessfully to contain the damage.

All in all, women found that while their new social role liberated them by giving them their long-sought freedom, at the same time it also complicated their personal lives, bringing about an uneasy marital stability and an alarming increase in the divorce rate, which in turn created emotional and social problems for their children. Against this confusing social background, social intercourse between men and women has become distrustful and volatile.

Some, afraid to commit to marriage, are looking for transient solutions to satisfy their need for sex and intimacy. They try to postpone marriage by substituting it with serial affairs, while others settle for long periods of cohabitations. These arrangements can be terminated on short notice or without warning; a switch of feelings, a change of mind, a promise for more fun, or a hope for a better life could terminate a love story or marriage which to outsiders might have appeared indestructible. In this context, romantic love has become gradually interchangeable with erotic love, which has dramatically affected long-term relationships between the sexes. It is all part of adapting to the new social paradigm.

Passionate, erotic love searches for temporary intimacy expressed by a fleeting fusion of feelings and bodies. But, due to the highly emotional nature of the interaction, the lovers pay little attention to each others' true personality and as such try to avoid possible conflicts owing to their dissimilar needs and interests. Yet, some people maintain that even this type of love can overcome conflicts triggered by the potential different orientations of their personalities. Passionate love, with its mixture of bliss and agony, has become the much sought-after emotional state by most people otherwise bored with themselves, who hope that this strong emotional-sexual stimulant will give a boost to their lives. Most often these passionate affairs are short-lived. They melt when at least one of the lovers loses interest after getting to know the partner and starts to clash in the pursuit of satisfying other needs. The tribulations and the grind of daily living dissipate the passion and estrange the lovers, if not slowly turning them to resentment or hate. Emotionally divorced, each party, afraid of loneliness, looks for a new experience of falling in love and the cycle continues until they get wiser and become more realistic in their expectations. If they get married impulsively, they have just prolonged the agony until a salutary divorce sets them apart.

Most marriages based on lustful love suffer because of the partners' inability to switch from pure physical attraction, which is an expression of sexual desire for possession, to mature love, which is based on total acceptance of the other person. Erotic love, when it is taken for romantic love, has disastrous consequences on the marriage. Leaving aside the incompatibility of the personalities of the partners, which lead to disruptive marital arguments, their eventual divorce is often traumatic for the children. However, to justify to themselves and others that their divorce is not bad for the children, parents have tried to accept the gratuitous reassuring statements made by social activists and pseudoscientists about its beneficial effects on children.

AN EMERGING PSEUDOMYTH

Another myth is taking shape right before our eyes: that children "will do all right" after divorce as long as both parents shower them love and affection. The modern position toward marriage attempts to present its termination in divorce as a casual unworkable contract with no effect on the children if the hypothetical clause of love is met. Undoubtedly, in situations of persistent marital violence, chronic alcoholism, antisocial behavior on the part of one spouse, or totally incompatible personalities, the children are better off without the disruptive parent. But the new myth does not refer to such dramatic marital situations, which are mostly handled by court and social agencies. Many marriages are dissolved when one partner gets sexually bored or falls out of love. When the marriage collapses, the children may become a true casualty. Their lives may be emotionally disrupted, often ending up as pawns in the battle between parents who usually resent, if not hate, each other. There are a few scenarios, consciously or subconsciously played out by the divorced parents, detrimental to their children. All of them contain various degrees of self-deceit. One frequent approach, a result of the rivalry between the spouses, is based on an attempt to overbid each other in the expression of love to their children with the outcome of spoiling them. Since neither parent wants to be thought of as authoritarian and punitive, they consciously overlook the misbehavior of their children. Then, the children grow up with a faulty sense of discipline and tolerance to frustration, which in turn, as young adults, makes them poorly adapted socially. In the second scenario, the children grow up attempting to accommodate the mother's boyfriend(s) or a disinterested live-in stepfather, situations that may adversely affect their emotional development. The worst case is when they live at home without any regular adult supervision, due to a working mother who is either overtaxed by job obligations or unable to discipline them. In many cases the children's socialization is then left up to their peers and to a lawless street culture, which may result in their becoming social delinquents. Undoubtedly, there are other complex social factors contributing to this state of affairs. But, one fact is sure: love alone does not solve these children's problems.

In reality, in the new social conditions, even when both working parents stay together, the lack of supervision of the children may have the same disastrous effects, since society has not yet created the necessary social programs for the supervision of children during parents' working hours. Even when available, most of these programs are inadequate for the needs of the children. The idea that children become better adjusted socially by spending more time with their peers than their parents is far-fetched.

But, if modern love between the sexes does not seem to succeed in overcoming their dissension, at least there is a consolation in the popular belief that social conflicts between citizens can be peacefully resolved.

CAN THE CONFLICTS BETWEEN PEOPLE BE SOLVED PEACEFULLY BY RATIONAL NEGOTIATIONS?

This new pseudoscientific belief, supported and spread by well-meaning social activists, is that people can and will find peaceful solutions to their various financial, economic, or social disputes by just using common sense and having a willingness to compromise. After all, they argue, we are civilized people who can control our emotions, think logically, and find fair solutions to any issue. This sounds right, if we ignore the fact that we have serious difficulty in controlling our emotions, routinely surging during the process of carrying out our egotistical needs. Furthermore, the same emotions are responsible for distorting our judgment by making our conclusions subjective and mostly self-serving. In fact, most people use logic to rationalize their behavior and actions, which are strongly influenced by emotional needs. It is common knowledge that emotions play a significant role in the decision-making process. On the one hand, they motivate people's social achievements, while on the other, they are the main cause of personal dissatisfaction or frustration. Although it is expected and desired of the civilized, modern man to be ruled by reason, in reality, most people have difficulty always being cool and rational in their decision-making process.

However, the very concept of the rational man was advanced by rationalist thinkers like the English philosopher John Locke of the 17th century and François Voltaire, together with other French encyclopedists, of the 18th century.[18] They considered emotions to be signs of weakness that required rational control. Until relatively recently, psychologists obliquely supported this concept by describing emotions as specific states of feelings that disorganize behavior, visceral functioning, and conscious experience. But this has been a circular definition of emotions, adding to the confusion surrounding them. Psychoanalytic theory related emotions to instincts, hence placing their activity beyond any awareness or reason. This meant that emotions working on an unconscious level could dictate one's behavior without any conscious knowledge on the person's part. This approach switched the pendulum for the explanation of the role of emotions in human behavior to the realm of the irrational. Conversely, the modern cognitive school of thought reemphasizes our rational ability to control negative emotions, depending on one's perception of the event and ability to cope with it.[19]

The fact is that there are experiences and behaviors associated with neurophysiological reactions concomitantly triggering judgmental evaluations of facts or events, which are consciously identified as emotional reactions. Either way, emotions spring from the person's positive or negative appraisal of a situation, depending on his previous experience or lack of it in negotiating that event. Since the evaluation of the event is highly subjective, any attempt for an objective appraisal is almost hopeless. It depends on too many personal variables, from the degree of intelligence to correctly grasp the facts to the built-in biases related to one's view of the world, all of which color one's judgment and response to a situation. While on one level primitive emotions (fear, anger, bond-love) play an adaptive role for the individual (inducing responses of fight or flight), on the other they may become quite disruptive or unproductive in social interaction.

In general, negative emotions are triggered by situations perceived by an individual as threatening to his physical or social security or denigrating to his sense of self. His negative reaction will be provoked not so much by a realistic appraisal of the situation but more likely by the specific needs of his personality. Confronted by upsetting emotions, he will try to use reason to alter the event in his favor. The intensity of a conflict will be decided by various characteristics such as the strength of his adversaries, degree of false expectations, and the significance of the disputed issue. It will also be fueled by mutual aggression, frustration, prejudice, posturing, and defensiveness. The conflict will be potentiated by the social context itself, which can exacerbate interactional patterns of competition, control, or provocation. In fact, one can judge the escalation of the conflict by simply assessing the strength of these variables. The conflict can take many forms, from physical violence to verbal abuse or legal confrontation, but all pursuing the same intent, that is, to punish the opponent, to teach him a lesson of dire consequences. In this respect, the experience of Ron is illuminating.

Ron, a 50-year-old professional, worked for an institution affiliated with a government agency that had just appointed Bob as the new director. Bob was Ron's immediate boss. Ron, as a senior member of the staff, had been well regarded by the chairman of the affiliated company. He also was a member of an important advisory administrative committee. A conflict of authority about some administrative matters erupted between him and Bob, a political appointee. Ron and his committee opposed some of Bob's decisions as being political in nature. Bob ignored the committee's recommendations in decisive issues, indirectly affecting Ron and other senior members of the staff. Ron not only felt insulted by not being consulted in those administrative matters, but was also personally affected in his work. As a result, he vehemently complained to the executive committee of the affiliated company about various improper actions and abuses of Bob. In response, Bob dissolved the advisory committee and threatened more reprisals for their alleged insubordination. Ron miscalculated two things: First, the political power of the director, and second, the apparent policy of nonintervention adopted by the chairman of the executive committee. Ron lost the first round but thought he had not yet lost the war. He appealed to the union to embrace his cause, based on an administrative ruling error made by Bob. After some investigation by an arbitration agency, Bob was notified about overstepping his authority in that particular matter, but this did not bring any real change in the balance of power in Ron's favor. However, nine months later, Bob took advantage of a new downsizing policy of the corporation and eliminated Ron's job, together with that of the other members of the advisory committee. Ron decided to sue on technical grounds. Though he finally won, Ron experienced a lot of aggravation and had to look for another job. Basically, the conflict escalated due to the clash between two strong personalities. Ron's judgment was affected by miscalculating the alleged support from the chairman of the affiliated corporation. He showed a complete ignorance of the political game played by his bosses to maintain their own turfs of power.

This conflict was fought within an acceptable social framework, but other work-related conflicts, like union strikes, may escalate to physical violence, not to mention those bitter feuds between individuals that may culminate in murder. If most of the conflicts between people are not solved peacefully, then maybe our legal system is better equipped to handle them. This leads us to another belief.

THE PSEUDOMYTH THAT JUSTICE WILL TRIUMPH IN THE END

It is understood that the basic purpose of the judicial system is to impartially settle disputes between people in order to preserve the peace of the community. To do so it is assumed that the courts try to establish the truth within a framework of legal rules and based on an objective evaluation of factual evidence. It is not an easy task for the courts to be able to follow these two intertwining principles of the judicial process. First, there is the problem of legal rules, which sometimes are purposely made vague to permit lawyerly interpretations. This system also gives the trial judge ample latitude in determining their meaning in any particular case. Hence, the judge's real discretionary power lies with the interpretation of the facts. As Jerome Frank, distinguished jurist, stated a long time ago, the judge's liberty in using the facts at his discretion is almost unlimited.[20] Another component in the judge's decision is the testimony of witnesses, which could be truthful, inaccurate, or perjurious. However, even a frank witness could give unintentionally inaccurate testimony under the influence of the examining lawyer, who unduly stresses certain points favoring his client. At other times, a witness's testimony may be modified due to the lawyer's outright dishonest coaching. Furthermore, the witness himself may be swayed by the adversarial nature of the trial, causing him to tilt the testimony either by omission or by emotionally reshaping the facts in favor of one party. Also, some witnesses, due to their personality problems or cultural or racial biases, may mold the facts to favor one party. The fallibility of the witnesses can be compounded by dubious expert witnesses and the juries' difficulty in establishing the truth. It has been assumed that the juries are better at fact-finding than judges. This assumption is questionable, since they may interpret the facts through their own biases. The role of the jury, as Frank suggested, should be viewed to apply "the general rule of the law to the justice of a particular case" with its specific circumstances.[21] But for the members of the jury to apply an inflexible law to a particular case presupposes that they ignore to some extent the rules of the law presented to them by the judge. In fact, the jury is at liberty to disregard legal rules according to its subjective interpretation of facts. But this evaluation of facts is greatly influenced by witnesses, experts, and the persuasive arguments of clever lawyers. As a result, juries' decisions are emotional, capricious, and arbitrary, or in a word, biased. This seems to have been the case of the O.J. Simpson trial. Yet, with all its imperfections and abuses, the justice system may sometimes triumph. But for a stiff price.

Let us see how the "justice system" worked in the famous Florida sex abuse case, which started in 1984 as pure act of revenge of a policeman against another and in which small children testified as alleged victims at the advice of expert witnesses who took advantage of their suggestibility. Politically oriented prosecutors posing as defenders of morality and social justice jumped onto the bandwagon for publicity, supported by the public hysteria fueled by irresponsible media reporters, but without any valid documentation of their case. Were the accusers and promoters of this social madness believers in their arbitrary findings or outright liars? This case, which became a "cause celebre" because of the peculiar ways in which a politicized judicial process reached the conviction of the alleged sex abuser, may throw light on the tragic manipulations of justice.[22]

Mr. G.S., a policeman, was initially accused of molesting a 3-year-old boy who was under the care of his wife, who was running a small baby-sitting service. Two years later when he was brought to trial, the prosecutor charged him with molesting two other children, while the first charge was dropped for lack of evidence. Without going into the details of the trial, it is sufficient to mention that one accuser was a 11-year-old girl who claimed to have been molested at the age of 4 by Mr. G.S. The jury acquitted him because there was no evidence that they ever knew each other. With her prestige severely damaged, the state attorney later brought other charges against him, as already being in the file system, for other alleged sexual abuses and obtained his conviction. Instrumental in his conviction had been the testimonies before the jury of the prosecution's expert witnesses on child abuse. The trouble was that one expert had a degree in speech therapy and was falsely introduced by the prosecutor as a psychologist. In addition, the speech therapist's interviews with the children were based on leading questioning, which directed the responses about alleged sexual activities to confirm the allegations made. Before the trial, these questions had been again and again repeated to the children in rehearsals until the desired reply was obtained. (Example: Is it not true that on such day Mr. G.S. did so and so to you? Or did you not tell me so and so?) Another expert in child abuse brought in by the prosecution, a psychologist, terminated her testimony to the jury with the astonishing statement that 99.5 percent of the children making accusations of sexual abuse are telling the truth. The unholy alliance between an unethical prosecutor hungry for notoriety and power and some unscrupulous and outright dishonest alleged expert witnesses led to the man's conviction to a lifetime in prison. The case was recently reviewed by the 11th Circuit U.S Court of Appeals and the unanimous federal ruling reversed the conviction of Mr. G.S.[23] Yet, Mr. G.S. spent 12 years in jail to feed the political ambitions of the state attorney who, indeed, advanced her career beyond her dreams while the expert witnesses profited. The testimonies of these alleged behavioral experts suggest that their actions were, at best, motivated by a mixture of political and social biases and unproven theoretical beliefs, combined with a strong dose of self-serving dishonesty. It took 12 years and the crusade of a dedicated investigative reporter to reopen the case fabricated by an unscrupulous prosecutor with the help of a team of dubious expert witnesses.

In favor of trial by jury is the contention that the jury can offer protection from a corrupt or incompetent trial judge. This happens to be true in many instances, particularly due to the political system of appointing judges, which quite often disregards merit. At the same time, the jury acts as an insulator for the judge in the case of a high-profile social crime where the judge's decision may affect his career. In the final analysis, the carrying out of justice is left in the hands of "fallible judges and juries," as Justice Felix Frankfurter remarked some time ago.[24] This raises the issue of the judge's competence and honesty in trials without a jury.

Judges are not immune to political pressures in cases where issues are related to social policies endorsed by their previous political supporters. At the same time, no one should ignore the role of the judge's social and political background in his method of administering justice. The judge's own philosophy of life, integrated in his personality make-up, is reflected in his sympathy with or antipathy toward the contested issue before the court or even toward certain witnesses, which ultimately must affect any dispassionate evaluation of facts. These factors may explain why court decisions vary so greatly in almost identical cases tried in different courts. These conditions have been cleverly exploited the by the plaintiff's lawyers who have chosen to litigate big lawsuits in small county courts, where they can manipulate inexperienced or corrupt judges. This has become a new trend, particularly in class-action suits. For instance, one of the biggest consumer class action suits settled for $950 million against a plastic plumbing company, was filed at a Union City, Tennessee court, a town with a population of, 12,000. The obvious reason was the personal relationship between the local judge and one of the plaintiff lawyers, who had been a former law school classmate and friend. Before the Union City filing, a state court judge in Houston refused to exercise jurisdiction over the case. Another class-action lawsuit, against Prudential Insurance, was recently filed in Entaw, Alabama.[25] Do small-town judges have any experience in handling complicated megasuits, litigated by experienced, sophisticated, big-firm lawyers? As a matter of fact, these lawyers are attracted to the small courthouses because of the lack of experience of these trial judges, who have difficulty extracting the truth from convoluted and manipulated testimonies and contradictory technical documents. Their weak competence is compensated by a subjective evaluation of facts leading to distorted conclusions. Intentionally or unintentionally, the decision is, at best, reached less on the idea of establishing the truth and more on the judge's feelings about the case. And this presupposes that the judge is honest and without hidden motives to promote the interests of one party. As a law professor once said, "inevitably some trial judges will be slippery, prejudicial or otherwise unfit for the office."[26] Popular justice was done in these cases but less within the framework of law and more to fulfill personal gains or political aims. Regrettably, its biases can result in verdicts where the law is unreasonably misrepresented or ignored. In absence of well-defined statutes, the trial judge himself can liberally interpret legal rules that are vague and uncertain. However, his decisions appear logically and objectively presented, based on a careful selection of supporting evidence. The illusion of objectivity is maintained so as to justify a predetermined or sometimes even a bought conclusion.

The final result must be that justice is relative, depending on too many known and less-known variables. Yet, people go to court for resolving disputes thought to be damaging to them, believing that justice will prevail. To reach such a risky conclusion, one must either be misinformed about our legal system or believe in a divine intervention to ultimately protect his interests. One main reason for believing in this myth is the educational process of indoctrinating citizens with the idea that the law is impartial, objective, and rational, but not that it is perverted by men who manipulate the court system for their own benefit. Another assumption is that the truth will emerge and be self-evident to the judge or jury, since facts speak for themselves. People often forget that between the facts and the establishing of the truth are the intermediaries of the justice process: the witnesses, experts, lawyers, jury, and judge who intentionally or not will distort or pervert the facts to fit their own personal beliefs or needs. For example, many expert witnesses lack the conviction of their opinions and are easily manipulated by the lawyers to suit their defense. Worse, some are peddlers of "junk science." An investigative reporter describes a physician who testified in numerous class-action cases against silicone implant suits, misrepresenting the facts and presenting false data about research and about himself. In a single year, he made over $100,000 from his dubious testimonies, favoring the lawyers who hired him.[27] The fact is that people who blindly believe in justice as the final arbitrator of truth may have a rude awakening, finding out that justice quite often will elude them regardless of the truth.

A NAIVE BELIEF: HONESTY AND GOOD DEEDS ARE REWARDED

Realizing the limitation of the fairness of justice, one may also understand the fallacy of the popular belief that honesty and good deeds are ultimately rewarded. In a recent survey of 1,300 employees conducted by the Ethics Officers Association, about 50 percent admitted committing at least one act of "unethical or illegal behavior" in the last year. The justifications varied from stress at work to coping with family problems or incompetent bosses.[28] But what about the fate of whistleblowers who publicize the wrongdoings of their companies? If they are fired by their company, in most cases, according to the company policy, they must take their grievances to arbitration. This policy places them at a great disadvantage since the arbitrators look at the issue as an employment dispute in which mutual allegations are made. Their final decision is not explained. Basically, it deprives the whistleblowers of an open court forum where they can air the true reasons behind their dismissal to the public.[29] So much for honesty in the workplace.

Honesty is highly praised by all societies as favoring a better interaction between individuals and between them and the state. However, if this assumption of honesty in social interaction is indiscriminately applied, it could also create serious problems for people. It rarely worked among individuals because of their inborn drive for self-preservation, striving to win by any means. In this sense, honesty is appreciated by an individual as long as it does not antagonize his interests. Undoubtedly, it is more welcomed if practiced by others in relating to him. Often, it might create serious problems. Take John, an employee for a small company in his late thirties, who is an example of a good citizen. He is married with two children, gets along well with his wife, is active in the affairs of his congregation, and is liked by coworkers, his manager, and his neighbors. His relatively peaceful life was shattered when he witnessed a terrible two-car hit-and-run collision. One small truck moving at high speed powerfully rammed into a limousine at a street intersection. The truck speeded away after the accident. The limousine was crushed and its diver apparently badly hurt. John called the police from the scene of the accident. No other witnesses were present. John's impression was that either the truck driver was drunk or he deliberately smashed into the limousine. He had noticed the characteristics of the truck, part of its license plate, and had even gotten a glimpse of the driver. One week after the accident, John was called in by the police after the truck was identified as belonging to someone associated with organized crime. Next, he had to identify the truck driver at a police line-up. Then the court action started. This required him to depose before the defendant's lawyer, which demanded more time off from his job. The defense lawyer deliberately postponed his deposition three times under various pretexts. This created problems at his job. His boss warned him he might be replaced if he continued to take too much time off from work. John wanted to get out of this mess, but he was subpoenaed by the district attorney's office. Finally, the "rewards" for being a good citizen started to pour in. First he received a couple of threatening telephone calls, which frightened him and forced him to send his wife and children to stay with a relative. A couple of days later he found his parked car with the tires slashed and the hood clubbed. He reported this to the police but they claimed that they could not establish any link between his testimony and the act of vandalism. But, one day after work, he was ambushed by a guy, who hit him hard and told him to "get lost" if he wanted to stay alive. He again reported the incident to the police, who wanted to place him under police protection or relocate him. John felt that his life had become a nightmare. After another telephone call telling him that "the best is yet to come," he decided that the time had come to forget about trying to be a responsible citizen. Truly frightened, John refused to testify, further claiming emotional strain with impairment of memory. So much for indiscriminate honesty.

In reality, honesty is used by people in a very discriminating manner, depending on circumstances and their impact on them. Like most other moral values, honesty depends on the person's judgment of the situation, which makes it of interpretable and relative significance. Even after carefully appraising a situation a person tries to act honestly, to the best of his knowledge, his perception of reality still may slant the facts or conclusion. There is no guarantee that other people's assessments of the situation will come to the same conclusion.

As a matter of fact, there is no absolute guarantee that anyone reaching a conclusion about someone else's actions can determine the facts with any certainty. This is exactly what happens quite often with "expert" witnesses who give testimony to the court in favor of either defense or plaintiff. One set of experts has to be wrong (assuming that they are not corrupt). This was the case with some experts hired by the defense in the O.J. Simpson trial.

In the daily interaction between people, honesty is even more difficult to assess, since it has so many nuances and gradations. After all, indiscriminate acceptance of people's honesty in any relationship hinges on naïveté if not poor judgment and may lead to possible self-destruction. For example, Janet, an elderly lady, truly believed that her neighbor, a young married woman named Julie, had a lover who came to her apartment in the afternoon when her husband was at work. In fact, twice she noticed them kissing in the doorway before he left. Because Janet liked Julie's husband, a straightforward man, she was revolted by the ostensible affair and wanted to do something about it. Janet approached Julie one afternoon and invited her in for coffee in order to start a conversation about the lax morality of today's women, hinting that she knew of the situation. The discussion did not strike a chord in Julie. Later, Janet decided to send an anonymous letter accusing Julie of immorality with threats of telling her husband if she continued seeing the presumed lover. Since no change occurred in Julie's behavior, Janet decided to stop Julie one day on the stairs to speak to her about the handsome man who was visiting her, but to her embarrassment she found out he was her brother who visited her during the day because he had a night job.

If honesty is subjective, relative, and sometimes detrimental to people, then what can be said about the belief that good deeds are rewarded? This is a problematic issue since good deeds may not always be perceived in the same manner by all parties involved. A case in point was that of Mike, a good Samaritan, who while walking over a bridge saw a man dangling over the rail of the bridge, ready to jump off. Shouting to stay still, Mike ran up to the man, caught him by the arm, and saved him. The man was apparently ready to commit suicide. He was despondent over intractable pains from a terminal illness. Since his condition could not be medically controlled and he knew he was going to die soon, chances are this man would try to take his life again. From the ethical point of view, Mike did a good deed; yet, the suicidee thought otherwise. It only prolonged his agony. Even from a simple community perspective, good deeds may not be rewarding for the individual. We may remember the case of an innocent guy who during the Atlanta Olympic Games in 1996 gave the first information to the police about a bomb that exploded not too far from the place where he happened to be at that moment. He became the prime suspect! It means that the idea of associating good deeds with rewards is not necessarily always a sound one. Society promotes this idea, since it is beneficial to its members, though not always advantageous to the doer.

In reality, most good deeds are done in specific circumstances that are appraised as meaningful by the doer. The act itself satisfies an emotional or social need for the doer. When someone is questioned as to why he did that particular good deed, the answer can be reduced to either one of two general, indefinite statements: "It made me feel good" or "It was my duty to do so." Moralists would ascribe good deeds to an ultimate moral imperative, meaning to the spirit of being humane and showing empathy for our fellow man. This behavior may be valid in selective cases, as for example when one is in mortal danger and a stranger comes to the rescue. However, in daily interaction, while people struggle to survive, most good deeds are done when viewed as beneficial by the doer.

If the above social pseudomyths are not critically evaluated by citizens, they may have a negative impact on their lives, leading to unnecessary frustrations or even serious problems in the process of coping with social conflicts. In general, indiscriminate acceptance of any of these social beliefs leads to a distorted view of human interaction, resulting in a poor appraisal of how to confront difficult situations. In addition, people who ignore the effects on their social interaction of the new social conditions caused by the powerful political and social changes of the last three decades are ill-prepared to relate to the raging moral relativism. Many people are unaware that this ambiguous morality formulates the concept of truth and falsehood according to the interests of specific social or political segments of the population. Those who downplay the new rules of social conduct, which ignore or bend the truth by imposing new concepts of right and wrong and views of societal order and justice, may become casualties. Ill-informed and ill-prepared, they are more vulnerable to the machinations and deceptions of others because of their naive adherence to social pseudotruths and beliefs, which hinder their public competition and interaction.

NOTES

1. C. Mackay, *Extraordinary Popular Delusions and the Madness of the Crowds* (New York: L.C. Page, 1956), pp. 462–564.

2. R. Frank, "Big Pyramid Schemes," *Wall Street Journal*, August 6, 1998, p. A1.

3. R. Kostelanetz, ed., *The Edge of Adaptation* (Englewood Cliffs, NJ: Prentice-Hall, 1973), p. 81.

4. J.K. Galbraith, *The Good Society* (Boston: Houghton Mifflin, 1996).

5. G. Heriot, "Doctored Affirmative-Action Data," *Wall Street Journal*, October, 1997, p. A22.

6. Editorial, "A Color Blind Constitution," *Wall Street Journal*, March 22, 1996, p. A12.

7. M. Perlmutter, "Why Lawyers Lie." Online. *The Institute for Central Conflict Resolution*, 1997.

8. H.W. Whyte, Jr. *The Organization Man* (New York: Anchor Books, 1956), pp. 449–456.

9. C. Sherman, "'Industrial Psychopaths' Can Thrive in Business," *Clinical Psychiatry News* (May 2000): 38.

10. R. Petras, & K. Petras, *The Stupidest Things Ever Said by Politicians* (New York: Pocket Books, 1999).

11. B. Russell, *A History of Western Philosophy* (New York: Simon & Schuster, 1965), pp. 684–701.

12. Ibid., pp. 617–640.

13. M. Twain, *Following the Equator* (New York: Dover Publications, 1989).

14. T. Sowell, "Criminals and Court," *New York Post*, June 9, 1995, p. 23.

15. R. Ardrey, *The Social Contract* (New York: Atheneum, 1970), pp. 77–79.

16. S. Stecklow, "New Era's Bennett Near Sentencing," *Wall Street Journal*, September 17, 1997, p. B10.

17. L.H. Block, *Psychic War in Men & Women* (New York: New York University Press, 1976), pp. 90–106.

18. B. Russell, *A History of Western Philosophy* (New York: Simon & Schuster, 1965), p. 596–664.

19. G. Serban, "The Process of Neurotic Thinking, "*American Journal of Psychotherapy*, 1974, 28(3), pp. 418–429.

20. J. Frank, *Courts on Trial* (Princeton, NJ: Atheneum-Princeton University Press, 1963), pp. 165–187.

21. Ibid., pp. 131–147.

22. D. Rabinwitz, "The Pursuit of Justice in Dade County," *Wall Street Journal*, October 28, 1996, p. A18.

23. Review & Outlook. "Reno Overturned," *Wall Street Journal*, February 20, 1998, p. A18.

24. J. Frank, *Courts on Trial* (Princeton, NJ: Atheneum-Princeton University Press, 1963), p. 87.

25. R. Schmitt, "Big Suits Land in Rural Courts," *Wall Street Journal*, October 10, 1996, B1.

26. J. Frank, *Courts on Trial* (Princeton, NJ: Atheneum-Princeton University, Press, 1963), p. 224.

27. M. Boot, "'Expert' for Hire," *Wall Street Journal*, August 22, 1996, p. A14.

28. H. Fountain, "Of White Lies and Yellow Pads," *New York Times,* July 6, 1997, p. 7F.

29. A.M. Jacobs, "Arbitration Policies are Muting Whistle-Blower Claims," *Wall Street Journal*, August 6, 1998, p. B1.

Chapter 3

Lying, an Adaptive Strategy

Take note, take note, O World! To be direct and honest is not safe.
Shakespeare, *Othello* 3.3.378

TRUTH, HALF-TRUTHS, AND LIES

Nobody contests that whether intentionally or not, justifiably or not, *everybody* has lied at one time or another. In fact, nothing has changed about human behavior since Diogenes's times. Diogenes, a Greek philosopher who lived in the beginning of the 3rd century A.D., to make a point about people's dishonesty, walked through the city of Athens one day with a lit candle in his hand, looking for an honest man. He has since been considered a cynic. In view of our historical and present knowledge of Man, perhaps we should call him a realist!

Lying is universal; it coexists side by side with the truth. In one way or another, lying is used daily in our social interactions. According to a recent survey, 91 percent of people lie regularly.[1] Lies permeate every aspect of human endeavor, from the media manipulating information, to the government's deliberate misrepresentation of social policies for political gain, to corporations promoting dubious products and/or releasing misleading financial reports. Lies are routinely used by people in their daily trivial pursuit. In a recent study conducted by DePaulo and colleagues, the subjects, college students, voluntarily acknowledged lying at least twice a day, or a minimum of once in every four social interactions. Their reasons for lying varied depending on the nature of discussions or transactions under consideration.[2]

Though lies are a part of our daily existence, we often have great difficulty recognizing them because of the myriad forms and disguises in which they are presented. Contrary to popular belief, lies are not necessarily the opposite of truth. Quite often they intermesh with the truth, filling in gaps of unverified knowledge, while at other times they are mistakenly or deliberately appended to the truth. For example, most people are unaware of the misleading nature of the social pseudotruths-beliefs that are part of our social and moral traditions, cultivated by society and incorporated by the masses as guiding principles for proper public conduct and potential self-realization. Constantly extolled by society, their recognition is tacitly implied by most common people in their social transactions. However, sooner or later, they learn that others do not always respect these "ideal" rules of interaction but, on the contrary, manipulate them for their own benefit. Furthermore, these societal beliefs that subtly influence our decision process may not always be beneficial for people. Why do people need to lie?

People lie and cheat for a variety of reasons, from avoiding embarrassment or humiliation to gaining recognition, power, or money. In general, lying is used by men to help them cope with events and situations for which they have been unable to find acceptable solutions, partly because of their unrealistic expectations, such as in disruptive marriages, lack of competency for work assignments, or as part of a strategy to ensure physical or social self-protection. However, lies told for the purpose of political manipulations or business scams are used for unlawfully gaining money, power, or both.

A closer look at the "smart" manipulators, the ones in positions of social leadership, ranging from policymakers to media communicators or financial operators, shows certain general pattern of manipulation of truth. They use specific methods of recasting the truth in order to deceive others and meet their aims. One is to dissect, fragment, and eviscerate the truth of its substance in order to recombine it with pseudotruth and unverifiable projections in a new formulation beneficial to them. This semblance of truth, at best plausible, is sold to other people as unadulterated truth. To create the impression of legitimacy is an art in itself, acquired by the people who understand that there are nuances in the interpretation of truth that may blur the distinction between facts and assumptions. For instance, the obfuscation of truth mixed with denial and a recasting of facts has been used repeatedly by the White House staff to deflect various attacks against their alleged illegal actions. Since telling the truth could have jeopardized their status, self-esteem, or their jobs, misrepresenting the facts enhanced their self-defense. This approach was used during the famous political scandals and trials like Watergate and the Iran Contra operation or recently by Clinton's staff in their famous "spinning" of facts, which successfully diffused issues associated with the interminable political scandals.

Another method used by the authoritative and respectable public figures who manipulate the truth is based on a classical principle that the redefinition of a situation within a new conceptual framework will give new meaning to that situation. This equivocation of the issue slants its initial context and changes the focus of attention to a secondary aspect of it. This method was successfully used during the heated Congressional debates about the budgetary problems related to various entitlement programs such as welfare, Medicare, or social security. The reshaping of the argument in emotional terms and the reconstruction of truth by the opponents of any budgetary restriction changed the substance of the debates and persuaded people to support their nonfactual position. However, they won. There are other forms of blatant deception used for quick financial gain that amount to outright fraud. It is widely practiced by crooked promoters who develop sophisticated fraudulent marketing schemes as subtle and convincing as gospel truth or by rogue brokers posing as financial investment experts while fleecing the naive. Disingenuous but elegant presentations of facts, interspersed with well-designed lies, have always succeeded to manipulate people financially or socially, mostly for the advantage of a few dishonest political or financial power brokers. It is amazing the unbelievable degree of misdirected inventiveness used in the service of these planned deceptions and also the degree of determination and unscrupulousness involved in their execution. Why all these efforts? Because most often deception seems to pay off.

Greed leading to the equivocation of truth and dishonesty, lately a standard method of winning in certain occupations, apparently did not spare professions that rely on high moral values and/or scientific knowledge and verifiable documentation. One would like to believe that those careers sought by men who have professed to dedicate their lives to the pursuit of truth, such as clergymen, rabbis, scientists, researchers, and judges, were free from the temptation of greed and lying. Yet we find some who are unable to resist cheating and lying for financial gain or power. Take for instance the embezzlement of certain great fundamentalist preachers or rabbis who used their spiritual power over the faithful for a more mundane and lucrative goal, that of enriching themselves.

Even among men of science, dedicated to the pursuit of truth, we find ones who sometimes cannot resist using deceptive approaches to enhance their self-esteem and gain recognition. If history can offer any clue about the behavior of scientists, then the alleged conduct of several giants of science from the past is quite revealing. Two brilliant men of science, one of the 17th century, physicist Isaac Newton who formulated the law of universal gravitation and the other Gregor Mendel, the 19th-century founder of modern genetics, have been accused of fudging and/or finagling some research data to fit their respective theories.[3]

Medicine, though a less exact science, has also had its share of cheaters both in research and in clinical practice because of the same uncontrollable drive for success and recognition from peers. From Mesmer, the discoverer of animal magnetism and the founder of the medical current known as Mesmerism[4] to the 19th-century itinerant "snake oil" salesmen, all boasted extravagant healing miracles while relying on human suggestibility and deceptive practices. The difference in their cheating styles is almost negligible when compared to the present peddling by quacks of esoteric cures for cancer. Even in our day, frauds are sometimes brazenly committed in research. For instance, in 1974, a skin immunologist had partially faked the results of his experiment, in order to get credit for what would have been a revolutionary discovery.[5] This transplant research fraud has become known in immunology as the "painted mouse claim." Another recent fraud was committed by a research professor of psycho-pharmacology who was convicted for running a fraudulent clinical drug testing operation. The motive was his insatiable greed. He filed false clinical reports about drugs allegedly tested on patients as required by the research protocol, while deceiving the college and pharmaceutical companies of millions of dollars.[6]

Interestingly, lying and deceit have always been quite commonly used as part of the methods of the healing process, whether for physical or mental illnesses. There are strong psychological reasons for the use of deception in the curative process. As inherited from tribal shamanism, it is still practiced in its primitive form by some ethnic groups in this country or in a more elaborate approach by some pseudopsychotherapists using arcane therapeutic techniques. In fact, Claude Levi-Strauss, a French anthropologist who described the healing methods of a famous South American shaman, compared the mythology of its cure with that of psychoanalysis.[7] Shamanism is based on using blatant deceptions combined with supernatural incantations to enhance the healing power and obtain the confidence of the shaman's ill clients. In Levi-Strauss's view, psychoanalysis also attempts to heal "by recreating a myth which the patient has to live or relive" but without resorting to deceptions. For Levi-Strauss, shamanism "lies on the borderline between our contemporary physical medicine and psychological therapies as psychoanalysis." It is an interesting comparison of mythologies since Freud, in the absence of any psychological evidence to support his pivotal theory of the Oedipus phase in the psychosexual development of the child, attempted to draw one from anthropology. However, he advanced his own fictitious explanation. According to him, somewhere at the dawn of history there was a primal horde, controlled by a despotic father who kept all the women for himself and forced his sons, as they grew up, out of the horde. One day the rebellious sons killed the father to have sexual access to women.[8] Although disproved by anthropologists, this mythical explanation became the bedrock of a chain of theoretical inferences and rationalizations about human behavior.

Our ability to separate the truth from lies has been seriously tested in modern psychology, in one of the most recent crazes of our time: the legal accusations that some people, most of these later proven innocent, had sexually molested or raped their children, or children entrusted to them. While some accusations have been legitimate, as a rule they have been obtained by leading questions and pseudoscientific interpretations gradually metamorphosed into facts of "recovered memories" by the disingenuousness of biased or poorly trained therapists. Their needs for quick professional recognition or financial gain led them to these "discoveries" based on the dubious, unproven technique of uncovering so-called "repressed memories related to sexual abuse" by free associations and far-fetched interpretations. Mind you, poorly trained and/or dishonest mental health professionals have implanted in the minds of suggestible unhappy women or those with certain personality disorders, during the therapeutic process, the belief that they had been sexually abused by their fathers or other significant persons in their childhood. These highly susceptible patients, who were seeking desperately an answer to their emotional difficulties, developed false memories based on the therapist's suggestions. These "memories," uncorroborated by independent evidence, became the basis for legal action. And the witch hunt started. These court cases mainly relied on the subjective psychoanalytic interpretation of dreams and symbolic assumptions concocted by professionals of debatable knowledge and suspected integrity. The accused father or other man who claimed innocence was arrogantly denounced by the therapist as "being in deep denial" and recommended for intensive psychotherapy until the "sexual abuser" recalled and admitted his criminal behavior. This was exactly the case of Mr. D.N., who was found guilty of alleged sexual abuse of his older daughter, K, based only on the allegedly retrieved repressed memories during her psychotherapy, which she was undergoing for totally different reasons.[9] In fact, she was sure that her younger sister had been molested, though the sister denied it. Certainly, she also allegedly suffered from "deep denial!"

Unfortunately, there are many similar cases that seriously call into question the integrity of those therapists treating patients for alleged repressed memories, which in reality are "false memories" induced by their methods of treatment and exploited for a professional advertisement or financial gain. One of the most bizarre cases, settled in court, took place in a Texas Psychiatric Hospital where a patient, L.C., and her two children had been hospitalized for years for treatment, based on recovered memories of alleged satanic ritual abuse, rape and so on, though no evidence was uncovered to justify it.[10] The patient later sued the hospital and won a substantial settlement.

The mixture of truth, pseudotruth, and fabrication still goes on today in many areas of borderline knowledge. We still have strong believers in counterfeit science like extrasensory perception, certain odd cures of alternative medicine, reincarnation, UFOs, impregnations of women by alien creatures, and so on. Do they truly believe in their ability to relive their alleged previous lives? Do the women truly believe they had been abducted and sexually used by aliens? Are they not exploiting certain beliefs for their shock value, getting attention and money?

Although it may seem baffling that people need to lie in their most intimate relationships of love and marriage, they do it for a variety of reasons. In the past, people lied and cheated on their spouses, though they pledged devotion to each other when they exchanged wedding vows, because most marriages were arranged by parents for business or social alliances, regardless of the feelings of the betrothed. The lying and deception in this most intimate area of human interaction has been from time to time, acknowledged by writers in jocular and entertaining form.

For instance, Boccaccio, an Italian writer of the 14th century, described the hypocrisy and deception in marital life and love affairs of the Florentine bourgeoisie in his well known book *Decameron*,[11] while Casanova, in the 18th century, wrote in his *Memoirs*[12] about the same situations taking place in France, Italy, or Germany. Although these authors lived four centuries apart, their reports on amorous intrigues and marital duplicity expose the lying that was going on in relationships between the sexes in the name of love or within the sanctity of marriage do not differ from the practices of our time. It shows how faithful commoners have always paid lip service to the Ten Commandments. A more realistic approach to marital interaction seems to have been taken by the Talmud, the Hebrew codification of religious moral traditions, which permits marital lying in order to keep the family peace. It also permits lying for other reasons, categorized either under the right to privacy or to secure peace. It means that since tribal times, people have realized that certain forms of lying help them function in the community.

Lying, as a product of human creative thinking for personal gain or self-protection, "has a hundred thousand faces and an infinite field," as Montaigne, the 16th-century French essayist, has wisely observed.[13] Lying is an integral part of human interaction and conflict, influencing the way people relate to others or even to themselves. In our highly competitive society, lying may signify for many the difference between frustration and fulfillment, between emotional death and gratification, between social recognition and fading in to oblivion. For some, it is the only way of winning a prized objective and the only route to avoid failure and loss of self-esteem.

Although lies may complicate if not aggravate human relationships, they also can smooth over some rough spots by reducing the friction and tension inherent in conflicts between people. As such, lying plays an important role in man's coping in society. No one is immune to lying.

LYING AND THE HUMAN CONFLICT

It is no secret that people in pursuit of their needs antagonize each other to the point of creating various degrees of conflict. Otherwise, lawyers would have been out of business long ago. Conflict is an inherent part of human interaction and lying plays a meaningful role in its resolution. In a broader perspective, we have to admit that the settlements of social or personal conflicts are not necessarily reached by friendly, honest negotiations. Man's need for securing what he deems to be his right to possess or fancies he must get, is too strong to always be controlled by decency, common sense, and respect for others. If people were always honest and reasonable, wars, revolutions, murders, treachery, frauds, thefts, and all other types of unimaginable crimes would not take place every second, simultaneously, in one part of the world or another. And in all these social conflicts, lying is part of the process either by triggering or heavily influencing its course and outcome. Whether the conflicts are between countries, institutions, governmental agencies, or individuals, the adversarial parties most often stake their winning on their ability to combine the most persuasive lying and treachery with any means available to take advantage of the opponent. There is no need to further elaborate on the amount of distortion, deceit, betrayal, perfidy, and clever lying used in any social, political, or business conflict in which each party claims to be fighting for the right cause. In fact, this situation has been aggravated by the new social paradigm created by the political and social changes of the decades that increased competition for jobs among various segments of the population.

The psychodynamics of the conflicts between individuals are quite interesting when one considers the variety of underlying motivations triggering them. The inner drives of an individual not only compete within oneself for priority in gratification, but may clash with those of others because of their potentially adversarial nature. The result is pitting people against each other in bitter struggles for self-affirmation or fulfillment of their wants. Most common conflicts involve competition, control, or provocation that determine the initiator to use a wide variety of legitimate and illegitimate stratagems to win, since winning is the final goal.

On the other hand, the person's methods of coping under attack depend on his perception of the degree of threat posed to him by the demands of the conflicting situation. This, in turn, is determined by many factors, from the hypothetical degree of perceived damage to his life to the available means of fending it off. In this case, he has the option, depending on his personality, either to accept being at fault or to fight the conflict by deceptive means. If he acts honestly, it may require accepting his " losses," and temporarily resigning himself, at least, to the situation, while waiting for better conditions. He may go a step further, and try to compensate for his setback by redirecting his efforts and attempting to succeed in a different area. Unfortunately, most people become more frustrated, resentful, or hostile against their adversary when they have less of a chance to favorably solve a conflict. To increase their chances for winning, fueled by their tendency to overreact emotionally, they attempt to use from the outset of the conflict devious strategies favorable to themselves. This presupposes that either one or both antagonists may negotiate the conflict in bad faith by using half-truths or outright lies, which change the framework of the argument and distort the parameters of dispute with the result of minimizing or magnifying the issues at stake. This is also facilitated by the fact that to some extent any conflict contains in its content twisted views, subjective interpretations, and personal beliefs. While the core of the issue under dispute may be real, the layers of assumptions and misrepresentations can totally obscure or minimize the substance of the conflict. These tiers of subjective argumentation, which represent the "gray area" of the conflict, are already distorted perception and arbitrary interpretations equivalent to discreet lies, though the person arguing the issue may deny any intentional deception.

This example will show how the decision of the contestants to lie or not in a conflicting situation drastically changed the outcome of the potential dispute. Let us discuss the different approaches used by two employees, John and David, in their attempt to secure a leave of absence from a reluctant boss. The employees had similar jobs and working responsibilities and reported to the same supervisor. John decided to ask his boss for a couple of days off after the completion of a difficult project, which had practically exhausted him because of the long hours of overtime required. He had some doubts about his boss's willingness to approve his request, but wanted to negotiate a reasonable amount of time. Since he felt that his demand was fair, he decided to make his request without any subterfuge. Any fabricated stories about the urgency of his need for time off would have been beneath him. As a straightforward man, he did not believe in using deviousness to secure a legitimate request. Unfortunately, his boss flatly denied the request on the grounds that it might interfere with another project, which in his opinion should be started immediately. Though upset, frustrated, and resentful, John was unable to argue with his boss, as he was fearful of incurring his boss's wrath, with its unforeseeable consequences. On his way home, John tried to think up a decent explanation to give his wife and son, with whom he was supposed to spend a short vacation. He decided to tell his wife that he had to postpone their short vacation because a major project would require his presence in the office. To his son, he decided to say that the trip must be put off because of some important legal obligations. He could not tell him about the job problem, since he had disappointed him in the past with the demands of his work. In addition, he had to enlist his wife's support for his story. All these tales would represent a slight departure from the truth, used as save-face devices.

At home, his explanatory scheme did not work out as he had expected. His wife had serious doubts about his commitment to the projected vacation, since in her opinion, he did not stand up for his rights. His son was disappointed because his father had again broken an important promise. John felt miserable and ineffectual. Basically, he manipulated his social milieu poorly because of his inflexible, dogmatic concept of his rights and ethics.

David, the other employee, was also concerned about whether his boss would accept his request for time off, but tackled the issue differently. He told his boss that his father had fallen ill and needed his presence for a couple of days but that he would work overtime when he returned. The boss grudgingly accepted the situation. An outright lie worked well for David.

Should we consider John an ethical man and David a shameless liar? According to a strict moral code, this evaluation is correct. However, from a problem-solving point of view, a different picture emerges. John handled the confrontation miserably, while David was able to successfully work out a deal. Practically speaking, David adapted better to the working conditions than John. Yet some might argue that, in the long term, John's straightforward approach will be recognized and rewarded by his boss. This is highly conjectural. If John acted as he did in order to please his boss with ulterior motives in mind, such as a salary increase or a promotion down the road, then he took a calculated risk. But this was not the case, since apparently he thought of himself as an ethical man. Had he taken a calculated risk, his decision still might not have paid off if his boss had left the company, John had been laid off, or anything else had gone wrong. In the real world, regardless whether or not we like it, the fact remains that sometimes various degrees of deviations from the truth make life more bearable.

In this case lies have been used as a "quick fix" for a problem where no favorable solution seemed available. The reality is that in most social conflicts the manipulation of truth is the norm of conduct. Social competition is not an exception. The game of telling the truth versus distorting or obfuscating it is part of the social competition for winning.

LYING IN THE SOCIAL COMPETITION AND PURSUIT OF SUCCESS

In general, success is viewed by ethicists as antithetical to moral norms. Achieving corporate or political success is often viewed as mastering a game of competition in which the rules of fairness are broadly outlined with lots of room left for free manipulating of fact often to the point of unscrupulousness.

This means that any adult who wants to be socially adept has to make the effort to become familiar with man's duplicity toward truth in the game of societal intercourse and competition. In finality, the test of his social proficiency is measured by his ability to negotiate social transactions in his favor by manipulations of others, approaches that correlate in most careers with degree of success.

At the same time, he should know that success at work is not always achieved by the ablest, but more often by the one who handles job situations more cleverly and less scrupulously against his rivals. In addition, anyone in the game of work competition has to reckon with the new special exceptions from the merit rules made for the affirmative action contenders. Playing by the old rules by sticking to conformity and hard work with hopes for recognition is not necessarily the road to success. This formerly "correct" conduct of playing the social game of success is helpful, at best, but social upper mobility in many professions requires, more often, something else, namely, a flexible attitude toward one's own integrity. In general, there is a conflict between success and classical values. This was recognized for a long time and popularized by novels like *An American Tragedy*[14] or trade books like *The Pyramid Climbers*.[15] Lately, these issues have become part of a growing genre of books that advise people on how to succeed. Learning the right way to compete for success is very important to anyone in pursuit of social climbing.

If a young person in the workforce wants to climb the corporate or business ladder and does not know how to outdo or outsmart his rivals in any significant competitive work decision, his chances of winning are slim. He also has to understand that to be a winner, one must either neutralize any amount of dishonesty involved in competitive situations, either by relying on his excellent qualifications or by attempting to top others' claims with better personal manipulations of the truth, if not with outright deceit. He must at least know how to blur unfavorable facts and be ready to negotiate the integrity of his beliefs and sometimes of his social allegiance according to the situation. In due time, the whole repertoire of lying, misstatements, and duplicity will become integrated into his social approach. As such, deception becomes part of his coping style either in dealing with unfavorable social events or in increasing his chances of success.

Furthermore, attaining corporate or bureaucratic success requires another chameleon-like quality: that of adjusting one's personality to the emotional needs of his boss. Most often, it is not good enough for someone to be bright, conscientious, and a good worker to get ahead, it requires ingratiating himself with the boss, which means pleasing him "beyond the call of duty." It also presupposes getting along with associates and superiors. This is attained by creating an image of oneself that displays charm, courteousness, tactfulness, and above all, loyalty. A success-driven person needs to convey these qualities, regardless of whether he possesses them or not. The ingredients for climbing the social ladder, as promoted by various teaching courses on this subject including those of Dale Carnegie, can be reduced to a simple philosophy of developing the ability to hypocritically charm others for personal advantage. This assumes an ability to dissimulate any true personal feelings, to be deceitful, opportunistic, conniving, and feigning modesty in the presence of one's superiors. However, above all, the success-driven person should simulate sincerity and convey trustworthiness to his superiors. He must tactfully show his admiration for his boss and try to emulate him, so as to gain his confidence. As we may see, "in achieving success there are no ethics," as Mark Caine, author of *The S-Man*, said a long time ago.[16] Conversely, this may explain why throughout history so many national leaders have been betrayed and torpedoed by their most trusted men.

Some may argue that this is a very cynical view that does not consider the idealism of some young people who fight for truth and social justice. This objection would seem to contradict the previous statements about the general acceptance of lying and deception by young people. Not quite. It is true that many young people are, by and large, aware of the unspoken rules of social conning, and are revolted by social injustices. A minority of them may even try to fight for the underdog; however, when they reach maturity, if they achieve any social status their idealism slowly dissipates. To maintain the gained status they may grow at best indifferent and detached, or, at worst, manipulative of others, as most social climbers do. Many alleged social activists, populists, and union reformists are good examples of changing lofty social goals of helping the disadvantaged for fixation on control and power, cynically exercised in their name.

Yet a small minority of more idealistically "committed" young adults may persist in their naive beliefs beyond their youth, only to be socially maneuvered by their admired leaders. In fact, their problem is that of not having acquired the necessary social skills or the experience needed to detect the fine inconsistencies in the sophistic arguments of their social idols. If they do not grasp the inherent ethical contradictions of the political system within their society or the hypocrisy and cynicism of the politicians, they are socially handicapped and they become the losers, or in psychological terms, less adapted.

The reality is that most people attempt to reach a degree of recognition within their field of work/activity which makes it a necessity for them to acquire a minimal mastery of the rules of social competence. Since it is very easy for someone by his frank behavior to either antagonize others or to make them into enemies, the idea of learning a bit of social diplomacy may be quite helpful. By the same token, ambitious people have little chance to become properly socially adjusted if they ignore the rules of social maneuvering, which may help them to disguise their hidden personality drives. The social climbers instinctively know or have learned from experience, the rules of moving forward to achieve their goals. Even the ones who may initially hesitate to lie under circumstances where lying might be useful because of their moral beliefs in the end change their minds and lie. Caught between social pressures and their obsessive ego needs, they resort to lying as the ultimate solution. They are able to dismiss or ignore their doubts about their otherwise dubious moral integrity and sustain their promoted self-image by employing convoluted rationalizations. With the use of "creative justifications" about the significance and consequences of their lies, these people are able to overcome any moral objection. In finality, the proof of people's adherence to the truth is uncovered in the process of their coping with social competition. In this case, they feel compelled to manipulate situations beyond the loose social rules devised to check any inordinate cheating into the domain of outright deception. The rules themselves have been endlessly bent and changed to meet new social and political realities. For example, let us examine Mike's dilemma.

Mike, in his fifties and married with two children in college, is a middle-level manager at a medium-sized company. He is favorably viewed by his bosses and his job seems to be secure. The problem is that the company is not doing too well. The stockholders are unhappy with the performance of the company, and its shares of the market are down. To improve the company's image in the market, the chairman and his executive group decide to hire an investment firm for a posssible sale of two divisions. However, these divisions have serious financial problems. Mike is in charge of marketing their products. He is supposed to present a glowing report about the future of these divisions, while he knows that their sales accounts and inventories have been fudged. Basically, he has to lie. His dilemma is a serious one: If he tells the truth his job is in jeopardy, but if he does not he may be accused of misrepresentation. He cannot resign either: he needs the money and there is no other job lined up for him. Also, he hates to lie, particularly for the benefit of others. But, after soul searching, and at the advice of his lawyer, he decides to go along with his bosses as long as he does not have to discuss the divisions' creative financial accounting with the potential buyers. The net result was that he embellished the potential marketing of the divisions' products, and omitted any presentation of their finances. This meant double lying. However, he secured for himself a future with the company. Is he an isolated case? Apparently not. Only recently a big company, Cendant, after merging with another one, CUC, found out that the accounting books of CUC had been forged. The financial consequences were devastating for the shareholders. The indicted executives of CUC claimed that doctoring the books was part of company culture.[17]

Now, we can better understand why many ambitious people striving for success and power learn to manipulate data and behave hypocritically in order to move ahead. They also have to selectively ignore their conscience, the otherwise extolled guardian of morality. Anyone watching the degree of redefining truth in the social and political arena sooner or later learns that people who smartly eschew the truth or replace it with credible distortions and a semblance of truthfulness in critical issues are more often successful in reaching their objectives than others. It strongly suggests that clever lying is profitable. Even society, which repeatedly sends messages to individuals about its "unswerving support" of the truth, has its own caveat in dealing with it. The current acceptance by society of multiple truths based on a multicultural, subjective perspective of human interaction has brought new dimensions in obfuscating truth. This biased view only reinforces the fact that the self-centeredness of the individual seems to be the key determinant of the usefulness of truthfulness. This is not surprising considering that people have learned from experience since childhood that sometimes honesty and truth can only be self-hurting or painful, if not outright self-damaging, while lying may be saving face, salutary, and even rewarding.

THE ORIGINS OF LYING IN CHILDREN

If lying is universal, it is important to know when and how people learn to lie. The emotional and intellectual growth of the child will give us the clue to this puzzle. It all starts in early childhood when the world of reality and fantasy are interwoven in the mind of a child. His needs, rooted in his egocentric way of thinking, are not clearly distinguished from those of others. Depending on his age, he gradually becomes able to see the causal connection between his actions and their outcome. Jean Piaget, a French-Swiss research psychologist, while proving the relationship between the age of the child and his stage of intellectual development, has also shown the emergence and formulation of lying. His findings have documented that the thought processes required for an adult logical interpretation of the world are gradually formulated by the age of 12 to 14. He suggests that lying is part progressive socialization of children's thought processes.[18] Piaget argues that lying cannot be present at an early prelogical stage of a child's intellectual development when reality is perceived in simple anthropomorphic projections and where all objects are animated and integrated in magical participation (causality is understood in terms of a fantasy construct). Since the distinction between reality and fiction is blurred, a child is unable to lie or understand the meaning of a lie.

Children between the ages of 3 and 5, in their magical stage of mental development, believe that they can modify reality according to their wishes and fantasy. At this mental stage the responsibility for an act may be shared in a child's mind with a toy, pet, or playmate who is not there, depending on the whims of his imagination. During this stage of magical thinking, the

truth is mixed in his mind with subjective assumptions and misrepresentations, which might be called by adults' lies, but the child does not have a
clue that he lies. A child of 4 or 5, who has no inhibition about making statements that do not conform to the truth, is puzzled by the indignation of
adults who tell him that what he has said is a lie. In fact, he is not quite sure
about what is perceived to be the untrue meaning of his statement. For example, if he played with a watch and broke it, he would believe that what
happened to it was not directly a result of his actions but that it just stopped
working by itself. As a matter of fact, at this age, it is very difficult for him to
understand the difference between a mistake and a lie, that is, between an
intentional act and an involuntary error.[19] This is the main reason why children in the early prelogical stage, or particularly in the magical one, are unreliable witnesses in the court of law, as evidenced from many fabricated
child abuse cases. In addition, they are very suggestible to adult questioning, which makes things more difficult for establishing the truth. Not until
the age of 5 or 6 is the child able to discard causal connections, understand
elementary causality, and identify a lie. Toward the end of the first
prelogical stage, the lie is understood as a nontrue fact.

This distinction gradually becomes more evident in the prelogical stage,
that of middle childhood, which ends by the age of 9 or 10 when his appraisal of actions and events slowly changes from a subjective interpretation to a more objective one and are based on more complex causal
relationships. During this time, he develops a fair amount of causal understanding and knowledge about the meaning of a lie, defined as an affirma-
tion that does not conform to the facts and is as such known to be wrong. Yet
the child will deliberately lie, most likely when the reality does not conform
to his needs. For instance, if he is responsible for material damage, like the
breaking of an object, he still will deny having done it, but, in this case, to
avoid punishment. Paradoxically, punishments for wrongdoings imposed
at a very early age by parents or outside authorities may have a harmful effect on the child's ability to be truthful. Unfortunately, at that early age and
level of reasoning, the adult punishment makes little if any sense to the
child. To escape being hurt or deprived of immediate gratification, he simply denies any responsibility for his wrongdoings. In this way, he may inadvertently be starting what may become a life-long pattern of selective
lying, if not one of habitual lying.

Two important factors act as a gatekeeper against the child's tendency to
lie defensively whenever the adult reality opposes his needs. One, already
mentioned, is adult constraint against lying. Sooner or later, the child real-
izes that sometimes lying may be counterproductive, and may lead to just
what he wanted to avoid, either punishment or withdrawal of love. Initially, the child is puzzled and for a while has some difficulty figuring out
how his parents are able to uncover his misdeeds, most of the time. However, he slowly learns by trial and error that he cannot lie when factual evi-

dence (there are no more cookies in the jar and nobody was there to eat them except him) is present that points him out as being guilty. Certainly, he knows by now to separate the truth from his own fabrications created to meet his needs, and he also recognizes what is right and wrong. In addition, persistent adult intervention against lying helps the child to tell the truth even against his desire. This is the beginning of the child's sense of moral realism, that is, a morality based on adult constraints, imposed upon him to control his natural tendency to fabricate his own version of truth.

In passing, it should be mentioned that Freudians relate the beginning of morality to the process in which the child learns to control his bowel movements under constraints imposed by the parents. These adult restrictions are responsible for the development of what they call "sphincter morality." Regardless of the validity of this assumption, the fact remains that the child will continue to struggle in the course of his daily activities with the restrictions dictated by adult rules. Quite often he will resort to very ingenious subterfuges and will fabricate elaborate stories to avoid being punished by the authority, be it parental or academic.

Importantly, a different degree of acceptance of right and wrong predominates in a child's game-play with other children. Learning to respect the rules of play with other children represents the second component of the gatekeeper against unrestricted lying. The interesting fact is that the child voluntarily adheres to some rules of ethics in his dealings with his peers. Most often these rules are learned in the course of playing social games with other children. The rules are handed down, during play, from children who know them to children who are new to the game. The rules are fully accepted by all participants and all children are able to respect the rules of the game without cheating. However, according to Piaget, the stage of a child's development determines the rules and the concept of the game played. For instance, between the ages of 2 and 5 a child is too self-involved to adhere to any rule. He makes his own rules and he does not play to win. After 6 or 7 he starts to play as a part of a team and tries to win. This new condition requires unification of the rules of a game to make playing possible. The participation is still limited, since the spirit of the team is not fully developed. Only around the age of 9 or 10 is there full cooperation among players and the rules are enforced against any attempt to cheat. In summary, two overriding rules seem to govern the games of children of this age group: one, the game is played by strict rules for the purpose of winning and second, cheating is not permitted. However, some more ambitious children will attempt to break the rules and cheat in order to facilitate winning, a pattern that may remain for a lifetime.

For example, David, a 7-year-old boy with no siblings, had problems playing with other children on his street. His parents recently moved to this neighborhood and David attempted to make new friends on his block. However, after a while, other children refused to play with him because he did not respect the rules of their games or because he tried to cheat when he became too frustrated by losing. Repeatedly thrown out of the game by the other players, he complained to his mother, crying that children did not like him. His mother sought the help of his teacher. His teacher suggested that David be taught in school on how to obey team rules in order to play with other children. Soon, David was again playing with his schoolmates after learning to be a team player, free of any need to cheat. This example is not an isolated situation among children. Children who do not obey the rules, bully others, or cheat are either disqualified or worse, rejected by peers. This situation offers us a beautiful example of how children learn to accept and obey a set of self-imposed moral rules. The fear of rejection by peers seems to be an essential factor that controls the natural egocentric tendency of the child, and may deter him from lying.

As previously mentioned, a different response is elicited when the child is confronted by adult constraints on the gratification of his egocentric needs. The child may rebel and try to do what he wants. In order to have his way, he will lie, hoping not to be found out and/or forced to suffer unpleasant consequences for his behavior. Other times, due to the previous punishments, he will think twice before attempting to satisfy a need against adult prohibition, afraid that his attempt to cover it up by lying will not work. By the same token, the development of his moral judgment may be derailed by his own moral mentors. Even during his prelogical stage, he may start to notice that the adults, including his parents, are lying in front of him or teaching him to lie in some circumstances. Adults tend to ignore the fact that the making of untrue statements in front of children has a negative effect on them. If the parents make deprecatory comments about "Uncle Joe" in his absence, while praising him when he is present, this is enough to confuse the child about being truthful. In due time, he will learn from his own experience that sometimes it is undesirable to tell the truth and it is preferable to lie. He will also notice that many times lying goes undetected and is even rewarded.

COPING WITH THE TRUTH DURING A CHILD'S SOCIALIZATION

It is well known that a child's learning about moral values takes place within the process of his socialization, which is dependent upon his family's concept of morality, his education, and peer enforcement of right and wrong rules of behavior. In addition, the neighborhood and street culture has played a significant role in his moral formation. The result, quite often, is at best confusing, at worst ambiguous or contradictory.

Let us take a typical example of a young man, Jim, 30 years old and a high school graduate, who works for a large company. He believes that the moral code learned in childhood from various sources of authority has been most often confusing. During his growing up years he attempted to reconcile mentally the observed contradictions between the real facts and untrue adult statements. Over time, a conclusion became inescapable to him: namely, that the truth was quite often used according to one's needs. Jim also learned, that, on occasion, if he told the truth about his misdeeds, he was punished anyway. He was able to solve his dilemma in only one way, namely, by being more careful about the circumstances in which he chose to lie. In other words, he learned to lie better. By trial and error he found out that he had to tell the truth only when he believed that his chances of avoiding unpleasant consequences by lying were slim or nil. By using this defensive reasoning, Jim gradually learned to tell the truth selectively.

Jim further thinks that his school experience did not help him to become more truthful but only enforced his ambivalence toward telling the truth. In fact, the doubts about always telling the truth, which started at home, were considerably reinforced during his school years, as a result of his interaction with his peers and school authorities. During that period of his life, he felt the pressure of deciding between telling the truth and lying in various social situations were in conflict with his emotional needs. Jim slowly understood the undesirability of sticking to the truth in situations where his allegiances to a set of beliefs or friends were seriously being tested. He remembers having to make decisions about whether or not to squeal on a friend, who might have committed an illegal act either in school or in the community when he was pressed by authorities. Other times, he had to decide whether or not to accept punishment for an act that he did not commit when he knew who the real culprit was. During all these years he was confronted with hard decisions when he had to choose between telling the truth, at the risk of alienating his peers and lying, which meant losing the favor of his teachers. He admits that he found an answer to all these predicaments by thinking selfishly of his needs, including that of acceptance by his peers, even though these approaches might conflict with the moral principles he had learned at home.

Certainly, for Jim, as for most youngsters, other psychological and social factors had contributed to his decision to manipulate the truth. In addition to the already mentioned family and school friends, his neighborhood, with its specific street culture, played a powerful role in his development of a code of ethics. Jim recognizes that the street "culture" had influenced and shaped to a great extent his decisions about telling the truth or lying. Often, there was a clash between the moral values developed in his family and the immediate social realities of his need for acceptance by his peers. In cases in which his peers practiced deception as part of the street culture, Jim's dilemma in making the right choice became a serious one. All these contradictory factors further contributed to his ambivalence toward a consistent approach to morality.

By his own admission, Jim's strategy for coping with moral conflicts developed gradually, sometimes by doing the right thing, other times by doing the opposite. Throughout the course of his school years, within his social milieu, he had lost some friends, had been cheated by others, and had sometimes been unfairly punished or treated by peers or authority. However, he had also won a few rounds by not always telling the truth. The net result has been that Jim has developed selective patterns of being truthful, which have guided him in dealing with conflicting situations at work or in his private life.

In addition, Jim, as part of the new cybergeneration, has been exposed, due to the Internet and to all multimedia communication, to the rapid proliferation of debates about political and social dishonesty, which has further reinforced his reservations about people's morality. Consider how much the media bombards people with avalanches of information about scams, spinning, and dirty deals and one may get a clear idea of the mistrust that the new generations have toward the alleged guiding moral values. What is even worse, under the new moral standards they have also watched crooks, swindlers, and even murderers receiving convictions equal to a slap on the wrist or even being set free by the very political arbitrary interpretations of justice. This murky moral landscape has become even clearer to him while competing against others for jobs and promotions, conferred not necessarily based on merit. This has only made Jim, like other people, skeptical about the wisdom of always telling the truth, particularly when daily realities teach him differently. In general, for any adult, the ethical experiences of his formative years represent only a background, quite often modified by the relativity of social truth in his daily living.

THE ADULT DUPLICITY OF THINKING TOWARD TRUTH

The pertinent issue is finding the puzzling human mental ability to reconcile one's social obligation to tell the truth in his adult transactions with the necessity of lying in the pursuit of gratification of his needs. How is he able to do it when in the process of social interaction an adult does develop a need for cooperation with others, which precludes lying and deception? The solution to this dilemma is facilitated by the mind's underlying capacity to retain in its evaluation of reality various degrees of magical thinking—pseudological remnants of childhood—which, due to their emotional nature, may heavily influence the decision-making process.[20] The result is a slanted view of reality tailored to fit people's emotional needs. We should not be surprised about this peculiar mixture of logic and pseudologic in adults if we remember that, to a higher degree, this kind of thinking has been at the core of primitive reasoning, which still can be found among less socially developed countries or ethnic groups.

In this respect the thinking of the primitive man may give us some insight into how people attempt to reconcile their daily life situations with their personal explanatory beliefs and fantasies. It does not mean that even though modern man's thinking is not as mythically and magically controlled as that of the primitive one, his mind does not make inferences based on its own beliefs or prevailing social myths. Most modern men, to a lesser extent than primitive men, still tend to attribute most of their actions for which they do not have reasonable understanding (now loosely identified as unconscious) to either "mysterious causes" or to unexplainable phenomena, which rest beyond their control (now delegated to extrasensory perception, cosmic activity, etc.). The significant distinction is that primitive thinking was less able to clearly separate the natural from the supernatural, subjective from objective, and magical explanations from truth, and as such was mentally operating on an interchangeably dual level. In their evaluation of facts and, in general of reality, they took justification for explanation and effect for cause. An example, given by French anthropologist Lucien Levy-Bruhl, may elucidate this duality of reasoning.[21] According to a story recounted by him, an Indian accused a missionary of stealing a few pumpkins from his garden and asked to be paid for their value. The missionary denied the theft and argued that, at the time, he was at least 150 miles away. The Indian agreed with him, but persisted in asking to be indemnified for the loss, based on his evidence of a dream. He had a dream the previous night in which he had seen the missionary entering his garden and stealing his pumpkins. To him the dream was real. It is important to note that he believed both in his dream and in the assertion of the missionary. While these two statements are incompatible with each other on a logical level, they could coexist in the mind of the Indian. They may represent a physical impossibility but not a logical contradiction if one accepts the idea of supernatural multipresence of the body or spirit endowed with special power.

Within the same framework of duality of thinking on a pseudo and logical level, Levy-Bruhl reports of the Bororo tribe, which believed that men of another inimical tribe, Trumai, were able to sleep at night at the bottom of a nearby river. Bororo people recognized the Trumai as men like them, who could not sleep underwater under normal circumstances. Yet they insisted that the Trumai had this special mysterious power to do so. For them the conclusion was self-evident: the Trumai were endowed with supernatural power. As we may see, the distinction between truth and fantasy can be blurred by the belief that supernatural powers can direct, control, and miraculously change the course of an action. But the reason behind their justifications was unmistakably clear, the attempt to survive by staying alert against any surprise attack from the other tribe, who may hide underwater. In a way, this type of thinking reminds us of the absurd accusations made against witches, like that of flying or inducing death by distant incantations, while remaining unable to free themselves from the hands of inquisitors during trials that took place in Europe and in America between the 16th and 18th centuries.

Most of the time, primitive man believes matter of factly in the intervention of supernatural powers in shaping his fate, while modern man may retain similar beliefs, but on a more sophisticated level by relating them to the vaguely defined notion of luck or God's will. However, men quite often, whether primitive or modern, appeal to these mysterious forces for justifications of their actions or for seeking relief from a threatening situation.

Let us take the case of a sorcerer who one evening did not come back to where the tribe was located. The tribesmen, together with Levi-Strauss, who was living with the tribe at the time, looked for him with no result. In the early morning he was found in the vicinity of the encampment almost naked, shivering and speechless. Later, he volunteered a bizarre explanation: during the previous night, when it was rainy and thundering, he had been lifted by thunder and taken far away. His explanation was believable and acceptable to most tribesmen, so long as it was in line with the prevailing beliefs of his community. Only some of his rivals doubted his story because of their suspicion of political intrigue with another tribe within the vicinity. It is quite possible that he started to believe his own stories, since he thought that most of his actions were determined by powerful inside forces connected to supernatural ones. His mythological process of thinking, with its free invocation of occult forces, made any objective evaluation of his reasoning almost impossible.[22] If this sounds fictitious, think about the current claims of intervention of extraterrestrial power in the lives of some people today.

The concept of supernatural power, miracles, or omnipresence of gods, now reduced to one God, has been accepted by believers of all modern religions, and, though considered to be beyond logic, their validity is found in faith. All these beliefs are based on the duality of thinking of these people, thinking that may affect their actions in two ways: on the one hand, it makes them susceptible to exaggerations and misrepresentation of facts, and on the other, it makes them an easy target for deception. For instance, it has been recently reported by the media that a minister of the Pentecostal church claims to have the power to exorcise demons, and heal amost any disease for a sizable fee.[23] As a result of this ability, churchgoers are submitting to the rituals of "casting out the inside demons." The people believed themselves to be possessed by evil spirits and asked for the pastor's help. The reasoning of these people is not so different from that of primitive men. A moot question is whether or not the pastor believes in his holy power. However, as long as he is not accused by the city of "healing" without a proper health license, he will do all right.

Finally, within this framework of duality of thinking we can better understand how men are able to manipulate the much-praised conscience, the inner censor of right and wrong.

PEOPLE'S MANIPULATION OF THEIR CONSCIENCE

This duality of thinking can explain why people are able to justify their actions, which are not in accord with either the prevailing social morality or with that of their own. Depending on the individual's degree of mixing in his thinking, hard facts and/or biased perceptions will be his interpretation of the truth. This potentiality of thinking leads him to experience events on a logical and/or pseudological mode (personal convictions and internalized subcultural beliefs), subsequently directs his duplicity toward his moral judgment. In this context one may be able to ignore selectively his "social conscience" as developed in the process of his socialization and yet be aware of its existence. His motives for doing so may be hidden under rationalizations and beliefs that may overrule moral considerations. In many instances, he would claim that he acts truthfully when he does not. In other situations, he knows that admitting and/or fighting for the truth may not be beneficial. In finality, most people manipulate, consciously or subconsciously, their social conscience, as dictated by pressing circumstances. Their mind's dynamics only attempt to obfuscate the truth in the pursuit of self-interest. Some people learn the hard way that others have a flexible attitude toward their social conscience that is often dictated by their interests. This was exactly what Judy learned painfully in her dealings with an alleged honorable academic faculty purportedly dedicated to the social welfare of people.

Judy, in her early forties, after successfully bringing up a child by herself, decided to pursue a career as a social worker. She had previously held part-time jobs that were community-oriented, and she enjoyed helping and working with people. Judy fought hard to obtain a scholarship to a school for social work and took her studies seriously. In her second year of field placement in a hospital, she was appalled by the lack of interest on the part of the staff for the field training of the students and for the care of patients. She expressed her concerns to her supervisors who, unfortunately, were part of the problem. After a few of her negative remarks about the patients' neglect by staff, she found herself attacked for surpassing her responsibilities because of her unwelcome overconcern with her cases. In due time, the whole issue was cleverly changed by her superiors into her having a personality problem. As a result, her supervisor raised doubts about her ability to become a social worker. The explanation was cleverly couched in psychodynamic interpretations of her alleged problems with "countertransference," an unverifiable charge. In other words, she allegedly identified herself too much with the patients who were in any case too demanding and ungrateful. Never mind that her direct supervisor was un-informed about the condition of her patients for whose caretaking she was being paid. The naive student, emotionally devastated, threatened with being thrown out of the school and lacking the money needed to hire a lawyer, accepted her "errors" and the punishment of taking extra courses even though this meant graduating later. Ultimately, Judy failed to see the arrogance of the faculty staff, who, although neglecting the patients and the training of the students, thought to be beyond any criticism. Then, when they felt they were being attacked and that indirectly their power was being questioned, they swiftly defended their turf with countermeasures and blatant lies.

Now we understand how it is possible for people to suppress their conscience, the alleged bedrock of one's morality that supposedly guides one's actions. Indeed, it seems that it has lately acquired, in most people, a chameleon-like quality. It is too often manipulated for the benefit of one's version of the truth. Unfortunately, the deterioration of the collective social conscience (as expressed in social morality), which too often disregards or reconstructs the truth, has also eroded and weakened people's conscience, the internalized repository of the social code of ethics. This may explain why shame is a waning emotion. Even if an individual does experience pangs from his battered conscience, most often he tries to appease them by rationalizing his lying for his own peace of mind. Sometimes he will justify himself as being forced to act deviously for self-protection. Other times he suspends any critical judgment about his deception and substitutes for it a convenient, flexible concept of morality formulated to fit his immediate goal.

The lesson for anyone is obvious: the social drive for status and the need for control over others, acting together or separately, are the moving force heavily weighing on any decision-making process regardless of the underlying moral issue. Practically, personal moral norms of conduct are disregarded or reinterpreted by most people to fit their social agenda. This has been helped by the erosion of the work and family values provoked by the new social paradigm, which left open to subjective interpretation the notions of right and wrong or true and false.

People who refuse to accept the current social realities are at great disadvantage in coping with or negotiating their social activities. This also applies to those conducted by high moral principle who dare to question the policies of their superiors in the name of establishing the truth and extirpating corruption. It is an old story that whistleblowers most often end up fired, demoted, or ostracized because of trumped-up charges.

Is this duality of thinking also responsible for man's duplicity toward his religious values?

RELIGION'S AMBIGUITY TOWARD LYING

Leaving aside politicians, who attempt to justify their lies and deceptions as being necessitated by circumstances beyond their control or even being justified by the fancy idea of safeguarding the public interest, most people defend their lying by invoking self-protection. Self-protection, however, is meant in the most general sense and includes all actions that may be perceived by the individual as damaging or threatening to himself. The argument of lying for self-protection or for the safeguarding of others has preoccupied philosophers, legislators, and priests since antiquity. The oldest known penal code is that of Hammurabi, the Babylonian king, who lived approximately 2,000 years before Christ; the best known religious moral code is obviously the Ten Commandments of Moses, the Hebrew prophet and leader. Both codes, from different perspectives, secular and divine, take strong positions against lying and deception. The first heavily penalizes the deceiver or the cheater in this world, while the latter threatens him with divine and possible after-life punishment. Yet neither of them stops people from lying. Why? Because neither one found a satisfactory solution to the human need to lie, as a means of coping with threats to what he perceives to affect his survival or self-protection.

This may explain the fact that we find, in the old Scriptures, a few lies related to these issues and other associated feelings. According to the Bible, a woman lied to protect the lives of two wanted men (Joshua 2:4–6). In another book we are told of a spirit that informs God of his intention to lie in order to entice Ahab, and God approves it (Kings 22:21–22). What is indeed fascinating is the impression that the story of mankind, according to the Bible, began with lies, was followed later by a murder, and continued with more lies and deception. As we know, Satan, disguised as a serpent, deceived Eve. Cain, after murdering Abel, lied to God about the fate of his brother Abel. But what about Joseph, who was sold in slavery by his jealous brothers while claiming that he accidentally died (Genesis 37–50). With these facts in mind, some could argue that with such "criminal genes" in our background, mankind has such poor psychomoral beginnings that our future moral survival is in question.

Nevertheless, the early Christian theologians attempted to address the issue of unrestricted lying in light of their new vision of eternal life and of man's belief in the divine retribution. St. Augustine thought that all forms of lying were sinful and endangered the individual's immortal soul. However, he recognized that under some conditions people may not be able to tell the truth, basically to shield others. He believed that all lies were sins and he graded them on a scale of one to eight with only two types of harmless lies: one, where the intention was not to deceive, and the other told to protect someone from physical harm. These two categories were supposed to be treated lightly. What is important is that St. Augustine attempted to separate the intentional and harmful lies from the unintentional and harmless ones. Ultimately, he offered believers a moral approach to their social conduct in accordance with their aspiration for eternal life.[24] Nevertheless, there was still a full prohibition against lying, which was extremely frustrating to the members of the Church, who were unable to obey these strict moral prescriptions in real life. This meant that even devoted followers of religious dogma could not go through life without lying, at least when necessitated by extreme life-threatening conditions. They needed relief from the anguish induced by the conflict between the fear of the apocalyptic consequences of lying and the reality of surviving in a ruthless medieval social system. The man who understood them and responded to their emotional torment was Thomas Aquinas.

Thomas Aquinas, a medieval Catholic theologian, modified and simplified the religious doctrine forbidding lying by qualifying that only malicious lies told with intent to harm someone are mortal sins. He categorized all other types of lies, which were sinful but pardonable, as officious or jocose, since they were considered either helpful or harmless.[25] This reappraisal of the moral prescriptions against lying has had vast implications for both social interaction and for the Church. It officially recognized the human need to lie, at least under specific circumstances, and it attempted to socially regulate lying by distinguishing the acceptable from the malicious lies. The unforeseeable result was that the Church's forgiveness, when extended to certain types of possibly harmful lies, became gradually abused. People told all kinds of lies while thinking of appealing to the Church for forgiveness. Once again this proves the boundless need of people to lie, though now it was facilitated by the Church offering of protection from celestial wrath.

It is puzzling to examine the logical subterfuge offered by the Church for its absolution of some types of intentional lies that led to the opening of "Pandora's box" with respect to prevarication. The concept introduced by the Church has been that of "mental reservation" based on the principle of permitting someone to tell an intentional lie as long as he qualified it, in his mind, with a statement that changed the meaning of that lie and in this way made it true to himself. If the untrue statement, by a kind of mental gymnastics, was recast in the mind as true, then the burden of "misintepretation" has been placed on the deceived. If a man lied to another about doing something contrary to their previous agreement, all he needed to say to himself was that he had not done that activity at another time, when indeed he had not done it. According to this skewed logic, that person did not lie. Unfortunately, this approach has given people a free license to lie, free of the fear of eternal punishment. Yet, these excesses did not stop here.

People were ready to lie and deceive not only to protect their interests, but even worse to enhance their social gains and status at the expense of others. They wanted the Church's absolution for more serious deceptions. The Church met their demand by selling them certificates of forgiveness for various types of deceptions. These indulgences granted remission of all penalties to the soul for an amount of money paid to the Church by the sinner. The reformers indignantly reacted to these mercantile or twisted moral practices by the then existing religious authorities. One of the reasons for Martin Luther's rebellion against the Catholic Church was precisely this selling of indulgences, which he regarded as a corrupt practice and a doctrinal abuse. This finally led to the splitting of the Catholic Church by the reformers. From a sociological perspective, this abuse shows the extent of man's propensity for corruption, in this case exploited by misguided clergymen. Did the reform change human morality? Not for a long time. In the name of the new morality imposed by the reformers, intolerance flourished, followed later by religious persecutions such as the Salem witch trials, when the truth was shamelessly abused.

Interestingly, people who continue to express strong religious beliefs and attend religious services regularly may also twist the moral code in their favor when faced with hard personal decisions, to the point of deceiving or even committing murder justified on questionable religious grounds. The recent case of anti-abortionists who resorted to violence and murder in support of their "sacred cause" amply documents this point. The reality is that throughout history, religious fanaticism has had its share of responsibility for political and social violence, murders, and wars, all instigated in the name of God and allegedly fought for man's eternal salvation. The political killing of Itzakh Rabin in 1995, at that time the prime minister of Israel, is the latest unfortunate occurrence of these misguided religious beliefs. But the secular society's arbitrary discrimination between allowable and nonallowable lies has not been more successful. Inadvertently or not, it does attempt to a great extent to "legitimize" lying.

Admittedly, the power of religious morality in Western societies has been slowly declining and the historic role of the religious man as social mediator responsible for enforcing the proper behavior in the community has been waning. The proscriptions for trespassing upon social customs as codified by laws are now supposed to be implemented by the law enforcement agencies. Only the punishment for disobedience of religious rituals has been left in the hands of priests and of God. However, both forms of morality, religious and secular, have been intertwined to a great extent throughout history, simply because they have been working together against the same enemies, namely, human selfishness, greed, and a tendency to exploit others.

Since religious morality and secular ethics are addressing different levels of interpretation of reality, it is interesting to see how the mind tries to integrate them in dealing with the hard facts of life. While both types of morality should work synergistically, they are in fact separately manipulated by the individual in his construct of reality. Basically, both attempt to induce fear in people who defy either the assumed divine code or the social laws. People clearly differentiate between the potential effects induced on them by ignoring the intangible divine power and by manipulating the secular laws. Then the question is whether or not fear of divine retribution has any power to restrain people from inducing conflicts with the prevailing laws of the social order.

This leads us to the issue of finding how originally the religious moral constraints used to work. They were based on the fear of breaking "taboos." A taboo was a prohibition against the use of an object or an act, such as killing of a specific animal or bird, or anything else that by tradition gained tabooed status. Taboos were believed to have been controlled by supernatural forces; they were holy, sacred, and feared. Any transgression of them automatically brought supernatural and social proscription. Although sometimes taboos were manipulated by priests or chiefs who arbitrarily bestowed taboo status on a favored person, they served as a method of ensuring conformity and obedience to the imposed social order of the tribe.

Certain loose taboos, often fear-inspiring, are still present today in some remote parts of the world, although much less often in the Western countries. Beliefs maintaining only the flavor of the old concept have survived today in our "civilized" societies, mostly as superstitions. The fear that "bad luck" may be incurred by, for example, an "evil eye" cast upon another still can act as a force to change one's immediate behavior. Today, some old taboos like incest have been integrated into laws, others have survived as social conventions subject to the collective consensus, while still others are part of a popular repertory of superstitions or personal beliefs that occasionally influence the decision-making processes of the believer.

At the same time, let's keep in mind that our social "taboos" do not stop anyone from relentlessly pursuing his ambitions and wants. From our daily experience, it seems that religion, with its moral laws as written in the Scriptures, exerts little power over the human conscience. Man apparently pays little attention to the preaching of organized religions, which have already been compromised by their past actions of lying, deception, and violence. The latest case of Rod Wright, an English bishop who fathered a child by a parishioner and after leaving the priesthood because of his affair with another woman sold his story to a tabloid, is a very disheartening example of the lack of moral scruples of some high representatives of organized religion.[26]

Regardless of some of their past detestable political or immoral activities, all major religions are still trying to be guardians of the moral ideals in their respective societies. Although religious morality, incorporated into societal ethics, tries to act as a guidepost for human conduct in social interaction, the divine proscriptions are a weak deterrent against deceptive actions and behaviors. The conscience that is supposed to inhibit among other things people's propensity to falsehood, dishonesty, and deception is ineffectual. Worse, people may still think of themselves as honest and lie, justifying the lies as having been compelled by unusual and unfavorable circumstances beyond their control. And herein lies man's perennial duplicity toward morality.

Consider David's morality. He is a successful businessman in his mid-fifties, a solid pillar of the community, a congregation leader involved in his community's affairs, a family man who prides himself on his integrity, self-discipline, and moderation. David thinks of himself as an ethical man. In fact, he is concerned with the existing moral laxity of our society as evidenced by declining work ethics, family disintegration, and juvenile sexual permissiveness. His problem is that his sister-in-law fell in love with him and after a period of innocuous flirtation and months of alleged moral reflection, they ended up in each other arms as lovers in a country motel with a romantic setting. This happened three years ago and the passionate affair continued unabated until recently, when it broke down due to his sudden health problems. Forget about the lies required to carry on the affairs or about the underlying conspiratorial duplicity, but just keep in mind that she is his sister-in-law. Yet, he claims to have been spurred on by extenuating circumstances, her aggressive pursuit of him, and the uncontrollable emotional explosion of passion within himself, which he had not been aware of possessing prior to this affair. The drama has unfolded itself for years, filled with more lies, deception, pains, and absurd rationalizations. The only positive note in this moral quagmire is his ability to terminate the relationship.

It is a fact that people tend to rewrite for themselves and sometimes for others when in a position of authority the social moral codes according to their pressing emotional needs. In other words, most people are pursuing, by and large, a selfish-hedonistic morality. This is a subjective morality, directed by the principle of self-gratification and justified by subtle self-serving explanations. It is facilitated by the moral relativism emerging from an opportunistic philosophy of life.

To this philosophy has contributed Man's realization of a few unsettling things in the process of coping to survive and protect himself. He has lately begun to notice that his conviction about God's role to protect him against life's adversities, including his enemies, in exchange for his duty to worship the Lord and obey His rules, did not work out well for him. He feels left at the mercy of natural and societal forces that have always tormented his transient and hazardous existence. The fear of God's punishment for disobedience of His laws, while still recognized by Man as a distant possibility, has gradually been relegated to the remote recesses of his mind. Man has identified his life's priorities as the struggle for survival and defeat of rivals, competitors, or enemies by whatever means he has available, while paying lip service to any thought of divine intervention. And here is the wrinkle.

For too many the social or personal moral code has become too lax and ambiguous to control their selfish needs. Neither the fear of divine retribution nor that of social disapproval, rejection, or even penalty is sufficient to make most people abandon their self-indulgent pursuits, often sought at the expense of others. This is well reflected in the attitude of the baby boomers, who feel, to a great extent, that the ethical values of the past era have little relevance for them.

THE MORAL RELATIVISM OF SOCIETY

What did happen to our society to find itself in this predicament? What social forces have contributed to the disintegration of its moral fiber? After all, there is nothing new about lying in our society. What is apparently new is the change of public opinion toward lying. It has become socially accepted, as factored into the course of human communication or transactions. The clever liars are applauded, the bad ones are ridiculed. Exposed liars show no shame, successful liars and deceivers look down on their victims. It is a reversal of moral values with a serious impact on the social regulation of lying and deception.

But how do our governmental institutions deal with this moral malaise? They seem to be part of the problem. The powers that be, while taking grave liberties with the truth, still try to sway the public into accepting their version of fabricated truth in order to stay in power. To convince the public of their credibility they hire expert "truth-spinners" who twist the facts in order to create a semblance of truth from outright lies and deceptions. They know that, ultimately, they have to get the approval of the ordinary people who determine the degree of acceptance of social morality and the support or not for its laws.

Take for example the recent prosecution by Congress of President Clinton for his sexual misconduct. One may think that the Clinton–Lewinsky sexual scandal, with his later admission to the nation of having lied, compounded by his perjury under oath, might have negatively affected his image of moral integrity. In reality, partly under the persuasion of "spin-doctors" and lawyers, public opinion turned in Clinton's favor, as shown in national polls. And the polls decided the outcome of the case by indirectly forcing Congress to acquit him. Certainly there were other political reasons why the majority of the public did not consider his misconduct and lying as punishable by removal from office. This was also helped by the sapping of our moral standards, particularly reflected in the collapse of family values that has been at work for some time that made his affair and adultery meaningless. This social background of moral laxity and confusion highly undermined the ability of a great number of people to make moral decisions.

The general perception of a justice system oriented toward social activism and inclined to favor social explanations for the crime instead of factual evidence influences the ethical behavior of many people. They do realize that regardless of how much these laws might, in principle, protect the right of the people, their execution depends on institutions run by politically elected officials who decide their interpretation.The decisions can be selective, depending on many political and social considerations that render the laws meaningless. Worse, the code of justice is also twisted by various interest groups. Yet most people do not care. Why? Obviously, it has to be related to a change in society's attitude toward lying and deception. How did it occur?

Exploring the ambivalence of the social institutions toward lying, analyzing the major reasons that motivate people to lie, finding that throughout mankind's history there has been a continued use and abuse of lying in human interaction, still would not explain what brought about the deterioration of our moral standards. It may only be a consolation to know that from Biblical times to the present lying has been well integrated into the social fabric by fulfilling the important function of helping people to cope with real or perceived adversities.

To explain our present moral predicament, we have to acknowledge first that there has been a consensual universal social policy toward judging lying in terms of permissible and nonpermissible lies. In general, lies have been considered permissible as long as they did not interfere with the functioning of the community. In this respect, the degree and types of lies permitted by societies may have fluctuated from time to time, and from one culture to another, but the main criterion for determining the acceptability of a lie has been its impact on the welfare of the community and state and rather less on the individual. And for good reasons. Excessive and grievous lying has always been considered damaging to any society because it destabilizes human interaction and makes any meaningful social intercourse almost impossible. Imagine a society in which everybody distorts or denies facts according to his immediate needs or retracts statements made in the course of doing business or pursuing personal activities. The confusion would be so great that it could bring that society to a standstill. The impossibility of making any decision would be so taxing it could result in violent, destructive reactions.

The obvious dilemma for any society has always been that of attempting to reach a balance between the people's need to lie and its own interest in functioning with a minimum of social disruptions created by lying and deception. Since the balance is a precarious one, the debate between society and individuals for establishing the truth and obfuscating or suppressing it goes unabated. Expediently it is solved in the favor of the class or political elite in power.

At this time, in our society the balance between permissible and nonpermissible lies has been destabilized and distorted by powerful social forces, which while attacking the social-economic structure of society by clamoring for a new social egalitarianism have also called into question the values of the old morality by favoring a more flexible one that would make more acceptable their social demands. The balance is heavily tilted in favor of obfuscation of previous social truths in certain areas of interracial and gender conflict, which surreptitiously expanded the concept of permissible lies by incorporating in its domain many types of lies previously considered as nonpermissible. This was based on the new concept of viewing lies and deception as politically correct or incorrect (a concept borrowed from the ideology of defunct Communist states). A new relativistic morality emerged, facilitated by the access to power of people earlier deprived of it. The result has been the blurring of distinction between true and false, between right and wrong.

Historically, this social-moral relativism has evolved in this country under the impact of the massive popular unrest and discontent of 1960s, which assailed the old ethical premises of fairness and biased justice while demanding significant social-political reforms. The outcome has been a new concept of justice and morality. In the process, society has even exhibited some degree of pathological behavior that is tolerated or encouraged by the new power elite in its efforts to enforce the new version of the moral code. A new loose concept of morality, politically inspired, slowly emerged that has reconstructed the notions of right and wrong to favor racial demands and gender rights. The elected leaders became less principled and more pragmatic than the previous ones, in an attempt to please their new rebellious constituents. Gradually, they ignored the old ethics and adhered to a new code of moral relativism. The powers that be have attempted to justify a new set of ethics, even twisting some basic Constitutional principles. The issue is whether or not this new morality will create a more ethical, more egalitarian society with more honest and fair citizens. Past and recent examples from the history of major religious reforms to that of Communism do not give us any encouraging positive answer.

Ultimately, the change in morality gradually has led to a new, flexible approach to the truth, dictated more by hedonistic, narcissistic, and guiltless gratification. This new morality is also influenced by the late extraordinary scientific developments that led to a novel view of the universe and Man. From this perspective, Man perceived as a product of evolution is reduced to the role of a smart and selfish animal at the mercy of his brain's chemical reactions, which frequently get out of control. As a result, he is often unprincipled and unpredictable, while he tries to cope with his cruel and chaotic environment. This means that Man is born neither good, some philosophers believed, nor wicked, as some religious doctrines try to preach. Man is both, depending on social circumstances and his perceived interests. In this context, for most people faced with a society in social and political transition, successful adaptation has become more a matter of ability to master duplicity and equivocation to either win or to protect themselves from other liars. For many, lying has become an easy way of coping with the new world in the making.

In conclusion, it would be fair to assume that most people function socially on the assumption that everyone is either to some degree a liar or has the potential to become one if necessary. Yet, daily life places in doubt this inference because people who know that others may lie or cheat often fail to protect themselves from liars.

Here is one great paradox of man's social behavior: while he himself may lie and deceive others under various circumstances, he has difficulty keeping in mind the possibility of being at any time the prey of a better schemer or more sophisticated liar.

NOTES

1. M. Perlmutter, *Why Lawyers Lie*. Online. *The Institute for Central Conflict Resolution*, 1999.

2. B.M. DePaulo, S.E. Kirkendol, J.A. Epstein, et al., "Everyday Lies in Adolescent Life in Sex Differences in Lying," in *Lying and Deception in Everyday Life*, edited by M. Lewis, & C. Saarni (New York: Guilford Press, 1993), p. 128.

3. H.C. Kraemer, "'Lies, damn lies and statistics' in clinical research." *The Pharos* (Fall 1992): pp. 7–12.

4. R. Darnton, *Mesmerism* (New York: Schocken Books, 1970).

5. "Was the Painted-Mouse Doctor Right?" *Medical World News* (April 1977): 28.

6. "Former Professor Admits Diverting Research Funds," *Wall Street Journal*, December 19, 1997, p. A11.

7. C. Levi-Srauss, *Structural Anthropology* (New York: Doubleday, Anchor Books, 1967), pp. 193–200.

8. S. Freud, *Totem and Taboo* (New York: Random House, 1946), pp. 151–207.

9. E. Loftus, & K. Katcham, *The Myth of Repressed Memory: False Memories & the Accusation of Sex Abuse* (New York: St. Martin Griffins, 1994), p. 103.

10. J.M. Grinfeld, "Criminal Charges Filed in Memory Case," *Psychiatric News* (December 1997), pp. 1, 3, 5.

11. G. Boccaccio, *Decameron* (Berkeley: University Press of California, 1966).

12. G. Casanova, *The Memoirs of Jacques Casanova de Seingalt*, tran. A.A. Machen (New York: C. Boni, 1932).

13. M. Montaigne, *Essays* (New York: Penguin Books, 1981), p. 31.

14. T. Dreiser, *An American Tragedy* (New York: Signet-Penguin, 1964).

15. V. Packard, *The Pyramid Climbers* (New York: McGraw-Hill, 1963).

16. M. Caine, *The S-Man* (New York: Houghton Mifflin, 1961).

17. F. Norris, & B.D. Henriques, "The Culture of Fraud that Shrank Cendant," *New York Times*, June 15, p. C1.

18. J. Piaget, *The Moral Judgment of the Child* (New York: Collier Books, 1962), pp. 163–194.

19. Ibid., pp. 42–65.

20. G. Serban, *The Tyranny of the Magical Thinking* (New York: E.P. Dutton, 1982), pp. 24–39.

21. L. Levy-Bruhl, *The Notebooks on Primitive Mentality* (Oxford, England: Basil Blackwell & Mott Ltd., 1975), pp. 7–11.

22. C. Levi-Strauss, *Structural Anthropology* (New York: Doubleday, Anchor Books, 1997), pp. 163–164.

23. L. Italiano, & M. Alvarez, "Devil Gets the Business on Mondays," *New York Post*, July 24, 2000, pp. 4–5.

24. St. Augustine. *Lying Treatise on Various Subjects*, edited by R.J. Deferrari (New York: Catholic University of New York America Press, 1952).

25. T. Aquinas, "Whether Lies Are Sufficiently Divided . . . Summa Theologica," in S. Bok, *Lying: Moral Choice in Public and Private Life* (New York: Vintage Books, 1979), appendix.

26. M. Bunting, "Bishop Branded as Judas for Betraying Catholic Church," *The Guardian International*, September 23, 1996, p. 1.

Chapter 4

Self-deception

Self-love is cleverer than the cleverest man in the world.
La Rochefoucauld, *The Maxim*

THE ROLE OF SELF-DECEPTION IN SOCIAL ADAPTATION

Carol (47 years old and divorced for 12 years): "I have a full social life ... I have a good job, a few friends, and men flirt with me all the time, at parties, social functions, even at the office. ... Men find me very attractive, classy, entertaining, and desirable. ... I go on dates only with successful, accomplished men ... I am waiting to meet the right man. ..."

Reality: Carol is a moderately attractive career woman, showing her age and living slightly beyond her means. She spends quite a bit of money on clothes and is constantly in debt. She flirts whenever possible with men, cajoles acquaintances to invite her to social events and has had short-lived sexual affairs but she does not have a steady boyfriend. Still, she hopes to marry a high-level executive, a successful professional, or a wealthy businessman. Is she realistic about her self-appraisal or is she deceiving herself?

David (middle-aged litigation lawyer who works for a mid-size law firm): "My senior partner too often misses important subtle legal issues, which I have to bring to his attention when we are preparing big corporation cases for trial. He relies on me to solve subtle legal points of defense. I even have to correct his legal correspondence, which is often rambling and confusing. Sometimes I have to tell him off. Quite often, partners in the firm come to me for advice in handling their cases. It may be flattering, but after a while it is annoying."

Reality: David likes to talk about the brilliant strategies he has developed in his defense in court cases, which have raised substantial issues of jurisprudence. He peppers his stories with his alleged successes in court, where he has crushed the arguments of the opponents with unbeatable, sophisticated counterarguments. David did not receive any increase in salary for the last two years because his billing was below the projections of the firm. He was unable to bring in any new clients. He has lately settled two cases contrary to the expectations of the firm's clients. The senior partner has gradually used David's services less, replacing him with a younger partner. David's explanation for these happenings, that he has been too busy to be bothered with internal politics, is weak and unsatisfactory. Does he believe that his assessment of his position in the firm and his interpretation of facts is the correct one? Is he kidding himself?

One of the most fascinating traits of the human mind is its ability to falsify reality to suit one's needs. The mind does this not only for the benefit of maintaining an internal consistency between unequally opposing drives within an individual, but also more often to present itself in a particular light to others. It is easy to understand the reasons that compel people to lie to others, but it is harder to imagine why they need to twist and distort reality for themselves.

Lying to oneself means going beyond indulging in daydreams about possessing qualities and talents that one never had or fantasying about being that terrific hero who performs daring acts that are out of character with his/her personality or his/her daily routine of life. There are very many degrees of lying to oneself, but the most accomplished self-deceiver reinvents himself by ignoring or denying the true self. While the daydreamer knows when he has escaped into the world of fantasy and is able to separate it from the real self, the same is only partly true for the accomplished self-deceiver. This individual, who wants to be what he is not, does not jokingly pretend to exhibit his invented skills and qualities; he tries to imagine that he has them and reinforces them by acting accordingly. Is he truly twisting the truth about himself or is he revealing another facet of himself as required by the circumstances?

From the point of view of classical psychology, people develop a coherent and cohesive sense of self-identity. Any crack or split in this self-identity represents a failure of personality integration, which results in various degrees of pathological mental states, from neurotic to psychotic. The habitual self-deceiving is considered a mild deviant personality formulation in response to coping with a developmental negative view of oneself. At a closer look, the self-deceivers are neither imposters who deliberately lie about possessing professional degrees or special training, nor braggarts who just knowingly exaggerate their role in various events to impress others. In a sense, the self-deceivers, by artificially adding attributes of personality to their self-image that they like to believe they possess but in reality they do not have, place themselves between imposters and braggarts. While they do not pretend to be from a different social position or status, they do brag about intellectual qualities that they do not possess to that degree or boast about achievements that may never have happened within the context of their relayed version. One basic difference between them and other categories of liars is that they tend to identify on one level of consciousness with their newly fabricated image. Their presentation of themselves may appear to others as incongruous and artificial, if not fake, but for self-deceivers, it is defended when dealing with others as the only acceptable reality of themselves. Yet it is a brittle image, poorly integrated in their mode of being and quite often betraying its artificiality.

This reconstruction of personality is part of the person's process of adaptation to his environment, which can either be quite successfully undertaken by building self-confidence or at other times it could go awry by integrating into it nonexistent qualities. Any individual in the process of socialization instinctively tries to enhance his ability to cope with challenging events and to successfully compete with others by improving the traits of his personality that favor his success and reduce those viewed as hindrances. Yet, self-deceiving is not a simple form of bolstering self-image. Building self-confidence presupposes improving the view of oneself by reinforcing positive traits that, in exchange, may increase one's motivation to achieve more. But, how can someone know that the self-esteem he has built is not blown out of proportion regarding his true abilities? If the person has overcompensated for his real or imaginary deficiencies while striving for betterment and as such has increased his expectations of himself beyond his true abilities, then he has started to deceive himself. He has overdone the process of tuning his coping skills to the point of magically ignoring and/or suppressing unwanted traits of his personality and gradually replacing them with desirable but imaginary qualities that he would like to have. The puzzling issue seems to be the ability of someone to deny knowledge about oneself which at the same time remains known to him. There are many hypothetical explanations offered by various psychological schools of thought, but all are wanting. Seemingly, the most logical explanation is offered by framing this phenomenon within the processes of the adult's mental dynamics, which retain strong elements of a child's magical thinking. There are two main issues raised by the mode of thought and behavior of self-deceivers. One issue is in regard to their duplicity of reasoning, that is, an ability to integrate within the self-image exaggerated attributes of personality by reinforcing them with favorable interpretations of selective experiences. This capability is related to a second trait of their duality of thinking, which permits their emotional judgment to overrule reality. The lack of critical judgment about themselves leads to persistently exhibiting types of behavior that make them look quite often awkward, if not phony, in social situations.

In this context, there are complex psychological factors responsible for the development of this distorted perception of oneself. In many cases, it can be traced to one's early years of socialization, to that stage of life when the child has gradually started to assess his intellectual and physical abilities by comparing them with those of other playmates and children at school. At this time, by participating and competing in games or academic activities, the child has received the first hint of his strengths and weaknesses that may have led him to wish to be different. In this situation, there are two social forces acting in opposing directions which influence and shape a child's responses to his milieu. One is represented by the parents, who may unrealistically boost the child's expectations of himself. The other is related to his interaction with his siblings and peers, who may ruthlessly ridicule his faults and shortcomings. Supported by his parents or others influential in his life, he tries hard to do better in order to escape other children's abuse and humiliations (putdowns). Gradually, the child may learn, by trial and error, to overcome some of his most suspected undesirable traits either by working hard to improve his skills or by avoiding to exhibit those shortcomings while pretending and acting as if he possesses the desirable but lacking traits. If he is overambitious or desperately wants to please the significant figures in his life but does not have what it takes to change, then he slowly falls in the latter category of pretending. He emulates others whose qualities he admires and wants to possess. He would like to be like his model, though he falls short of being able to fully incorporate the desired attributes. Nevertheless, over the years, these newly assumed qualities, which portray the ideal image of a desirable self, have magically become a part of himself, attempting to determine his actions; they are, however, only partially congruent with his true abilities and hence, poorly integrated into his personality. And here begins the social problem for the self-deceiver, who may have even achieved a degree of social success, namely, the difficulty in bridging the gap between the extreme qualities that he strives to be accepted by others and the real self with its true shortcomings. In addition, in the process of socialization, self-deceivers have learned to reject or deny not only some unfavorable aspects of their personality but also to claim that those negative traits are misperceptions or malicious views owing to the envy of others. The duality of their thought, with its logical and pseudological intertwining processes, is responsible for this mind's gymnastics, which have succeeded to suppress the truth about themselves and to accuse others of finding imaginary faults with them.

Their obsessive need to be recognized as having those ideal, unreachable attributes is so overpowering that it supersedes the acknowledgment of the existent qualities that they possess. The desire to impress others with their intellectual wit, talents, and cleverness is overwhelming to the point that they risk appearing overbearing or conceited. In general, these people talk mostly about themselves and of their real or invented achievements to impress others, regardless of the evidence contrary to their assertions. Although this behavior could temporarily discredit them, it does not stop them from continuing the same pattern of phony self-promotion. Paradoxically, these mentally convoluted processes indirectly reinforce their deep-seated feelings of insecurity, which they have initially tried to overcome by adopting their self-created image. Because of their inability to think realistically of themselves in their interactions with others, the conflict between what they display and what they are more painfully emerges, causing most of them to act incongruously and inappropriately in critical situations. This may explain why during a difficult transaction or discussion, when all means of persuasion of the other party have failed, some self-deceivers get angry and resort to various types of objectionable behaviors from an arrogant patronizing attitude to bravado or insults.

The seemingly mystifying issue is why people who appear to be intelligent and otherwise reasonable resort to dubious tactics and artifices to convince others of their alleged superior intellect and cleverness. It is obvious that someone would not have this need unless he was attempting to compensate for harboring feelings of real or imaginary intellectual or physical inferiority. Some may have adopted a new self-image to enhance their ability to cope with those social events and people who do not yield to their emotional needs. Then, one may say they are just posturing. Is this true?

This assumption about their behavior seems to be in line with a new concept of flexibility of self touted by the postmodern humanistic school of psychology, which questions the validity of the classical integrated self. The new approach to self claims that an individual can function with various presentations of his social self and all be genuine parts of the same self because the self is flexibly influenced by others in a given situation.[1] According to them, no one has a coherent, stable sense of identity. This means that an individual can present many versions of truth about himself, which all depend on his perception of reality at the time. In this context an individual considered a self-deceiver by the classical psychology is just spontaneously presenting a different self as required by the circumstances. The new perception of self has been induced by a different mode of viewing reality. This is like someone looking through a Lavoisier mirror, which because of its concavity collects light from an object and returns it so that the object outside the mirror is seen changing its image with any shift of the eyes. But this is an optical illusion and the viewer is aware of it. What the postmodern "science" of humanistic psychology fails to tell us is the processes of consciousness associated with the emergence of this new self. If it is a conscious response to the new circumstances, then it is an intentional act that suggests posturing. If it is not so, then one may think of a dissociative process, which is not the case. For the self-deceiver the imposed perception of self is constantly fighting the old one like unruly tidal waves. Furthermore, his new image does not change in response to new situations; on the contrary, its rigidity and persistence is a source of difficulty for him. His inner ambivalence makes his awareness of his self-deceiving often appear in the twilight zone of consciousness.

People with self-deceiving tendencies exhibit varying degrees and shades of self-deceit, from the simple need to automatically exaggerate personal contributions, some notable deeds or creative, brilliant concepts to remaking reality to meet their needs. Some go so far as to imagine possessing and acting as if they have those desired outstanding qualities or talents, which they like to brazenly demonstrate in any situation, regardless of its appropriateness.

SELF-DECEIVERS "BEGGING" FOR RECOGNITION

Most self-deceivers like to think and sometimes convince themselves that they are different than they suspect or deeply know that they are not. But the most engaging task is to persuade others that they are not what they are afraid or know that others may think they are. While emotionally they have gradually succeeded in blurring the distinction between the truly achieved changes in themselves and those that they aspire to convey to others, on a critical level of conscious the doubts still haunt them. In other words, on one level of consciousness, which deals with their pseudoreality, the magically fabricated new image of themselves is fully accepted and supported by pseudorational arguments. However, there is the other level, which handles the factual reality more critically and objectively and where their beliefs and rationalizations are not enough to give them emotional comfort. Hence, they need the confirmation of others. The belief that maximizes the self-deceivers' ability to cope with their environment sometimes turns out to be quite troublesome for them.

Take, for instance, Jay, a young professional man, who thinks of himself as being brilliant but is afraid that his intellectual smartness might not come through in his interaction with others. He even is unsure whether his clever and catchy statements made in conversations with peers, friends, or casual encounters are properly appreciated. Jay unequivocally wants to get recognition, to be relished and admired by others for his allegedly high intelligence as displayed in what should be his thought-provoking and attention-grabbing statements. He would like to be the center of attention with his allegedly sparkling remarks and comments. This problem has haunted him since his pre-high school years when he became obsessed with the idea of not feeling accepted as equal in intelligence by the elite in his class. In order to prove his equally high intelligence and to impress them and his teachers, he would interject in casual conversations with them quotations from various classical writers learned specifically for this purpose. In the same vein, his school achievements had to reflect his brilliance, which required sustained hard work at the expense of any meaningful social life. His attempts to bridge the gap between his idealized image of superiority and its translation in his work performance became an almost Sisyphean task. Any lessening in his academic efforts would automatically increase his anxiety about his ability to preserve that image of excellence. During his college years his capability of maintaining a sustained effort in the service of that image faltered and he failed to meet his self-imposed standards, to his own chagrin. He was plagued by "unexplainable" anxiety in carrying out any assignment with the result of postponing it to the deadline. During his graduate-school years he continued to be consumed by the need for revalidation by others of his brilliance, which made pursuit of the degree an exhausting experience.

Finally, after years of tremendous intellectual efforts and sacrifice of his social life, he became a junior corporate executive, still obsessed with the elusive goal of being admired for his doubted brilliance. However, he found the rules of success in the business world to be different than those of his school years. It required more spontaneity, more creative thinking, faster decisions, and high flexibility in organizing his work. He had a difficult time in meeting all these new demands, which made it harder for him to prove his intellectual superiority. In his corporate career hard work was not enough; he was supposed to develop new strategies, which to a great extent were difficult for him. His justifications related to his lack of work discipline or need for more experience to master the assignments were unconvincing. He had to work harder and harder to maintain his elusive "status." Unable to shine at work, he looked for comfort in recalling the alleged glorious past of school achievements when he was praised and admired. Gradually, Jay started to interject extraneous and hyperbolic tales about his previous scholastic successes in his business discussions with his colleagues. The unexpected twist was that at the same time he bragged to his friends about his alleged successes at work. Did he lie to others in a deliberate manner or did he lie to himself? Both. From the point of view of classical psychology, he was lying to himself about his alleged brilliance. However, from the relativistic position of postmodern humanistic psychology one might say that Jay's perception of reality led to the projection of a specific self-image that was not a fabricated self-image but simply a reactive one to the realities of work. The trouble with this sophistic approach is that it does not fit the reality. Jay not only habitually responded to social situations with the same distorted self-image but he promoted it, while often "subtly" asking others for its confirmation: "I bet that you like the way I handled him.... You should have seen the surprise on his face when I told him about the inconsistency of his explanations.... They don't know how really sharp I am...." The reality is that while fishing for praise, he knew that many of his

statements were exaggerations, if not pure fabrications. Though this bragging supported his baffling belief in his superior mind, deep down he
tried to believe that these self-serving statements could be close to the
truth. The next question is whether his lies to himself and others were socially productive. Partially, they were. They increased his level of diligence in support of his competitiveness. It energized him to work hard to
try to reach his goal of becoming a respected executive and, he accomplished it to some extent.

SELF-DECEIVERS "INFATUATED" WITH THEMSELVES

Many self-deceivers are truly narcissistic people who convince themselves to be these terrific selves and hence, to try acting according to their
newly created social image. Certainly, the newly invented traits based on
wishful thinking are either compensatory for the ones missing or overblown exhibits of the existing ones. But, the new alleged qualities are only
superimposed on the suppressed traits that they would have liked to discard. This creates a confused coexistence of opposing drives, which are
maintained at best in an unstable equilibrium. Practically, it may lead from
time to time to inconsistent behavioral responses induced by the underlying basic traits of personality that may surface against the image projected
for the benefit of others. The more they overstate their true abilities as part
of their self-fabricated image, the larger will be the magnitude of the gap
between their achievements and aspirations. The more their conceited personality takes hold of them in their social interaction, the more artificial become their relationships with others. In addition, their fanciful image has
raised false expectations for themselves and for others about their potential
achievements, unsupported by their real capabilities. Driven by their grandiose ideas about their capabilities, they may get involved in the wrong
deals or social situations. Furthermore, this illusion of high ability and the
pursuit of high social standing, combined with the craving for the admiration of their associates, compel them to take credit for the successful activities and the smart ideas of others. The same devious approach, taken in the
context of a business transaction, may sometimes lead to embarrassing situations in which they are unable to logically document the reasons for supporting a particular position. Other times, they act impulsively in order to
convey determination and leadership but are unable to objectively evaluate the pertinent facts. Instead of sticking to cold facts, they undermine
their doings by acting as grasping situations that they do not understand.
Sometimes their responses are at variance with the demands of the negotiated situation but brought about by frustrations leading to inappropriately
suspecting others of attempting to exploit negative traits of themselves and
undermine their positions. What is worse, during a stressful critical situation they are not always aware of these background negative feelings that

may interfere with any proper decision. Otherwise, their social responses are almost predictably in line with their new image. A case in point is offered by a relatively successful businessman who has always fancied himself as having a high social standing and recognition beyond the factual reality.

Bob came to the United States in his early twenties to study for a graduate degree and elected not to return to his native country. After receiving a master's degree in liberal arts from a prestigious college, he decided to try to get a job in business. He changed jobs a few times until he found the right one with an insurance company. He learned the business of insurance and after finding a partner, he opened an insurance office. With a flair for business and hard work, he became moderately successful, only to suffer a serious setback after some bad business deals generated by his partner, who had failed to fully disclose to him their shaky nature. This lead to a break-up of the partnership and almost to a liquidation of the business. Interestingly, he placed much trust in his junior partner, who while making a routine of praising him for his flair for business was cutting dubious self-serving deals behind his back. A determined man, he started the business all over again. Single-handedly, without too much capital, he successfully rebuilt the business to a respectable size. Yet, on and off, he still got involved in bad business deals promoted by untrustworthy associates who in the end took advantage of him. Importantly, all that these slick characters had in common was their smooth talk combined with enticing schemes. They were charming, easy-going, excessively flattering, and subtle persuaders. During negotiations of their schemes, they always stressed the need of a business leader of his caliber for the success of the deal. According to these promoters, the opportunities for striking it rich were almost unlimited under Bob's guidance and alleged business skills, provided that he supplied the initial money. Furthermore, Bob often fell for the flattery of his own staff, who supplemented their mediocre performance with praise for his acumen in business and his ability to solve intricate problems with clients. What may appear puzzling at first sight is why Bob, an intelligent man with relatively good business sense, savored these cheap expressions of admiration offered either by these promoters with suspect business records or by his mediocre staff.

Bob fell prey to his own need for flattery, recognition, and desire to be held in high esteem. His misjudgment of people was not due to any naïveté or ignorance but to an overwhelming need for being admired, if not revered. He wanted to impress others by his cleverness and business acumen, which he enjoyed expounding with a myriad of embellishments. At the same time, to enhance his image of success, he surrounded himself with various prestigious consultants who were paid to evaluate deals that never materialized but rather were set up to give him the appearance of importance. He enjoyed to maintaining the illusion of being thought of as a wheeler-dealer, part of the "big league" boys' network. Most of the time these deals were beyond his financial resources or domain, yet he talked about them only for the purpose of enhancing his status in the business community. In the same vein of aggrandizement, his consultants were employed to bolster his appearance of cleverness and expertise to others, by using their advice and insights at his meetings. In addition to boosting his ego, this pretense of participation in big deals was feeding his fantasy of being thought of as a significant "player" in the financial markets. It suited him well, since his ultimate dream was to convey financial and political power. After achieving a moderate degree of financial success, his life became directed toward combining business with politics in his final scheme of reaching power. Thus, he "bought" political contacts with hefty contributions and became involved in political manipulation and in the election of candidates whom he cleverly used to enhance his business, all interwoven in the grand scheme of feeling important. Unfortunately for him, he remained at the fringe of real power. His illusion of power was maintained in direct ratio to the amount of money contributed to various elections and political fundraising dinners. On the positive side, the business drew a handsome amount of cash to support the money spent in politics and still gave him a comfortable living. Yet, he liked to think of himself as a powerful figure behind the political scene in addition to being a successful businessman. In reality, his level of success was below his claims and his political influence quite limited. Anyone faced with this discrepancy between the factual reality and the gross exaggerations of Bob's statements would wonder whether he was a blatant liar or just a guy with a distorted view of his social status. Bob seemed to be a mixture of both. Sometimes he was posturing, but most often he tried hard to identify himself with his projected image of power and success. For anyone listening to him it was very hard to separate fact from fiction in his stories. Bob had an irrepressible, compulsive need to bolster his image or to absolve himself even in situations where his business blunders and mistakes were self-evident. One might wonder whether he believed to any extent his convoluted explanations in justifying his self-evident faults. As a result, he was unable to change his style of interaction with other people regardless of the frequent disappointments and setbacks he experienced in dealing with unreliable politicians or sleazy promoters. Could he have dropped this pretentious, grandiose self-image? The boasting, the self-aggrandizing, and the constant need for adulation were expressions of the same craving for recognition of what he wanted to appear to be. Obviously, he was not fully aware of the suppressed inner conflict brought about by a dramatic and turbulent adolescence, although the dormant feelings were there. Most of these were painful memories of humiliation and a fight for survival, which were buried but not totally forgotten. Yet he was not aware of the causal link between his earlier years' experiences and his fabricated self-image. He was unable to see that the compensatory reparative process of affirming himself fulfilled a very important psychological function for him: it attempted to thwart off those suppressed negative feelings about himself. The trouble was that his attempts to redress the balance went too far into the other extreme, hence unnecessarily complicating his life. He sometimes payed dearly for his need for recognition, when he was misled by devious promoters or insincere politicians. His problem was compounded by his conviction that he could spot any unreliable or dishonest businessperson or politician. His blind spot was his need to prove his superiority, which led to misinterpreting significant factors involved in business negotiations, making him easy prey to the manipulations of others. Did he properly cope with his business activities? Partly. He had successfully manipulated and outsmarted many clients. The undisputed fact was that Bob was able to successfully compete in his own business, though within a limited range. Yet his overblown ego held him back to some extent from achieving his true business potential because of the amount of energy and time spent away from his core business in purposeless deals. However, the same self-deceiving, which made him ignore some sensible rules in selecting partners for business, was the source of his success in his main business. His ability to boast and distort helped him create an illusion of political and business power with customers, which served him well in his own business. Did he have a multifaceted consciousness that was able to present alternate views of himself, as the constructionist psychologists claim? If this were the case, then he would have suffered from a dissociative state of personality, which was not so. It means that regardless of his strong belief in his inflated ego, even against proof to the contrary, he was also pretending and posturing, hence lying.

Let us see if other ways of lying to oneself can offer even better degrees of social adaptation for the individual.

SELF-DECEIVERS DEMANDING UNCRITICAL ACCEPTANCE

Some people, while fighting to prove their superiority, have a need to aggressively assert themselves or attempt to impose their point of view, disregarding the opinion of others. Furthermore, they have to show how good they are by putting down others. Most often they exhibit an attitude of arrogance mixed with outright insolence in support of their otherwise relative competence. They fancy themselves as being very smart and shrewd, capable of easily controlling and imposing their judgment on others. They exude confidence. The need to be right makes them distort and twist facts to fit their preconceived conclusions. Admissions of judgmental errors are most often considered by them as a sign of regrettable weakness. The same applies to any display of negative emotions, which in their mind conveys lack of control and an expression of a need for sympathy or support from others. Any exhibit of any form of emotional weakness is considered damaging to the self-esteem and puts that person at a disadvantage in dealing with other people. In fact, people cannot be trusted and must be viewed as potential adversaries.

Based on this pseudo-Darwinian philosophy of life, they see human interaction as being treacherous because people's emotional unpredictability is controlled by irrational needs. This is reflected in people's social unreliability or dishonesty. If people cannot be trusted, then everyone must watch out for himself. Naturally, according to these "elitists," the world is governed by those who trust their own judgment, are smart, unemotional, and in control of themselves. They are the elite because they are, in the end, the winners. These domineering, outspoken, aggressive individuals look down on others who are less combative and decisive. They are overassertive in order to intimidate others and prove their superior judgment and abilities. Plainly put, they deceive themselves by assuming that, by being loud and bullying others, they are superior. However, when things do not work out for them as they would have liked they do not take responsibility for their errors, but rather accuse others for their failure. In any failure, they simply cannot tolerate being wrong, they become very defensive, and blame others to the point of a touch of paranoia. Basically, if they had accepted being wrong, they would have shaken the very base of their carefully built self-esteem and undermined the whole support for their confidence with disastrous social consequences. Their relentless drive is to succeed as proof of their alleged superiority and in the process may pursue goals beyond their true abilities, sometimes leading to setbacks. Are these people dogmatic social elitists or unscrupulous self-deceivers? Do they truly believe in their inborn superiority, which has given them true knowledge about the world? In reality, their behavior is a result of their twisted view of the world, as we can see in the next example.

Mike, a two-year college graduate in his forties, decided after years of abortive business trials to become a telecommunication products distributor. He realized in the process of doing business that the most effective sales of his products were made when buyers were pressured to make fast decisions under the threat of possible loss of a deal to a next-door competitor. To complete a sale, he had to be assertive, convincing, and pushy. He was all of the above and much more. In the process of a sale, he used any imaginable stratagems to control and decide the outcome of the negotiation. Sometimes he literally refused to leave the buyer's office unless he secured at least a strong commitment from that person. In order to sell his product, Mike most often had to convince the potential buyer that in his refusal, either he was not acting in the best interest of his company or presumably he did not know what he was doing in his job. In case of further resistance on the part of a buyer, Mike would become indignant, raising his voice while making clear to the buyer that his lack of appreciation for a product that was offered to him before his competitors because of their long-term business relationship was an indication of the buyer's poor judgment. He would stress the fact that the buyer's alleged inability to see the value of a product would put him in a bad light in the industry, implying that he would let the fact be known to his competitors. In some cases, he went beyond a veiled threat and took up the issue of an unresolved sale with the buyer's boss. Some buyers dreaded doing business with Mike but since most of them thought they might occasionally need his products, they felt compelled to deal with him. At the same time, they were afraid of being bad-mouthed by him and of the possibility of having unverifiable terrible stories about them spread throughout the industry.

Mike always displayed an air of unshaken confidence and undisputed excellence in carrying out his business assignments. He considered most other people in his business either less knowledgeable or mediocre. In contrast, he thought of himself as very intelligent and cognizant. His unorthodox method of selling was carefully orchestrated by him to make it possible for him to control the sale's negotiation process, even if it required innuendos, disguised threats, or outright verbal abuse. His approach was based on a philosophy of the survival of the fittest, which he felt justified his actions. However, behind these elaborate rationalizations and display of self-assurance was a man tormented by insecurities and serious psychological conflicts. He was constantly afraid of losing sales and being forced to go out of business. While socially Mike successfully compensated for his fears with a mask of confidence and strength, in the privacy of his home he tried hard to dispel the self-doubts and self-incrimination by spending countless hours devising new plans and different approaches for generating business. Although he knew that he was playing a social game of intimidation that he thought was necessary for his success, in doing business he would not have played the game if he had not thought that he was better or superior to others. Mike's justification for his lies and outrageous behavior was the tolerance and emotional weakness of others. As long as they permitted his "psychological game," all was legitimate and part of doing business. Indeed, it was the main explanation for his success. Had he allowed his clients to attack or deny his alleged business superiority, his whole sense of power would have crumbled, exposing his true weakness and shallowness.

His private life was a different story. He did not have any close friends or anyone in which to confide. He was all alone because he was either disliked by business associates or he was unable to share any of his personal worries with someone else due to the fear of being taken advantage of. He lived for his business success, though it was clouded by the negative connotation given by his overaggressive, sometimes outrageous behavior.

Mike knew when he was lying and pretending, but he was less aware of the degree to which his behavior was offensive and appalling. To a great extent this type of behavior became part of his "normal reaction." This approach became part of his sustained effort at remaking himself for the purpose of hiding those weak aspects of his personality that he detested. From this point of view, the created image was a better one than the suppressed one, which was full of self-doubt and fear. The downside of this new image was its lack of flexibility, which was affecting his ability to develop social relationships. Otherwise, the public image, built on pretense, became the source of his pride and social recognition. From an adaptational point of view, his developed patterns of lying to himself and to others helped him successfully build a career but were not helpful in gratifying his personal life.

People like Jay, Bob, or Mike have gradually succeeded in hiding to a great extent some traits of their true self that they disliked and in replacing them with new assumed attributes, which resulted in a mixture of what they wanted to be and what they basically are. By doing so, they have become caught in a web of lies and pretense around which their social functioning revolves. In reality, they live an inauthentic emotional life, full of insecurities and self-doubt. They may try hard to harmonize their coping behavior with the social realities that do not conform with their one-sided view of human interaction. Their mastery of human relationships is a sham. Over the years, they have become aware that something is amiss because of the smoldering conflict between their old self and the new outward image. When suddenly faced with an unchartered situation, it instinctively triggers their old self and their behavior becomes incompatible with their promoted role. These inconsistencies of behavior are sometimes noticeable but unexplainable to them. They occur more often in their private lives. Many times their lies attempt to justify such behavioral contradictions, like a display of unwarranted arrogance or making impulsive decisions that are out of line with their regular mode of behavior. Yet they tend to ignore these behavioral incongruities because what these self-deceivers care about is social admiration for their cleverness and/or talents, proven in their various stratagems.They do not crave love; they want only to be respected and revered. However there are other self-deceivers who crave love. They may go to great lengths for the sake of buying love.

SELF-DECEIVERS "BUYING" LOVE

The mental attitude and behavioral expression take a different direction for the self-deceiver who indiscriminately yearns to be liked or loved by others. They seem to be as a norm agreeable, accommodating, considerate, and soft-spoken in their relations with people at work or in their circle of acquaintances and friends. They go to great lengths to please others even when those people seem to provoke them. These compliant people appear to be sociable, sympathetic, and supportive of others. They seem concerned about the misfortunes of casual acquaintances and certainly touched by unfavorable events in the lives of their close friends. Basically, they want to be liked, sought for confidences, and above all loved almost at any price. Any personal rejection from significant people in their lives takes almost calamitous proportions. Any slighting by coworkers or acquaintances truly upsets them, though they try not to show it. It takes them a long time to recuperate emotionally. They try to avoid any spurning or rejections, quarrels, and direct confrontation with colleagues or close ones. They prefer to be conciliatory even in disputes in which the evidence seems to favor them. What is quite amazing is the fact that they appear to rarely harbor any resentment against close ones who might have offended them. But this behavior is only a facade, a mask for social performance. The true feelings are shockingly different. To everyone's surprise, in situations that might appear as simple annoyances, these people suddenly overreact. A person who is usually seen as obliging suddenly becomes belligerent, if not furious, about minor issues. Their behavior becomes even more abusive in arguments with strangers. Someone might assume that a particular unrelated and unexpected distressful event might be responsible for their unwarranted reaction. Far from the truth. Their routine congenial behavior with close acquaintances and friends, regardless of displeasing circumstances, is a cultivated approach for the sake of acceptance, closeness, or for securing love. In reality, in situations in which they do not care to be accepted or liked, they might be quite callous, detached, even unfriendly. But even with close ones, toward whom they may not show any superficial resentment, they may still display at times deviant behavior that is at odds with their professed courteous manners. They may overreact and be a bit surprised themselves by their unwarranted unfriendly actions directed against their presumed close ones. In fact, these negative behavioral reactions would have been a routine part of their coping repertoire if they had not been indiscriminately seeking approval and closeness from casual acquaintances. For this purpose, they will go to any length to distort, lie, and cheat in order to maintain their illusion of being liked or loved. The self-deceiving done for the sake of wanting to be liked or loved may lead to misconstructions of their relationships with significant others. It creates false expectations in most interactions, leading to mutual disappointments. This was exactly Dana's predicament.

Dana, a moderately attractive career woman in her mid-forties, has been upset for quite a while about her mediocre achievements in her life. She is dissatisfied with her job and even more with her social life. Her boss and her coworkers like her because she is courteous, compliant, and easygoing. Dana is attentive, sociable, sympathetic to coworkers' problems, and ready to offer her assistance whenever possible. Whenever she is upset about a situation, she prefers to keep her displeasure to herself. She rarely complains or lets others know her true feelings. Acquaintances, friends, and associates at work like her because of her superficially pleasant personality and poise. Nobody suspects her inner turmoil that is related to her dissatisfaction with them and her intimate life. She truly feels that her efforts in her career did not pay off as she expected; she has gotten nowhere in her intimate relationships. She dislikes her boss and she does not care about her coworkers. Her relationships with men have always been unrewarding if not disappointing. Depending on her job for a mediocre livelihood, and without a man in her life, she has started to wonder whether her acquiescent attitude was responsible for it. Dana feels that the men in her life, starting with her ex-husband, took advantage of her by abusing her sweetness. In her opinion, they took her friendliness and kindness as a tacit acceptance of their right to pursue their egotistic needs, with little attention paid to her. Dana wants to be loved and what she has been able to secure from men has been transitory conditional love based on sexual involvement. With her coworkers, she resents pleasing them by performing services for them. The concessions made to boyfriends did not bring the expected love. Yet, if she refused to meet their demands she was afraid of being rejected. The affairs were short-lived, which was unexplainable to her.

Dana is unable to see that the cause of her poor relationships is related to her emotional withdrawal when others did not meet her expectations of total devotion to her. In fact, she had ambivalent feelings toward them, since they were not giving her the desired dedication and love. They were not paying attention to her needs and trying to please her. Dana wants to believe that some day she will meet the "right man" (handsome and successful) who will totally accept her, take care of her, and give her "unconditional love," which she thinks she deserves. One problem is the unreasonable meaning she attaches to so-called unconditional love. Does she live in a world of fantasy or does she kid herself? Certainly, she has been unrealistic in appraising her expectations in relationships with men. The insoluble conflict has been created by her emotional needs, on the one hand, for absolute love—the total dedication of a man to satisfy her wants; on the other hand, by her unrealistic belief that she offers something very special to men, which they obviously do not perceive in the same manner. Her self-deceit made her love affairs unsustainable and her relationships with others emotionally unrewarding. Furthermore, her overstated sense of worth in intimate relationships adds fuel to her problems, significantly affecting her social life.

PEOPLE SELF-DECEIVING IN EVERYDAY LIFE

In general, many people who are unable to meet their own unreasonable expectations often feel compelled to distort facts and events in their favor in order to preserve their image about their alleged abilities. Any failure is softened by elaborate rationalizations. Confidently, but self-deceitfully, they may try to convince themselves and others that things might have been different had they not been caught in some particular adverse situations that interfered with their ability to energetically confront those events that led to a justifiable failure. Their alleged interference may vary from an unexpected family crisis to a sudden financial problem or other dramatic happenings beyond their control. This is a common method of self-deceiving: using outlandish rationalizations in an attempt to restore a favorable self-image in one's mind.

A case in point is that of Rick, a college graduate who decided to take the LSAT for law school admission. Though he had studied for the examination, he was afraid of not being able to solve some of the test's logic problems fast enough, which would result in getting a low score. With these doubts in mind, he decided to accept a friend's invitation to go out together the evening preceding the examination. While he knew that he had to get up early the next morning for the test, he agreed to go to a party, where he spent more time than he planned. After going to bed late, he had difficulty falling asleep and woke up with a severe headache. The net result was that he did not go to the test. Was his previous night's behavior an intentional act to avoid possible failure or a poorly conceived attempt to overcome his anxieties about the examination? He of course denied the former assumption and admitted the latter as a possibility. Yet for the people who knew him, it was obvious that he sabotaged himself, afraid of failure. In reality, he lied to himself, though he would not think of it as a fact. And if this self-deceiving becomes a pattern, it may not help him meet his aspirations. Are his own fabricated or circumstantial explanations satisfactory to him? Apparently they are. To maintain his high self-image, he has gradually had to deceive himself even more, widening the gap between his achievements and his potential claims. In this sense, it is obvious that his self-deceiving hinders his ability to successfully adapt to his social habitat.

There are many other people who by the duality of their thinking have the ability to deceive themselves in critical situations that are viewed by them as either emotionally crushing or too difficult to cope with. A case in point is Dan. Dan believed that he was the best research technician in a division of a high-tech company. He had a very high opinion of himself and was convinced that his highly specialized work was indispensable to the good performance of the division. His evidence was that his superiors did not criticize his work. In casual conversations with his supervisors or coworkers, he believed that he was entitled to express his opinions about the alleged poor organization of that division and to mildly joke about its leadership. Dan was unaware that he alienated his boss and others with his unrequested criticism. Eventually, he found out to his own surprise that he had not been promoted as he had expected. He asked for explanations from his boss, convinced that it had been an oversight. On the contrary, he was accused of lacking leadership qualities and was advised to look elsewhere for a job. Upset by this rejection, he mulled it over and came to the conclusion that he has been persecuted because the boss was afraid of his superior skills. To make things worse, he complained to personnel about this injustice. Did Dan have an exaggerated sense about the importance of his skills and services he offered to the company? To what extent did he deceive himself? His personal history will give us a clear answer. A hard worker and convinced of his high qualifications, Dan always had attempted to impress coworkers and superiors with his job skills and efficient solutions as read about in various technological journals. But his ideas were often rejected because they were allegedly either too costly or impractical to implement by a given company. He ultimately had been forced to leave a number of jobs. His explanations over the years had been that the jobs did not meet his needs because of the companies' unwillingness to spend money on the latest technological solutions offered by him. He was unable to see that his expectations about the job were unrealistic and counterproductive. In this case, self-deceiving has seriously handicapped his career.

There are others who are unable to deal with dramatic events, which happen to contradict their unrealistic expectations and plans for the organization of life. The most common approach is to deny the undesirable events as if they never happened. Let us take the example of a young woman, Jill, who received the bad news that her fiancé had been killed in a car crash. While his name was incorrectly spelled by police, all other evidence pointed to the fact that he was the victim. She refused to believe this terrible news and asked for more detailed information, which was furnished to her. Yet she rejected all the documentation as inconclusive and requested to identify the remains. Unfortunately, the body was mangled and burnt beyond recognition due to the after-crash explosion, which made it impossible for any positive identification. The identification was done based on dental chart and a few items scattered at the place of the accident. Jill refused to accept the reality of his death, even after his family confirmed it. She wanted to believe that her fiancé had temporarily dropped out of sight to avoid some pressing financial problems and that the person who died in the crash was someone else who might have borrowed his rented car. In any case, she was convinced that her fiancé would call her when he was ready. It took her a long time to face the reality that her fiancé was gone forever and that she needed to reorganize her life. How can her reasoning and her irrational behavior be explained? Certainly there were hidden reasons for her inability to concede to the truth about his death. Among others, it was the feeling of an inner collapse, of the shattering of her expectations related to her planned marriage, which was the best hope for saving her from a marginal, drifting existence. She doubted how soon she might succeed finding another man to replace him.

Practically, these various methods of self-deceiving may help some individuals to overcome self-doubts about problematic abilities to cope with social conditions viewed as antagonistic or overwhelming. Jack's problems may illustrate this point.

After graduating from medical school, Jack had serious problems deciding which medical specialty to pursue. Finally, he settled for a residency in internal medicine, which he successfully completed, only to conclude that he was not professionally ready to enter into private practice. Doubting his knowledge to properly treat patients, he convinced himself to take two years fellowship in a subspecialty which was supposed to give him more expertise. However, after the completion of the fellowship, he concluded that further training would be beneficial for conducting a successful practice. He thought that another year of training in a close subspecialty would give the right knowledge for practice. In all these years of training he believed to have made the right decisions about a successful future career. Jack reckoned that more comprehensive knowledge would make him a better practitioner. Was it true or was he lying to himself, afraid to face the challenge of private practice? In fact, the learned subspecialties were of some help in solving the problems of a diversified private practice. Yet, after completion of all these studies, and after running out of all justifications for not practicing, the old insecurities and anxieties about improperly treating patients returned in full force. Solving his dilemma between entering private practice while doubting his ability to cope with it and that of taking a paid job in a hospital, where he could rely on the support of other physicians, was nerve-wracking. He opted for a paid job, claiming to be able in this way to practice better medicine. Jack could have reached the same conclusions after the completion his of internal medicine residency, but the extra training alleviated his anxieties and improved his chances for a better job. It seems more likely that the fear of failure, and the avoidance of any unpleasant consequences related to it, were his justification for the long training. For a need of internal consistency, he rationalized his actions as best he could.

To function socially, Jill or Jack had to deceive themselves with rationalizations and lies to bolster their egos. For instance, Jack, during his extended training, was forced to exaggerate his alleged interest in gaining more knowledge for practice or to outright lie about not minding having to work as a fellow at low pay and with irregular and extended hours. His claim that his sacrifice was worthwhile because it helped him become an accomplished specialist practicioner was weakened by his own final decision to take a paid job in a hospital.

In the same vein, Jill, who denied the death of her fiancé, was lying outright when she pretended to be unable organize her life because she was waiting for him to come back. In reality, she dreaded returning to the previous life of working in a low-paying job until she might succeed in finding another man to take care of her. However, one can see the mixture of self-deceiving and outright lies used to reconcile conflicting inner needs with stressful social situations and protecting oneself. Apparently these people never learned to objectively confront significant life events that potentially could have damaged their self-esteem. They do not see crises as challenges that require flexible solutions, including even the possibility of circumventing unyielding barriers. Their insecurities that emerge with any stressful situation lead them to an "ostrich policy" by which they disregard the self-evident truth and replace it with their flimsy version of self-serving statements.

One may argue that in their view of reality, their responses are truthful. In this context, they did not lie or rationalize because they allegedly did not make any calculated choice to deny the reality of themselves. Hence, they are not self-deceivers. At first glance, this may seem plausible, except for the fact that they know the nature of their insecurities and doubts of themselves, which they try to suppress with band-aid solutions. These contrived solutions may work for a while, that is, until they become incongruous with the ongoing demands of reality.

The fact remains that most people have a tendency for either not admitting their faults and mistakes or rationalizing their behavior as justifiable, even when evidence plainly shows their errors. They dread the projection of a diminished sense of importance in the eyes of others. They are eager to devise, one way or another, a variety of psychological defenses in support of the desirable image. The more fragile their ego is under a perceived attack, the more formidable is the barrage of defenses used, ranging from distortions or clever justifications to outrageous accusations against others. With the perception of reality highly subjective and colored by the superimposed fanciful image of themselves, the relations between cause and effect are continuously changeable, sometimes in reversible modes. Facts are sorted by preconceived ideas, which in the end replace any objective evaluation of reality. Truth becomes indistinguishable from the twisted, invented facts. A new fabricated reality emerges as a mixture of fact and fiction to meet their conflicting emotional needs, which, in turn, reinforces their ambiguity about their relationships with others. Ultimately, it may work against their sought-out support from others by mutually reinforcing the doubts about the sincerity of the interaction.

Self-deluding as a mode of seeing oneself is not restricted to either a particular group of individuals who attempt to compensate for real or imaginary inferiority complexes, or to some narcissistic people who need constant validation of their overblown self-image. Many people when confronted with critical situations that dramatically affect their self-image feel compelled to either deny the hard facts of reality or to reconstruct them in their favor. This helps them to cope with events viewed as unfavorable to their held opinion of themselves. Self-deceit is also frequently found among hard-core dogmatics who have naively embraced and uncritically accepted social theories or precepts as guiding principles for organizing their lives and who persist adhering to them even after evidence questions their validity. Excluding the opportunists and demagogues, these people may start out as idealistic social and political reformers and end up as self-deceivers. Their social and political ideologies developed within their cultural background or learned during the years of intellectual formation are viewed as articles of faith and are not questioned by them, even when the evidence suggests their falsehood. Why would someone who is relatively intelligent and well-informed cling to dubious social dogmas?

Let us take the predicament of Rachel. She is an intelligent woman in her early forties who divorced her husband, a successful businessman, because their style of social life interfered with her ideological convictions and career aspirations. She felt that they spent too much time socializing and partying with her husband's business associates and partners. Rachel was not interested in his financial investment business or the crowd with whom he was involved. Going to various glamorous social events bored and tired her. She would have preferred to meet her friends who were activists for social issues from environment causes to animals rights. In fact, she abhorred the idea that her marriage turned out to be an example of female emotional enslavement to the husband's needs in exchange for a comfortable life. Her past consolation for accepting this condition was her ability to contribute to these reformist social causes with the money of her husband, who had agreed to help them finance. However, over the years she changed her opinion, particularly since her husband wanted her to entertain more and spend less time on her social activism. This was the last straw in their relationship. She filed for divorce, to the consternation of her husband. However, her husband did not contest it and since they had a binding, enforceable prenuptial agreement, the divorce was swiftly granted but left Rachel with a modest income.

To explain her behavior we have to take a look at her life history. Rachel grew up in poverty and resented it. She put herself through college working as a clerk, a secretary, and a dance instructor. At one time, her dream was to become a professional dancer. Since she hated social injustice, she has been very active in various social reform groups fighting for political changes. Her life radically changed after she met her future husband at a dance. Rachel was impressed with his intelligence, success in business, and easygoing personality. After marriage, she became an upper-class housewife, dedicated to helping the career of her husband and marginally involved with her social reform groups. Later, since she did not have children, she became more active in various charitable organizations starting as a fund raiser, and finally ended up on the board of directors of a foundation that promoted causes for social reforms. All these activities had been financially sponsored by her husband and his friends. Despite all of it, at the time of the divorce she believed that she might have achieved her social goals as well without being married to him. Her reformist friends had supported this assumption. She believed that the combination of her charm and the importance of her social "causes" were sufficient reasons to attract the interest of important charitable people, although she was left with limited income after the divorce.

Was she self-deceiving about her social aspirations after the divorce? Was she so dedicated to the causes related to social reforms to warrant a divorce? Was she realistic in trading her marriage for an illusory life of a social activist? Apparently she miscalculated her true possibilities as a divorcee. She overestimated her social importance and her ability to influence people to support her causes. It was too late when she became aware that she had derived a great deal of satisfaction in being a "rebel," different from the rest of her husband's social crowd. She was the free thinker who disregarded social conventions, which automatically attracted the attention of others to her professed ideological bent, making her an independent wife. In reality, her support of some social causes and of some reformists living at the fringe of society gave her a sense of overblown importance. Now, the friends she had met through her ex-husband were no longer inviting her or answering her calls and her close associates at the foundation were no longer courting or deferential to her.

Although during her years of poverty her identification with the reformist causes was a normal reaction to the daily frustrations of poverty, after the divorce she realized that her pursuit of radical reforms had been her way of expressing her freedom from her husband and his social world. Her delusion was made even greater by her assumption that she could play an important role in changing society. This misconception cost her the marriage. Two years after the divorce, frustrated with her unfulfilling social life, she started to make attempts at a reconciliation with her husband.

There are other people who seem to have enthusiastically embraced various political ideologies, only to use them as a vehicle for self-aggrandizement. It is obvious that they act in bad faith by obscuring or hiding the truth from themselves while claiming total identification with the party's program. Although, owing to their social background, they may have some degree of genuine emotional affinity to the social programs promoted by that party, their political activity is directed by self-serving schemes of gaining power. An example is the union leaders who either become corrupt by power, embezzling union funds or betraying the interests of the workers by playing self-serving politics. The question is to what extent these people know that they lie to themselves in claiming to believe in what they are not. Certainly there are shades and grades of misrepresentation of their political motivation to other people. At most, they may vaguely admit to their manipulations in order to gain power, but at the same time they deny any personal ulterior motives. Are they telling us the truth? Try to think about a modern Communist in the West or Russia who has wholeheartedly followed the ideological party lines while seeing the Soviet bastion of Communism crumble, exposing the crimes committed against the system's alleged opponents and its exploitation of workers. How is he able to relieve his inner conflict, created by the discrepancy between the ideology and its practice? Will he still rationalize his allegiance to the party by claiming that the former Soviet society had been in a period of transition for 70 years, requiring the sacrifice of the working class, or blame it on the ineptitude of past leaders? Can he believe these far-fetched explanations? In the duplicity of his consciousness, either he denies the facts or he justifies them in order to defend his political commitment.

The mind has a few options to deal with this conflict of conscience created by his beliefs, which contradict realities. Practically speaking, he can either minimize or deny the conflicting issue, as Rick, Jill, and David did. Most people try to rationalize one's unacceptable behavior. In some cases it is combined with distorting evidence opposing one's beliefs, as in the case of Jay, Bob, or Rachel. In general, in order to maintain an equilibrium between their own image and the confronting realities, self-deceivers may use a combination of all these psychological stratagems.

But to what extent are they aware of their distortion of reality about them and others? In this context, any outside event that diminishes or disputes their wrought image is treated as others' misperception, which has to be ignored or discarded. Truth is reflexively twisted to conform to their views of reality and of themselves, otherwise their whole forged identity would fold like a deck of cards. At the same time, on a more critical level of consciousness, whenever their actions do not produce the desired results, they doubt the validity of their own opinions of themselves. Then to reinforce that illusory image, they, fully aware, lie or suppress the truth.

One may say that in fact most people tend to misinterpret reality to incorporate their own biases and to justify their actions according to their view of the world. In this sense, one's subjective judgment contains elements of duplicity. Is everyone a self-deceiver? The difference between a personal view of reality and the true self-deceiver is related to the degree and constancy of projection of one's own distorted self-image in that appraisal. The self-deceiver lies to himself because of his lack of objectivity to assess or accept his true abilities, created by the self-retouched areas of his personality. In finality, it places the self-deceiver at a disadvantage in his dealings with others who understand his poorly masked shortcomings and try to exploit them. He may also lose because of the inappropriateness of his claims.

Psychoanalysis has attempted to explain self-deceiving as an unconscious process concept, which in light of our present knowledge is scientifically unsustainable. It poses an insoluble dilemma, namely, if the consciousness is aware of the object of its repression, then the process is not unconscious and if it is not, then the consciousness has nothing to repress. More likely, the self-deceiver misconstrues the factual reality to support his twisted view of himself, developed as a compensatory mode of coping with personality shortcomings and fear of social rejection.

For instance, Jane, a young unmarried woman, comes to work seductively dressed. Her apparent intention is to look attractive and be noticed as tastefully dressed. She gets annoyed if an employee of minor status in the company compliments her for her taste in dressing and attempts to flirt. Why so? However, she would like to lure an eligible bachelor such as a desirable executive. She rejects the fact that her way of dressing implies the possibility of attracting the attention of any interested males. Yet she indignantly rejects any ulterior motive in spending her salary on clothes. This kind of duplicity is a common form of bad faith. This tendency to take out facts that are inconsistent with the intended act, in order to justify it in favorable terms to oneself, is at the root of the social misperceptions leading to conflicting situations. This happens to be the case of many situations leading to sexual harassment. The male may misread the equivocal nonverbal behavior of the woman, responding in an inappropriate manner. The indignant woman seizes the opportunity to claim that she was harassed in order to demand financial compensation. In other cases, the male abuses his position of authority and demands sexual favors from the woman.

As we know, most people act in bad faith in various equivocal situations perceived by them as gainful. On one level they pretend that their attitude or actions are the correct ones as required by the situation while on another, more personal level they question the validity of the stated position. Practically, they pursue the gain offered by their political "correctness." Examples of these situations are many. A good one is offered by the racial game of college admissions. Many members of academia pretend that test scores and academic records are inaccurate predictors for the scholastic ability of minority students, while they know that study after study has proved the contrary.[2] Yet this rejection of truth about the predictive role of scores is used as a political cop-out, a subtle form of self-deception, which results in misleading the public and only increases the rate of failure for unprepared minority students.[3] The problem, according to Shelby Steele, who wrote about this issue, is that people in academia do not want to be thought of as racists while minorities resent being viewed as allegedly inferiorly prepared. In reality, both sides are self-deceiving and the painful result is that minority children are not positively helped to work harder for a better education. To what extent do they distort the facts to themselves? It all depends on their personal underlying motives and interests at stake. Subjectively, each racial group may want to believe that their held position is the one closer to the truth. The vested interest in the issue precludes any objectivity and thus, they expediently try to achieve a social compromise, which automatically leads to more distortions and lies.

As we may see, self-deceiving in its various forms and nuances is part of a human, twisted attempt of adaptation to a milieu. Some self-deceivers, by their methods of lying to themselves and others, are enhancing their ability to cope with life situations, while others benefit less or not at all by the stratagems they use. Had they developed other psychological defenses in response to their psychological problems of self-image would they have fared better? This issue questions the value of self-deceiving as a positive factor in adaptation. In fact it is more likely a neurotic adaptation in which coping, most often, produces limited if not negative results. This thesis is apparently supported by a study done in attempts to bolster self-esteem.[4] It was believed in the past that high self-esteem is a predictor of success, until studies showed that criminals and juvenile delinquents may have a glowing self-esteem. While traditionally the concept of self-esteem has been highly appreciated in our culture as an expression of individualism and self-improvement, in reality, its pursuit may sometimes be self-defeating. Even feminists, for whom raising self-esteem of women in order to compete with men has been the cornerstone of their policy, now admit its limited value.[5] In fact, people with low self-esteem can be high social achievers. Thus, from an adaptational point of view, the successful self-deceivers are doing quite all right to the extent to which their limited expectations are in line with their achievements. For others who are not doing that well, there is an incompatibility between their expectations and their projected self-image, which is related to other factors ranging from that of intelligence level to cultural beliefs or other neurotic problems that may put them at a disadvantage. This disparity is more likely the cause of their lower degree of social adaptation.

NOTES

1. A. Samuels, *The Plural Psyche* (London: Routledge, Kegan Paul, 1993).

2. T. Sowell, "Academic Lies and Self-delusions," *New York Post*, May 26, 1997, p. 19.

3. C. Murray, & R. Herrnstein, "Race, Genes and IQ," *New York Post*, October 19, 1994, p. 21.

4. K. Johnson, "Self-image Is Suffering from Lack of Esteem," *New York Times*, May 5, 1998, p. F7.

5. Ibid.

Chapter 5

Types of Liars and Their Techniques of Persuasion

Let God be true, but every man a liar.
St. John, Romans 3:4

THE "CASUAL" LIARS

When perceived as necessary, most people, self-deceivers or not, tend to tilt the balance of their social interaction with others in their favor by retouching or reconstructing the factual reality. This is an easy way for people to either avoid an impending conflict or to possibly gain an immediate advantage over others. Practically speaking, most people lie whenever the external circumstances either contradict or do not meet their needs.

Jane, a market analyst, calls in sick. She knows that she is needed for an important meeting, but wants to take her daughter to a social event, which she considers important.

Geneva, a student, lies to her parents about passing some college courses that she never attended. She claims that she lied so as not to upset them.

Dan, a salesman, fakes sales reports for a quarterly meeting with the sales manager in order to impress him with his diligence and business skills.

Kevin, a lawyer, charges a client for 20 hours of services on a minor case which requires an explanatory letter and some calls to an institution. In reality, the time spent on documenting and editing the client's draft took him 6 hours of work at best.

Honorable Steve, a judge, pretends to be unbiased against a particular minority group, when in fact he dislikes them, as most of his decisions tend to reflect.

Ian, a dermatologist, professes to have informed a patient about the risk of a treatment procedure that ended up harming the patient. The patient denies any knowledge of its possible ill effects. Who is lying?

A congressman denies any wrongdoing about fundraising for his political campaign when there is evidence of his receiving illegitimate contributions.

White House consultants and staff, when faced with possible incriminating evidence of certain illegal actions, conveniently claim an inability to recall those events, though documents which surface later prove a different story. Worse, the president, in a televised address to the nation, admits lying about a sexual affair that he had previously denied, and is fined by a federal judge for perjury. Most people do not care.

These are not isolated cases of deception; they are routine lies used by most people from all walks of life in their daily interaction with others. They are part of our way of negotiating social relationships, from business to love affairs, from a vantage point. Most of these types of lies are subtle statements, a mixture of semi-truths or unverifiable assertions, which seem to be benign at first sight, but in reality are self-serving and quite harmful. A case in point is of a surgeon who in a book written for lay people, boasts of his ability to moderate the high pulse rate of a patient under general anesthesia or to control the arrhythmia of another patient on the operating table by whispering in their ears to decrease the pulse or to stabilize the heart's rhythm. All these hyperbolic statements, combined with his alleged miraculous methods for treating, if not curing, terminable diseases such as certain types of cancer, are part of a drive to promote himself as an innovator in medicine, an exponent for the power of positive thinking in healing.[1] Does he do a service to the public with his overblown statements about the healing power of love, or with his simplistic and inaccurate explanations about the causes of cancer as self-induced, a result of unresolved emotional conflicts, and an expression of guilt and sin. At first glance, it appears that his approach is an attempt to give hope to patients beyond help by the standards of medical practice. Yet in reality the disservice to these patients is immeasurable. It makes people feel responsible not only for causing their diseases but for failing to attempt to positively influence their course. Regrettably, these assertions were not made by a lay healer or a minister, as articles of faith, but by a surgeon who was supposed to maintain a higher respect for scientific knowledge. His esoteric treatment of cancer smacks of shamanistic divinations.

The interpretation of experimental data in medicine can sometimes be loosely used, particularly when there are underlying personal gains. Recently, newspapers reported about another surgeon who in lectures and articles persuasively promoted a new surgical procedure for the treatment of enlarged prostate that allegedly would improve patients' quality of life. While the unproven value of the device is still being debated, it surfaced the fact that the surgeon, who has been the main investigator of the device, was the paid director of the company that made it. This conflict of interests, undisclosed by the surgeon, seriously undermined his reputation.[2]

This fluid and casual approach to the truth has also been promoted by many healing or diet trade books written mostly by self-styled experts. This is a cheap form of self-advertisement and a way to make money by using half-truths, anecdotal stories, and unverifiable testimonies. In a way, they are similar to many Wall Street investment letters or weight-loss brochures, which promise a lot and deliver little or nothing. However, out of self-protection, all of them, while manipulating the facts, use disclaimers that tend to weaken the promises made about losing weight, getting better, or making money. Obviously, these escape clauses get the authors off the hook and allow them to perpetuate their deceptive games. Yet, this deliberate obfuscation and distortion of truth is socially tolerated under the umbrella of representing personal opinions and interpretation of facts subject to the follower's approval. It is assumed that any person has the common sense to critically evaluate the validity of their contention. However, these promoters, self-styled experts, and deft manipulators of the available data easily lure naive or desperate people looking for a solution to their problems and who tend to accept their dubious forms of counseling as articles of faith.

COURTESY LIES (WHITE LIES)

What is even more interesting is that society encourages people to lie in some situations where it is considered as advancing good will among its members. The most widely accepted "civilized lies" are the courtesy lies, or white lies. Courtesy lies are meant to fulfill a social function and as such are viewed as acceptable. In fact, these lies are not only admissible but deemed as desirable. For instance, it is impolite to tell someone that he looks sick or that he has bad breath. It would be outright inconceivable to tell the hostess at a dinner party that her prepared dishes are not quite tasty. On the contrary, the guests compliment her for her culinary talents. These lies are part of our social etiquette. But in practice, they go beyond the exchange of social pleasantries, being also cultivated in business interactions. No one in his right mind would tell his boss that his jokes are in bad taste and that nobody enjoys them or that his comments at the last office meeting were ill-advised and counterproductive. As a matter of job survival, subordinates ingratiate themselves and flatter the boss in an attempt to gain recognition from him.

All these courtesy lies are socially justified as necessary for maintaining people's self-esteem by not hurting their egos. But this protection of peo-

ple's ego fragility opens Pandora's box. Man, by and large, is neither inclined to take full responsibility for errors damaging to his self-esteem,
without diluting its effect with self-serving explanations, nor is he able to
accept his defects or limitations at their face value unless forced to do so. In
fact, these self-serving traits are the main problem of any self-deceiver. But,
for most people, the acceptance of truth can be limited to shades, which can
be acknowledged as long as they guard them from the full impact of facing
the unpleasant truth about themselves. Regardless of contrary evidence,
people will always attempt to find explanations or extenuating circumstances to justify their actions, if not to others, at least to themselves. The
brutal truth about oneself is for most people displeasing if not insulting.

Society, fully aware of people's partiality in facing their true selves, has
created an elaborate system of euphemistic approaches to reduce the blow
to their egos. The result has been that of institutionalizing the white (polite)
lie. By doing so, social hypocrisy has tacitly been legitimized. If it is socially
acceptable for someone to hide his true thoughts or intentions under the
claims of not offending the feelings of another person, then the license to lie
can be stretched to any situation, depending on one's perceived needs or
judgment. He will lie in any situation that he sees as contrary to his interests. If so, white lies are not as inoffensive as society tries to portray them;
on the contrary, quite often they are detrimental for the people at the receiving end.

Let us take John, a 35-year-old part-time teacher who has the ambition to
become a professional writer, though he lacks any outstanding talent. Yet
John is constantly encouraged to pursue his writing activity by his close
friend, Jack, who recommends patience and perseverence while John lives
on the fringe of poverty. But John holds Jack's opinion in high esteem. The
trouble is that Jack has serious doubts about John's skills, as he has expressed this fact to others. Yet Jack refuses to advise John on this issue, not
wanting to hurt his feelings. Is he truly helping John? On the contrary, he
supports John's lack of interest in pursuing a more rewarding career.

Mary's plight is no better. Mary apparently has poor taste in clothing,
which affects her physical appearance. However, her close friends, who admit among themselves her poor taste, praise her selection of dresses when
she asks them. Do her friends realize the extent of disservice done to Mary
by perpetuating her illusion of having a flair for fashion and being dressed
attractively? The practical result of their hypocrisy is that of negatively affecting her social image. It means either that her alleged friends do not care
enough about her to tell her the truth or that Mary's personality is too sensitive to any criticism, excluding her from any real sincere communication. In
this context, courtesy lies are mutually protective of an artificial relationship. Each person, in relating to the other, operates from a defensive position of mutually shared hypocrisy, respecting the other's self-imposed
limits of hearing or telling the truth.

EXCUSES AS A FORM OF SOCIAL LYING

If courtesy lies most often spare any embarrassment induced by one's own blunder, error, or manners that might seem inappropriate, and only indirectly protect the liar's stakes in that interaction, there is another type of routinely used lies, called excuses, which mainly tend to preserve the excuser's image. Contrary to courtesy lies, excuses often have a negative social connotation because they might question the excuser's sense of responsibility and credibility. Yet, they are highly used socially because they fulfill a double role: they support the individual's ego when it does not conform to the expected or agreed-upon terms of social transaction and second, it lessens the negative reaction at the receiver's end about the other's otherwise unjustified behavior. This face-saving device permits either party to continue the planned activity without any emotional interference from the tension caused by the behavior of the excuser.

Nancy, a graduate student, told a professor in charge of her doctoral thesis who also wanted to date her that she just got married and for this reason was unable to go out with him. The fact was that she was unmarried but not interested in having an affair with him. In fact, she was having an affair with another man. However, she did not want to hurt his feelings, which might have had unpleasant consequences for her graduation.

David told his client, "Sorry, I was unable to to finish the work because my computer broke down." The truth is that David had another job to finish but accepted the new job so as not to lose a client. However, any true admission of postponement would have made the client angry; instead, this excuse-lie, if accepted, permits both parties to do business in the future.

Society considers it very rude not to reply to an invitation, letter, or call from an acquaintance but at the same time, it leaves open the approach to be used for refusal. One common solution is to repeatedly ignore the solicitation by either pretending of not having received the information or not remembering to have seen it. This is one of the most commonly used lies, with the same degree of credibility as the classic lie "The check is in the mail." Excuses play a very important social role in keeping afloat otherwise jolted interpersonal relationships. Are all these excuses made with the intention to deceive? To reveal its reverse as a lie is not that hard. Simply, if the refusal is repeated too often the receiver can either stop the communication or confront the other person. In other, more complex situations, the excuses may be the only possible or acceptable response short of confrontation. In another case, someone may feel torn apart between two conflicting needs and he may decide on the spur of the moment against one in favor of the other. Then he might justify to himself why he made this decision and not the other, attempting to cope later on with its outcome. Under these circumstances, the distinction between the excuse-lie and a true misjudgment is a difficult one.

Jane thought that she had a date with Don on Thursday evening. It turned out that the date was for Friday evening. But, Friday she had tickets to go to a show with another man. She could not cancel on this man, whom she needed very much to enhance her career. However, she did not want to disappoint Don either, since she was romantically interested in him. Thus, she told Don that she could not see him on Friday because she had to be at her sister's supposed birthday party. Fortunately, Don believed her excuse-lie. In other situations the initial misunderstanding can lead to a cascade of lies in order to repair the first mistake. This happens quite often when an excuse is used as a way out of a miscalculation or doubt on the part of an individual who is afraid to confront a given situation.

There are other types of more refined excuses, in which one admits to having lied but only when forced to do so for the benefit of a social or political cause. Certain lies that are justifications introduced after the fact at a later date, and which contradict one's previous statements, are often political, or diplomatic lies, and are practiced under the umbrella of protecting national interests or a particular unexpected international crisis. In general, these lies may be accompanied by an apology in order to reduce the negative impact that they may have on the public. For example, President Bush made a promise during his presidential campaign not to increase taxes, which he was neither able to keep nor to successfully argue the reasons for his behavioral inconsistency. Later, he apologized for not keeping his word, but it was viewed by people as an awkward excuse. The result was a loss of credibility with the electorate, which somewhat contributed to his defeat for reelection.

SELF-SERVING APOLOGIES

There are many social interactions in which people voice an apology or a pardon statement, mainly intended to appease a hypothetically injured person. For example, "I apologize for not coming to the meeting but I did not feel well" or "I feel terrible for losing my temper but I was overstressed." Apologies like these are heard everyday as part of our routine social interaction. They attempt to justify a variety of behaviors that are allegedly beyond one's control or intentions and are in contradiction with a previous agreement between parties. The result is asking for forgiveness. In reality, the party apologizing might have disregarded the commitment for a variety of reasons: the pursuit of personal matters, disinterest in taking care of the matter under consideration, or at worst, avoidance of full responsibility after committing a reprehensible act. After hiding his true intentions and actions under fictitious explanations, the party serenely asks for forgiveness. Interestingly, this type of repentance-excuse is initially learned in the process of a child's socialization. When afraid to tell the truth about some nasty behavior, the child is coaxed by the parents into admitting it with an offer of extenuating circumstances, such as "You should feel sorry for talking back to your aunt, though she might have teased you." Some apologies are legitimate, but more often they are perfunctory statements that are accepted by people instead of crude denials of facts. Indiscriminate denials are viewed as a sign of immaturity, since this approach is used by children who tend to deny having done things that they were otherwise proven to be responsible for.

Society encourages admission of one's errors as a sign of the individual's maturity by being willing to take responsibility for his actions. At the same time, the admission of culpability reduces the burden of society to prove the guilt of the perpetrator. Yet, society reserves the right to punish the criminal offender who, after his admission of culpability, asks for forgiveness or at least for leniency. The punishment of the repenting guilty person may depend on the relative evaluation of circumstances in committing the offense and other arguable social variables, which may decide the degree of leniency accorded by society. However, in general, apologizing for relatively minor errors represents a form of social appeasement appreciated by people, regardless of how meaningless or phony it may be. The idea behind the absolution of the "sinner" after the acceptance of a social transgression, justified as unintentional and hence assumed of not being repeated, has its origin in the religious teaching of morality.

The admission of criminal guilt followed by profuse apologies is highly appreciated in legal cases. This method is widely used by defendants in court. During a recent trial, an army sergeant, accused of imposing his rank and having had sex with or raped some women trainee soldiers at a military training base, admitted his crimes while crying, banging his head against the witness stand several times and claiming that "the devil got into him."[3] The result was that he was convicted and sentenced to only six months in jail while another sergeant from the same military base who had previously been accused of roughly similar crimes, but who did not repent in court, received a heavy sentence. Was the former sincere while the latter a hard-core deviant? The religious concept of remorse on the part of the sinner followed by forgiveness by society is an acceptable tool for avoiding punishment. While in some isolated cases this defense may be justified, it is usually abused.

The gamut of socially admissible lying, from that of courtesy to those of excuses-apologies, has evolved in myriads of subterfuges and stratagems in people's attempt to negotiate truth. It may take the form of a denial of facts or that of selective omissions, including equivocal admissions of truth but sweetened with an invocation of extenuating or mitigating circumstances. Basically, all these approaches to shrouding the truth have in common an intentional element, that is, misleading others by equivocating the true facts under a professed pretense of frankness and candor. It is a pretense of being honest, which it is not.

Pretending is an important but sometimes confounding issue in human interaction since it is part of the process of make-believe. This game of pretending is an intellectual process in which reality is replaced by a self-made representation of it, where the restrictive constraints are removed for one's own needs and desires. This process takes place within the realm of one's imagination, which determines the quality of its outcome. It is an intentional remaking of reality for sheer pleasure. The ability of people to relate to and accept the virtual reality offered to them is rooted in and has evolved from the magical thinking of childhood. However, in the magical stage of thinking, the distinction between fantasy and reality is poorly delineated. Only after maturation of the mental process is a person able to separate fact from fiction. Reality and fantasy come apart and are recombined at will in the process of creating a symbolic reality. But these products of imagination would not have any meaning for others if people did not have the built-in capacity to switch to the state of make-believe in which these plots and stories are treated as real. Judgment of reality is suspended and the new "reality of make-believe" becomes the focus of attention. In fact, whenever they want, people can escape to the world of fantasy and pretense by creating their fictional pseudoreality. Adults can sometimes become so engrossed in fictional activities that they treat those activities as fleeting moments of reality. Quite often we see people on the street engaged in animated conversations with imaginary parties, whom they claim as being right there. Furthermore, fantasy and role-play have always held a significant place in the individuals's gratification in most forms of sexual activities from the masturbatory one to fetishism or transvestism, to mention only a few. The need to escape from reality into a world of fiction is so great that a whole industry of literary creativity, based on fabricating a pseudoreality, has been developed. The more it succeeds in appealing to the public's insatiable need for recreating reality in new dimensions beyond their limited existence, the more successful is the author of that fiction. It plays a crucial role in entertainment and theatrical settings, although the motivation is not to deceive. Here, the game of mutual pretending is staged by the actors who represent specific characters and by the audience who accept their roles as if they were real. Under a tacit agreement, people become engaged in a game of experiencing imaginary events and activities enacted for the benefit of pure mental pleasure. While the mental process of inducing a state of make-believe is the same in both situations, plays and lying, the intentions of the "acting" liars are different. This act of pretending runs through all types of lying from courtesy-lies to the most sophisticated and malicious ones. It gives credibility to the liar. No wonder that popular common sense lumps together all masterful liars, like sociopaths, imposters, and confidence men, under the symbolic notion of "con artists."

THE ROLE OF PRETENDING IN LYING

If elements of pretense and make-believe play a significant part in various forms of human activity, then it is easier to grasp their role in a variety of more sophisticated deceptions. Since individuals tend to respond positively to presentations of illusions that simulate reality and meet their needs, someone who knows well how to use the right illusionist game is a successful liar. Like a magician, he dazzles his listener, making anything possible and plausible. Ultimately, the skillful liar, intuitively realizing the power of pretense in recreating reality, uses it to connect with a potential victim in order to gain his confidence. A liar's pretense of conveying the truth becomes the springboard for obtaining the acceptance of the listener.

But first, to succeed the liar has to gain the confidence of his listener by imparting an impression of deep sincerity while delivering his fictional truth. The faster he is able to induce a state of make-believe in the victim's mind by appealing to his imagination to envision new and unseen possibilities that automatically suspend any critical judgment, the easier he will reach the intended goal of deceiving. This "acting," if successful, contributes to his further manipulation of truth by reducing it to the point of a simple game of smoke and mirrors. This game of pretending has been refined by crooks to an art in which fiction and truth become both equivalent and convincing. They become powerful tools used for sophisticated arguments for self-protection or for self-enrichment. In business transactions they may represent the difference between success and failure or winning and losing.

There are other classes of liars who pretend to be more qualified socially than they really are, claiming to be basically better than their competition; they lie to increase their social competitiveness. In a way, they appear to be socially insecure but, in reality, their calculated lies are used to advance their career and to gain a higher status than they deserve. These liars do not have any reservations about the legitimacy of telling a lie whenever they think that it is beneficial to them. While an honest person will adapt a strategy for reaching any projected goal within the limits of his true inner possibilities and external realities in order to avoid any embarrassments or ethical conflict, a liar will take the easiest and most direct pathway to achieve it. He will fill the missing links or absence of required qualifications to reach that goal with fabrications. In this sense the lie is used as a shortcut to secure a desirable goal.

This was the case of John, who claimed to have an master's degree from a midwestern university, when in reality he held a bachelor's degree in Business Administration. Later on, caught lying by pure chance, he justified his story by maintaining that he already had the work experience comparable to the degree and thought that the requested MBA was only an administrative formality. Furthermore, he felt that he was qualified, since other employees holding that degree were less competent than he was. After all, he argued, most people lie anyway to advance or to enhance their chances for a better job. The deceit was legitimized in his mind by embracing a twisted Darwinist philosophy of life, which would justify winning at any price against competitors. According to him, the driving force in life is the fulfillment of oneself, and any hindrance has to be removed even at the expense of others, as long as one can operate within a loose frame of legitimacy. Any moral scruple may limit one's ability to achieve his aims.

Recently, a financial newspaper reported claims made by a small pharmaceutical company about its success in developing a new skin graft, which was tested in a clinic by a research team under the direction of an "experienced research physician." Since the potential market of the new product was significant, the stock rose spectacularly. After some careful investigation, it was found that the chief investigator was neither a physician nor a Ph.D. in biochemistry, as he had claimed at various times. In reality, he had a master's degree in animal science. As a result, the stock took a dive. The legitimate concern of the stockholders was that the principal investigator might have difficulty with the FDA because of his unsatisfactory credentials. By pretending to be what he was not, this researcher had tried to make a fast career move and, ignoring the long-term implications of misrepresenting himself, he brought down the company. Examples like this one abound in all types of careers. While these people are not true impostors, their embellishment of credentials for personal gains makes them dishonest.[4]

This fraud is not so different from the recent prosecution of brokers and brokerage houses by the Manhattan district attorney. The operations were run from store fronts or apartment houses, using enticing names and addresses to sell phony stocks on the telephone by promising huge profits. In this case, the fraud was committed under a mutual pretense; the crook sold worthless investments as valuable as "gold" and the buyers pretended to know what they were doing in the stock market.

The element of pretense is not only widely used by con artists but also by people in their personal interactions, from love affairs to claims of self-protection. In fact, pretending is used as a powerful weapon for the justification of one's incriminating wrongdoing or criminal behavior.

PRETENDING SELF-DEFENSE

Quite often, elaborate manipulations of implicating facts by pretending to have a different knowledge of them is encountered in situations that are loosely lumped together by society under the general umbrella of self-defense. Self-defense lies are the most common protective methods used by people to get out of any minor or major troubles that are thought to have unpleasant consequences for them. These lies are frequently employed because they easily blend in with the concept of self-defense, which is morally and legally considered as part of the individual's indisputable

right for self-protection. Some of these pretend self-defenses are very difficult to detect since they are unverifiable, self-serving statements. While, in
principle, a legitimate self-defense is valid, most people use elaborated or
concocted stories to justify their behavior in situations where the alleged
self-defense was not the reason for their antisocial or criminal behavior

The following example of a legal case using self-defense is self-explan-
atory. A woman in New York State shot her husband in their bedroom in the
dead of the night, claiming to believe that he was an intruder. She stated
that she woke up in the middle of the night and saw the shadow of a man
near the window. Then, in a state of panic, she took the gun from her
nightstand and shot him. Afterward she realized that the alleged intruder
was her husband. No witness was present at the shooting. It was also true
that during this period a prowler had been reported to have been seen in
the neighborhood. However, there were a few intriguing issues contradicting her testimony. One was the fact that she might have had a motive: that
is, her husband had a lover, and he was considering a separation from her,
which she had known about at the time. In addition, there were further
questions about her financial situation if they were to divorce. Another unanswered issue was her skill as a shooter in the dark, which would have
presupposed a degree of experience in using a gun and also an amount of
self-control, especially since she was allegedly awakened from her sleep by
noises made by what she had thought to be an intruder. Was she telling the
truth or was this an act of jealousy or a crime of passion, skillfully planned
and executed? Many domestic disputes or conflicts among close acquaintances end in violent acts, which are justified by the perpetrators as an act of
self-defense. While there may be evidence suggesting some elements of
truth in their statements, the explanations for their violent behavior are fabricated to cover up for their uncontrolled emotional state, ranging from
jealousy and hurt to blind rage, which are responsible for the criminal offense.

The lie most often used when no other self defense is valid is that of temporary insanity. Here, the lawyer and the defendant conspire to manipulate
truth and justice by claiming that the accused had been emotionally unable
to distinguish between right and wrong because of a temporary clouding of
his consciousness that was induced, however, by an unverifiable physical
or mental state. A famous example is that of a young woman in England, a
barmaid, who in 1980 killed her co-worker during a violent argument. The
woman claimed that she suffered from severe premenstrual disorder
(PMS) which made her lose control over her behavior. Her defense
amounted to temporary insanity. She prevailed and was placed on probation. The diagnostic manual of the American Medical Association might
recognize this condition under the general heading of "personality change
due to medical condition" in which case PMS is associated with violent behavior but not with an altered state of consciousness. Ironically, a year later

she was arrested for assaulting police officer.[5] The same distortions of truth have been used by people who claim to have committed crimes under conditions of cloudiness of consciousness leading to a mental state described in the New York penal code as an "irresistible impulse." This argument is still introduced in court as a mitigating factor in a variety of cases, from exhibitionism to shoplifting, and in some other instances of antisocial and assaultive behavior against an ex-lover or spouse. The emotionally rejected partner claims to have had the urge to act in an antisocial manner and to harass, follow, or threaten a victim because of an uncontrollable obsession with that person. The element of obsession about the lost lover is real, the extent to which it is uncontrollable is arguable. For example, Joan, after a three-year affair with Peter, decided to terminate their relationship because, in her opinion, it was leading nowhere. Peter was not ready to get married and she felt that their emotional interaction had lost its passion. In fact, during any serious argument between them, he often suggested that they split up. When it happened, at first he was very upset but after she left, he started to call her at work, follow her around, and abuse her verbally, until one day during another argument related to his claims that she should pay some past debts considered by her as gifts, he manhandled her in front of her home. She called the police and obtained a restraining order, but this did not discourage him from continuing to call her. In court, he admitted to being fully aware of his actions but he claimed that he was unable to stop them. On a closer psychological inquiry he also admitted that he felt cheated of his emotional and financial investment in her. He felt that after "being good to her" during crises with her job, and after helping her financially, he deserved a kinder treatment from her. Now, he felt an inside rage that he could not control. He realized that his desire for revenge was mixed with that of trying to get her back and both were the motivators for his actions. The irresistible urge was more likely the result of a feeling of impotence over his inability to connect emotionally with her. Did Peter lie about the urge to talk to her? Psychologically no, but legally it could have been construed as harassment. While the pains of rejection gave him the drive to pursue her, it also unwittingly suppressed his critical judgment to evaluate the consequences of his actions. As a result, his judgment might have become temporarily "dimmed" by his "bleeding ego" and ensuing rage. The same psychological elements, but leading to more devious behavior, were responsible for the illegal behavior and actions of a well-known New York State Supreme Court judge against his former lover.[6] He was convicted for harassing his former lover and her daughter by sending threatening and obscene letters and by making similar telephone calls. Certainly, with some will power and less resentment, these two men might have controlled their objectionable behavior.

The same mental processes, except for the preexistence of any obsessive preoccupations, are present in cases of heavy marital or social disputes that trigger spontaneous states of rage in which the enraged person attacks the other party, claiming afterward to have vague recollections of the event. The court defense in these cases is basically the same as the previous one, but it is legally known as "diminished mental capacity."

A case in point is Rudy, who while serving a sentence for robbery had been befriended in the last leg of his prison stay by a woman, Vicky, who was close to his age and social background and who took an interest in him during some visits to the prison that were organized by a religious group. After visiting him a couple of times she gave him her home telephone number. During a number of telephone conversations while he was still in jail, she poured her heart out to him about her distress induced by the separation from her husband, who had left her for a younger woman, and about other intimate aspects of her life. Rudy, after being discharged from prison, called her at her consent. She happily received him in her home and they started to spend time together. A couple of days later, she invited him for lunch at her home, with the idea of spending the afternoon together. After being with her for a while, he became uncomfortable and decided to leave, even though she strongly objected. When he was trying to leave, she came over to him and embraced and kissed him, asking him to stay. He tried to pull away from her and afterward, he claimed to "have gone blank." The next thing he remembered was lying down on the floor while Vicky was on the couch with her blouse full of blood, crying. He assumed later on that he had been pushed down by her. In a state of panic, he got up and ran out. He knew he had suffered in the past from what he called "blackout" episodes, when he had been accused of assaulting people, although he did not have any recollection of those happenings. A couple days later, he was arrested at his home for assault and intended rape. A careful review of his history revealed episodes of past violent behavior. He admitted to having a "short fuse," but he maintained that only when he felt "stressed out" did he experience "blackout" attacks. There was no hard evidence to corroborate his story of these alleged amnesiac periods. More likely he had become easily enraged when feeling emotionally and sexually manipulated by Vicky, and had exploded in violence. Did Rudy lie about his "blackout?" Yes, in regard to his denial of any recall of the initial phase of their quarrel when he might have started to hit her. It is quite possible for someone not to remember for a while the rest of the details of an incident, though later on, those facts should have come back to him. There is, however, a psychiatric syndrome known as catathymia in which basically the offender commits a violent act with no rational motivation and with poor immediate recollection of his sudden behavior.[7] It is legally used sometimes as a variation of the diminished capacity defense. Generally, the inexplicable extreme violence, which is triggered by trivial events, is directed toward someone with whom he had previously a good relationship. The psychological explanation for this violent behavior is given as relating to an inner tension created by an unresolved emotional conflict, which is projected onto the victim when he has made unwarranted remarks or acted in an undesirable manner. The trouble is that Rudy claimed total amnesia for that event, which is a condition that might be triggered by a different set of mental processes belonging to dissociative reactions. The authenticity of this type of amnesia is very difficult to prove or disprove since only independent corroborative evidence comes from the person's history. These subjective defenses are still used by some lawyers in the hope that their claims will create mitigating circumstances for evaluating the crime.

There are offenders who use an unusual self-defense when charged with crime by claiming that they were not responsible for the act because of their inability to understand the legal meaning of it. Basically they plead legal insanity. The plea of insanity is accepted by courts based on the expanded interpretation of the McNaghten rule, which permits the assumption of nonresponsibility for the crime if the defendant offers proof "of not having been himself"at the time of the crime, yet not necessarily insane. One variant of this defense is claiming that the criminal act was committed by another personality unknown to them. One famous case is "the Hillside strangler." Kenneth A. Bianchi, the Hillside strangler, indicted in 1977 for strangling 7 women and 2 girls denied the charges and attributed the crimes to his other personality, Steve, discovered during psychiatric investigation. Allegedly, the alter-ego Steve killed in complicity with Kenneth's cousin Angelo. During the trial the criminal was able to convince a few experts of his alleged multiple personalities until it was found that he learned about this condition while having access the patients' records of a psychologist. Out of 18 pleas of insanity claimed by criminals based on their alleged lack of conscious control because an alter (other) personality was in charge at the time of the crime, only 3 were accepted by the court. While is very easy for an offender to claim having multiple personalities, it is difficult to support it without a history and corroborative evidence.[8] But some offenders try to fake it anyway.

However, for each liar caught claiming (pretending) self-protection, there are many others, as unscrupulous but more clever, who know how to take advantage of any situation and escape unpunished. And this raises the issue of the validity of social distinction in permissible and nonpermissible lies translated morally in right and wrong lies.

PERMISSIBLE VERSUS NONPERMISSIBLE LIES

Since our society arbitrarily differentiates between permissible lies, loosely identified as allegedly innocuous courtesy statements, and nonpermissible, malicious lies, it gives to the liars an advantage over their victims because it justifies their lies as possibly acceptable, regardless of their gravity. All permissible lies, deemed necessary for facilitating human interaction under unfavorable or compelling circumstances, are considered an integral part of normal human behavior. Society recognizes as natural the need of people to lie for their own good and also for the good of others. People prefer to hear a soothing lie to protect their ego or to get out of a troublesome tight spot than to face the consequences. While some permissible lies may be harmless, such as slight exaggerations of the truth, others are not. Even when they appear to be inoffensive they may be detrimental to the individual's social credibility. Consider for a moment only the lies of those allegedly amusing people who like to fancy the idea that they have achieved great deeds, taking part in glorious exploits that provoke the admiration of others. It makes their lives more pleasant. Though on the surface their tall tales seem to be harmless, they do represent a deliberate attempt either to aggrandize themselves or to make certain personal gains. It all depends on the circumstances under which these lies are told. If the stories are told to bolster their ego, at best, they should be treated as entertaining. If there is an attempt to enhance themselves for ulterior motives, then the result is a misrepresentation of themselves for illegitimate purposes. Their magnified social stature depends on the degree of earned credibility from their stories, though unmatched by their social performance. The credibility of these lies depends on the intelligence and creativity of its producer and also on the intellectual and emotional quality of the listening audience. If under scrutiny the "confabulation" misstates legal facts or issues, then it is a potentially damaging situation to themselves and to others. The uncritical acceptance of someone's fabricated stories leads to a social condonation of the person's tampering with the truth.

In realty, all types of lies are related to some immediate direct or indirect benefits and are triggered by the individual's perception as being helpful for the maintenance of his sense of well-being or self-protection, regardless of how arguable their moral value may be. But if they pass the test of credibility, they are morally acceptable. However, this dubious moral perspective inherently leads to an abuse of this type of lying. The best example is offered by protective lies that are necessary for his/her well-being in the opinion of the liar (e.g., Rudy's case or the British PMS case). Even the issue of right or wrong in lying is an artificial one. It becomes a question of an implied degree based on the intentional gains derived from deception. If society has more or less arbitrarily decided which lies are harmless and which are injurious, then they are automatically labeled as either good lies (desirable or necessary) or bad lies (harmful and destructive), which makes the truth highly relative. In general, except for legal issues where lying can be documented as financially or socially damaging for the victim, people find it difficult to immediately realize that most lies in routine social intercourse can also be hurtful and distressing. Lies easily recognized as harmful and malicious are those inducing losses of some nature to a person. Most often, they are identified as part of the arsenal of fraudulent business strategies to defraud corporations and to cheat the public financially, as done by swindlers, crooks, con artists, sociopaths, and imposters. Interestingly, all of them, to carry out their schemes, rely on various degrees of pretense, though the ultimate master of pretense is the impostor.

THE MENTALITY OF A MALICIOUS LIAR

A good, malicious liar has a philosophy about the nature of man and of human relationships that justifies lying in support of his drive to achieve his ambitions and/or social needs. There are a few basic operative premises that loosely guide the liar's manipulations of people. The first one is obvious, that is, most people are gullible and simple-minded. Basically, they do not protect their interests as they should when they negotiate their affairs. To make things worse for themselves, they do not admit how little they know about things that they have to decide upon. The liar knows that people who accept the reasoning of others before any careful evaluation and deliberation about the facts become easy prey to manipulations. If, at the same time, people are greedy and want to get something more or less for nothing, then they are inclined to believe almost anything that fits in with their secret fantasy of enrichment. It is well known that people tend to believe statements, stories, or pseudodocumentation that conforms with their beliefs, emotional needs, and fantasies. This is psychologically explained by the selective attention used during someone's presentation, which slants the way that information is processed. The selective attention directs and connects the incoming information with those areas of the brain that store either highly sensitive memories related to rewarding past experiences or to those that elicit high emotional interest. In other words, the victims have a set of mental "blind spots," which guide them to ignore information that does not fit in with their preconceived scheme of things. This also explains why some people, more than others, are repeatedly cheated since they do not learn from past mistakes, when they had been similarly cheated due to their overwhelming hidden needs. Ultimately, the combination of all these factors creates a psychological background that makes people liable to successful exploitation and manipulation by good liars.

The final argument of the liar for his deceitful behavior is that the success of any lie depends on its credibility, which, in finality, is decided upon by the listener. A credible lie, if viewed as truth by the other person, shows a flaw in his judgment for accepting it. Furthermore, a good liar argues that as long as he did not use any form of intimidation or outright coercion, the other person had the opportunity to refute or accept his claims. In this context, lying is viewed as a battle of wits between two contending parties, each one attempting to establish and interpret the facts as constructed or perceived by him. However, in this exchange, the liar has an advantage over the other person, since he intentionally has changed the rules of fair play by introducing false data in the negotiations unbeknownst to the listener. Fair play presupposes that both parties involved in the negotiating interaction adhere to the rule of reciprocity, which means communicating in good faith. However, the liar intentionally slants the information in order to convince the other person to accept his point of view or argument. This mode of persuasion departs from the normal expectations of truthful communication because of the liar's decision to distort, modify, fragment, embellish, or purely fictionalize the facts in order to produce the desired result. To proceed in this manner, the liar divests himself of any sense of guilt by not adhering to the generally held presumption that it is immoral to attempt to profit from the naïveté, negligence, or poor judgment of others. As such, he remains free to effectively argue his deceitful position.

Another condition required for someone to succeed in being a good liar is to believe in his power of persuasion, and in his ability to present a falsehood as truth. Without confidence in himself, the liar would not be able to carry out his schemes. He knows how to impart a sense of self-assurance, which implies expertise in the matter under negotiation and also lends authority to his argument. He tries to make his potential victim perceive his demeanor and verbal presentation to be regarded as a sign of his superior knowledge. This self-assurance is supported by his belief that his listener is less informed than him in the area under discussion and by his ability to detect and address the other person's emotional needs.

All these mental processes take place on two different planes of thinking. A good and sophisticated deceiver simultaneously operates on two mental tracks in order to entrap a victim. On one level, during the encounter (unless he already has prior knowledge), he assesses the potential psychological weaknesses of the selected victim by attempting to uncover his sensitivities and possible mental "blind spots." On the other level, he guides the thrust of his arguments according to the acquired knowledge or assumptions made about those areas of the victim's high emotional receptivity. This is not an easy task. This approach is well mastered by the promoters and dishonest businessmen.

RESPECTABLE LIARS IN BUSINESS TRANSACTIONS

To appreciate the smooth operation of these liars, let us follow a smooth social interaction leading to a business deal struck between Joe and Michael. Michael, a successful trade consultant and writer in his late forties, was approached at an upper-class social gathering by a promoter-businessman, Joe, an expert in the area of oil tax shelters. After some general conversation interspersed with personal data that established his business status, Joe began to discuss the profitable opportunity of investing in oil leasing fields in Texas. Michael appeared interested in the subject due to the potential for reducing his taxes. Later on, Joe, who was the president of a small oil and gas exploration company, convinced Michael, after a few telephone calls and lunch, to come for a meeting at his company where charts, maps, and documentation books were exhibited and presented to Michael, all supported by solid business references about Joe's professional integrity. Michael was still undecided because, except for tax deductions, he could not see how he would be able to recoup his investment. Then, after some reflection, Joe offered Michael a different deal that he claimed was only for investors close to him. Michael was invited to another meeting at Joe's company with other businessmen, already investors, where Joe and his associates made a full presentation of the final stage reached by a new business venture. Michael negotiated, as a first-time investor, to invest the minimum of a half share, which was still highly priced. Michael, after consultations with his accountant and lawyer, decided to invest because on paper the deal looked legitimate and potentially profitable. Everything seemed to be going smoothly in the leasing of oil fields, until a year later, when Joe claimed to have discovered that the geologist, his field man, had excessively overpaid for most of the land leases. To keep the operation floating, more money was required from investors or the deal would collapse, especially since gas prices had also dived. Joe himself put in an additional share of money to the amount of shares he allegedly held. He also admitted his error in overly trusting his irresponsible employee. The twist in the story was that Joe knew very well the value of leases, since he had himself worked in the past in those regions. In addition, he decided not to prosecute his employee, though he apparently got away with a significant amount of money.

Michael thought of himself as a knowledgeable investor who had the ability to understand a deal and had the support of his lawyer who read the contracts. The deal appeared to them to have been legitimate with the inherent risks related to this type of deal, such as variations in the price of leases related to changes in the gas market. Neither Michael nor his lawyer or his accountant suspected that a possible stratagem for cheating was that of inflating the price of the land leases since according to the terms of the contract, the prices were supposed to be within the market range, but subject to market variations. The escape clause for Joe was "subject to market variations," which justified any sudden potential increase in price. Joe's admission that the land leases suddenly surged did not fully justify the price paid by his leasing representative, the geologist. The overpayment in acquiring the leases was unfortunately followed by a collapse in the price of gas, resulting in a total loss of value of the leases. The partnership died since there was no more money for their renewal. The question that remained open was Joe's potential involvement in the leasing scheme or at least the extent of his possible "negligence" in carrying out his duties as a principal partner. Either way, it was hard to prove beyond any doubt his degree of deceit, if any. Michael and the other investors, regardless of their alleged business acumen, proved to be no match for Joe's smooth talk and possible double dealings. Michael made a grave judgmental error by believing in Joe's business acumen as suggested by his ability to get wealthy people to invest in his tax-shelter products. His assumption of understanding the unverifiable risks of the deal was fatal. Either way Michael did not realize that, after all, Joe was a very talented promoter who was a successful manipulator of investors. However, dubious business deals like this one or outright frauds are consummated every day between sophisticated promoters and pseudoknowledgeable investors, helped or not by inexperienced advisors.

A recently reported international scam will demonstrate this point. A group of international swindlers collected more than $60 million, defrauding over 400 people, by offering them venture capital loans after they paid substantial fees in advance for processing their applications. After the fees were collected by the promoters, the applicants were informed that they were supposed to sign contracts that required them to obtain a letter of credit from a bank for the amount of the requested loan. Had the potential borrower been able to obtain a letter of credit, he would obviously not have needed to use their services. After the venture-capitalist crooks were informed of the applicants' inability to obtain a letter of credit, they offered them a new deal that would allegedly facilitate the transaction under some terms and conditions for an additional hefty fee. But they still did not guarantee the approval of the loan. This is a typical business scam. Yet entrepreneurs from all walks of life—lawyers, doctors, famous stars, athletes, and businessmen—on the brink of bankruptcy or in need of expansion, were caught in the net. How is it possible that these supposedly intelligent, knowledgeable people could fall for a scheme such as this without some prior investigation of the alleged venture capitalist group? Was it because the smooth operators created the impression that the processing fee would automatically assure the loan or was it because of the victims' poor judgment due to their overwhelming needs, which superseded any thorough discussion of the terms prior to paying the fees? Did they truly believe that they would get the money from any bank without collateral assets or based on the simple guarantee of the schemers in the deal? After losing their initial fee of tens of thousands of dollars, any further involvement snowballed.[9] The combination of naïveté and greed seems to be financially fatal for most people, as illustrated by another massive fraud.

One of the most widespread frauds across the country lately has been that of some small Wall Street firms that had been promoting low-priced stock of poor or not performing companies. The brokers pitched the stock over the telephone as "the new Microsoft," while they knew that the phony stock in short time would be worthless. According to press reports, in 1998 alone people lost millions of dollars in this type of fraud.[10] This shows not only the extent of abuse of the public by deceptive stock brokers claiming stock market expertise but also the indiscriminate credibility bestowed on the brokerage houses and their salesmen by ordinary citizens. This mania to quickly get rich in the stock market is similar to the Dutch tulip mania of the 17th century, when people sold and cashed in their fixed assets in order to buy tulips at any price before the market crashed. The mania was produced by irrational popular beliefs and shrewd exploitation of crooks.[11] Comparable to other past popular delusions exploited by crooks would be today's frenzied speculations in penny stocks of gold mines due to the alleged sudden discovery of fabulous deposits of precious metals (e.g., the recent swindle of Canada's Brea gold mines) or the cheating promoted by some ingenious Ponzi schemes. The Ponzi scheme, named after its inventor, who defrauded 40,000 people of $15 million in the early 1920s, is a pyramid scheme in which investors are promised exaggerated returns on their investments. Early investors are paid with money received from later investors. Eventually, the funds are scooped by the founder of the scheme and all investors lose their money.

SOPHISTICATED CON ARTISTS

Most often, swindles and schemes are masterminded by corporate con artists who use their talents and imagination to cheat others. The main difference between the crooked business promoters and con artists is that of degree of pretense of legitimacy. While the former attempt to protect themselves with a variety of ambiguous documents, the latter do not bother, ultimately, with legal justification for their actions.

Recently the financial world has been shaken by corporate and investment enterprise swindles masterminded by allegedly responsible businessmen who cheated the public/corporations of hundreds of millions of dollars. Outstanding among these schemers have been John Bennett, Jr., of New Era Philanthropy Foundation, and Martin Frankel of Creative Partners Fund and St. Francis of Assisi Foundation. They cheated investors and corporations by their ingenious financial manipulations, which were basically Ponzi schemes. There are many other crooks who were either pure embezzlers or irresponsible gamblers trading in Wall Street with corporations' money (Baring Bank case, Sumitomo Bank copper case, etc.).

The thorny issue is whether these top swindlers believe that they will get away with their booty and enjoy a lifetime of luxurious living or they think that any received punishment in case of being caught will represent a small sacrifice in comparison with the reaped benefits from the crime. Are these liars-cheaters emotionally ill or are they daring opportunists who try to take advantage of social situations offering victims possibilities to make fast money? If the latter condition is true, then any encountered difficulty with the law is due to a simple miscalculation of the risk involved in pulling off their schemes. In this context, they acted as unscrupulous gamblers who believe in their ability to beat the law and they deserve to be severely punished. These particular types of crooks are mostly narcissists, belonging to a subtype known as "unprincipled narcissists"[12] who defy the social conventions and show a disregard for truth, although they try to keep their shady activities a step ahead of the arm of the law. They lack principles and tend to have a minimal or nonexistent sense of guilt and social conscience, enjoying outwitting and abusing others.

Con artists organize their life based on lying for material gain and as such concoct sophisticated and fraudulent plans to defraud people. They may use their own business or claimed expertise as a launching pad for their devious schemes and scams. Their initial approach is always business-like, which means they pretend to earnestly negotiate a transaction with a potential victim, except that later they misrepresent or disregard the terms of the deal. Even worse, they have no intention to deliver what they have committed themselves to do. These con artists are usually intelligent people who can make a decent living without preying on others. They prefer to swindle because they have become used to an easy way of life by cheating people. In addition, they get emotional satisfaction by proving to themselves that they are more clever than others. Some are true sociopaths, others are white-collar crooks. A case in point is Tev, an Eastern European immigrant who came to the U.S. after a short period of residence in France, where he did not fare well in his attempts to pull off some small business scams. He came to this country to try his luck, since he heard that here one can quickly get rich. After working for a while in a private investment firm, he decided to start his own business as a financial consultant. However, his business did not take off as he expected and the bills were piling up regardless of the help received from his wife, who was employed. By chance, he found out about the ease and laxity in obtaining government loans for minorities interested in starting small businesses and decided to earnestly pursue this activity. In the process, he realized the perfunctory control exercised by the official administration over the approval and control of these loans. This gave him the bright idea of submitting to the government valid loan applications mixed in with those for nonexistent businesses and then personally cashing the money for the fictitious ones. His living conditions improved tremendously, giving him access to frequent events in high social circles and meeting well-off professionals to whom he introduced himself as a successful private banker. These persons were the right targets for him. He wanted to do business with them because they were known as naive and gullible. Tev was delighted to have finally met these unsophisticated investors in friendly social interactions such as parties and personal introductions, where he could spin his stories of fabulous financial successes. Tev did not waste any time and started receiving money for investment in his alleged money-making deals. Unfortunately, he became too greedy and when he was unable to justify the fate of $500,000 that he received from a wealthy woman, his carefully built castle of cards started to crumble. Under investigation by the district attorney's office, it surfaced that he had bilked the Small Business Administration of millions of dollars, in addition to the unaccounted money taken from private investors who received phony investment statements. Tev jumped bail and left the country under an assumed name before trial. He was never caught and convicted. However, at that time, his swindles made the business page of the *New York Times*. Again, this goes against the popular belief that even the smartest crime does not pay off. This type of con game can be initiated by a swindler who may or may not be a sociopath. While he failed to observe the social norms of conduct by pursuing an antisocial behavioral pattern, Tev was carefully calculating his illegal moves in order to avoid any unexpected setback with his clients or the law. Tev was an unscrupulous narcissist who wanted to live high and get social recognition for what he thought to be his superior intelligence and social skills. He believed in his ability to "beat the odds" and he succeeded. His antisocial behavior cannot be considered in the domain of true mental pathology, since he pursued his deceit in a pure business fashion with the risk factored in. His attitude toward deception and swindling were for him the only way to achieve his goal of quick enrichment. He calculated the risk factor and he decided to go for broke. His behavior was antisocial but highly profitable to him.

TYPES OF IMPOSTERS

The number and/or the ingenuity of crooks cheating government institutions or corporations is impressive, yet the frauds that are committed are impersonal, permitted by the negligent or inept bureaucracy. In cases where deception takes place between private persons, the interaction is direct and each side is able to assess the possibilities of a fair transaction by actively and carefully examining the facts. However, there is a special category of deceivers who assume fictitious roles in life by identifying themselves with fraudulently chosen careers for personal gain or for noble causes. Most of them are con artists, but some are responsible citizens.

An imposter is the type of liar who lives a total lie by cheating people while adopting new social roles for himself for which he does not have qualified training or credentials but which satisfy his grandiose needs in addition to securing material benefits for him. At the same time, his approach to life represents an attempt to willfully deny the reality as is, for the main purpose of quick social gain. The skillful imposters portray the ultimate refined expression of misrepresentation the of truth. They may be pathological liars or men who live dangerously, executing special missions.

There are various degrees of impersonation, from that of occasionally assuming a different social role in order to obtain something that otherwise may be denied to that of living a lie by fabricating a new identity, which may change, depending on the demand of the circumstances. True imposters pretend to be socially what they are not. They usurp false identities, careers, and life histories, and act accordingly. They try to play highly lucrative social roles as if they are the real persons. Imposters may fake being physicians, lawyers, financial consultants, psychologists, and so on. The assumed careers they select may be influenced by some minimal experience that they might have had in that field, such as a position as a hospital attendant or a clerk in a law firm or in a Wall Street investment firm. These people are smart, intelligent, very creative, audacious, and clever. Some of them are con artists who in order to facilitate a swindling scheme, temporarily impersonate a legitimate profession or person, which can confer them the credibility and authority to execute it. Some use their impersonating talent for a national cause.

These are the people hired to take a different identity and infiltrate illegally a foreign business or governmental agency. They live under an assumed identity in a foreign country, but basically they are a genre of imposters. One famous imposter-spy master was Colonel Rudolph I. Abel of the Commisariat for Internal Affairs (Soviet Security Service). From 1948 to 1957, he lived in Brooklyn, New York, under an assumed name posing as a photographer while he was directing a spy network, comprising all of North America. He had a previous record of playing an imposter, during World War II, when he served as an intelligence officer for the Red Army and infiltrated the German Army posing as a chauffeur and with the necessary documentation of being German. He was decorated and promoted by the Germans to the rank of lance corporal. Basically, this man lived a great part of his life identified with different jobs than his true profession, adapting to the life condition of foreign countries, passing as a national of those countries while he did intelligence work for his own country. Was he antisocial? Obviously not, at least, for the Soviet Union. But he was an imposter for the country where he gathered intelligence information. According to the international rules, these imposters are heroes in their countries and labeled as villains in the ones where they operate.[13]

Other imposters are in business for themselves. An unusual case of impersonation has been recently reported by newspapers. The imposter was discovered by chance, when he attempted a brazen swindle. Posing as a wealthy businessman, Nathan—the imposter—wanted to cash a substantial amount of money from an insurance policy that was allegedly left to him by a brother who he claimed had died of AIDS. The insurance company suspected some irregularities due to the high amount of money involved in the policy and the unusual documentation that he, the apparent heir, had offered as proof of death. He claimed that his alleged brother, an orthodox Jew, was so upset about contracting AIDS that he went to die in Israel and asked to be buried in an unmarked grave. The investigation proved that the alleged brother had not died and was not secretly buried in Israel as Nathan had claimed, because he never existed. He *was* Nathan! Under closer scrutiny it was found that Nathan had impersonated another nonexistent brother in order to obtain a $1 million mortgage loan from a bank. Before his arrest, he lived a life of luxury in a 27-room mansion in a suburb of New York, claiming to be part of a large, wealthy family who wanted to use the house as a family retreat. Other swindles by assuming different names of nonexistent brothers for which he had forged documentation have also lately started to surface. Ironically, at the time of his arrest, Nathan admitted to being unemployed and without a career.[14] He is a con artist-imposter using invented identities of alleged close relatives, who are easier to forge and to explain to people.

But there are other true imposters who, after assuming a role of expertise in a particular field and gaining status and prestige, are able to function well within the boundaries of the impersonated profession without committing other frauds. Books have been written about these impostors.[15] One of the best known successful impostors was Ferdinand W. Demara, who pretended to be a Canadian physician during the Korean War. What is fascinating about this impostor was his success in treating Korean War casualties such as serious physical trauma related to combat action, which required difficult surgical intervention. He was able to perform complicated operations, sometimes extracting bullets lodged near vital organs, without having had any acquired formal surgical training. Before this he successfully impersonated other professions. Regardless of his unusual skill, he was still a fraud. He admitted in his own biography to being a brilliant liar who was consistent in his stories. As a departure from most imposters, he showed, by the nature of the profession that he chose to masquerade, a compassion and a desire to help people. In consideration of his outstanding medical work, when he was discovered, he was not prosecuted but simply discharged from the Canadian army. Most imposters are ordinary crooks who impersonate for sheer financial gains.

What has puzzled researchers in the field of human behavior about imposters is their preference to use their above-average intelligence and skill to fabricate or borrow professional identities instead of trying to obtain them on their own merits. Though there are various hypotheses to explain their behavior, the consensus seems to be that impostors are narcissistic people who lack the perseverence and tolerance for frustration needed to orderly pursue the training regulations of a career. In addition, they are audacious, adventurous, and imaginative in devising ways of impersonating others, exactly like actors on a stage, which results in their being able to live the chosen career role in real life. In this risky game, they are able to overcome issues of legality and morality based on their unshaken beliefs in their superior cleverness, which help them to navigate through the maze of legalities and to rescue them from any unexpected jam. The stakes are very high and they believe that they are able to win.

However, there are other types of crooks whose actions are prompted by uncontrollable emotional needs that suspend any judgment about the consequences who may be considered to belong to the domain of mental pathology. This is an arbitrary division from the first group of deceivers, since many con artists and imposters have serious mental problems. It is a controversial issue. It questions the validity of classifying certain liars as pathological based on their impulsive/compulsive lying and apparent self-destructive pattern of behavior.

TYPES OF PERSONALITY, THEIR PSYCHOPATHOLOGY, AND LYING

Popular empirical observations supported only later by psychological research have come to the conclusion that some types of personalies are more inclined than others toward lying and deception. Malicious lying has been mainly associated in psychology with specific types of personality disorders. While this contention holds a great deal of truth, the reality is that the distinction between the alleged normal personality, which may maliciously lie, and these specific types of personality prone to lying are far from being clear-cut. As a matter of fact, there is an imperceptible transition from those considered to have normal personality to the ones classified as having a personality disorder. Furthermore, personality disorders are not viewed by some theorists of personality as representing disease entities.[16]

At present, it is strongly believed that by assessing the cluster of basic traits of temperament and character, which together form a particular type of personality, one can predict its preferred mode of coping with the social milieu conducive or not to deception and maladjustment. In many cases, poor coping clearly suggests trends of specific psychopathology. What is important is the fact that the core cluster of traits, which identifies specific types of personality disorders, do not offer to these people a working foundation for a satisfactory social adaptation. Most often their handling of significant events in their life is either ineffective, unproductive, or outright destructive. The problem is aggravated by the actual gap between their unrealistic expectations and the limited ability and/or opportunity to pursue their goals. The combination of their inherited abilities (temperament) and of their developmental experiential learning (character) lead them to the formulation of inadequate coping designs to deal with the complexities of adult life. In general, the normal individual's coping style to life stressors and events can be reduced to either one of these all-inclusive pairs of responses: dependence or nurture, dominance or submission, assertiveness or avoidance, and competition or cooperation, all flexibly used and varying with the situation. The people with visible personality disorders misuse or confuse these responses due to the overwhelming imposition of the dominant traits of their personality that guide and direct the interpretation of confronting events in line with their needs. The response will attempt to satisfy the particular orientation of that personality, quite often in an inappropriate manner unwarranted by the situation. For example, a narcissistic person who is grandiose and hypersensitive to criticism may react with a high degree of defiance totally condemning the reprimand of his boss as unjustified and improper while a histrionic either may simply deny that it happened or may sulk. Certainly both these types of reactions do not help their standing with their boss and if often repeated may lead to their dismissal. However, the same people, when torn between their need of maintaining their cherished self-image and relating to the negative remarks of the boss, may try to soften the blow by defending themselves against his criticism with the help of distortions, misrepresentations, and fabrications. Anyway, these defenses, though used as rationalizations in support of their self-image, become part of their coping style. As a result, they perpetuate the same poor adaptive style that sometimes gets them out of trouble and most often interferes with their social functioning. The main problem with their coping style is that of being rigid, inflexible, and uncritical. They tend to respond to a set of interactions perceived as offensive in the same unsuited manner regardless of the circumstance or people involved. While their responses may be appropriate in some predicaments, most often they are harmful to themselves. Controlled by their unbridled emotional needs, they are unable to properly evaluate confronting events.

Let us take another example of a paranoid but not psychotic person, Jim, a 35-year-old, unmarried engineer, who is indiscriminately suspicious of other people's intentions and actions. He is convinced that "they" want to deceive him in any business or personal interaction. He does not trust people and he indiscriminately challenges them about the sincerity of their motives and veracity of their statements. At his last job, he had secretly tape-recorded the content of conversations with his boss to protect himself from being later accused of misinterpreting his orders. But, one day after a disagreement with his boss about the execution of some work directives, Jim confronted him with his own statements recorded on the tape, since this boss's dispositions were somewhat unclear, leaving room for interpretation. His boss blew his top and accused him of improper behavior. Jim justified his taping by claiming to suffer from attention problems, which was a lie. Two weeks later, he was fired for having difficulties in following orders and in relating and cooperating with coworkers. Looking for a job, it gradually became harder for him to find credible explanations for his past erratic employment record. Unable to concoct credible lies, he was forced to accept temporary assignments. While people do attempt to protect their self-image and interests from the attack of others, they simply are reasonably cautious and prudent in their dealings. Jim's overdefensiveness was counterproductive. The issue is whether he understands his problem of an inability to discriminate between situations that may require extreme cautiousness and others that do not. He claims that he does but he is misunderstood by others who distort the meaning of his behavior and sayings. In reality, his critical ability to correctly evaluate and reach the proper conclusions about the real dangers posed to his security in interactional situations is wanting. His lies, which attempt to correct, smooth over things, or redefine his behavior only succeed to complicate or aggravate his difficulty in his social functioning.

Most personalities are mixed cases with major traits of one personality and minor traits of another, not as "pure" as Jim's case. A narcissistic personality can have secondary paranoid, histrionic, or antisocial traits. A combination of diverse traits may affect the degree of social adaptability of the person. For example, both cases of Bob and Mike (in Chapter 4), described as self-deceivers, basically were narcissists. While Bob was boastful, pretentious, name-dropping, snobbish, and narcissistic, Mike a was more patronizing, haughty, hypercritical but suspicious person who sometimes entertained paranoid thinking. Yet both were successful in the business, Bob, the self-deceptive narcissist, was respected by the business community and Mike, who was more a reactive narcissist, meaning more autocratic in interaction with others, was accepted with reservations and most often disliked. Their social adaptation has been limited to business where their manipulative intelligence and endless fabrications have compensated for their personality flaws. Their private life has been less rewarding due to their lack of sensitivity and superficial emotional involvement with their wives and children.

However, other people with the same personality disorder may not fare so well if they lack compensatory qualities to help them to cope better with the various stresses of life and enhance their chances for fulfillment of their social aspirations. In these cases, the balance between rational thinking and their obsessive emotional needs becomes so tilted in the favor of the latter that any realistic appraisal of events is hopeless. The gap between the implacable reality and the one constructed in their mind to fit their self-image is bridged with lies. Reality is reconstructed, reshaped, and modified to support their unfulfilled but pressing inner needs in an attempt to stabilize their fragile self-image. For example, Tim, a 35-year-old college graduate, has been unable to find the "right" job for him. After graduating from an Ivy League college, he tried various lines of work that he found either too demanding or unappealing. He wanted a glamorous job where his talents and cleverness would be recognized. Articulate and exuding confidence, he was able to sell himself during the hiring interview to the employer as an ambitious, hard-working man who just wanted a chance to prove himself. But at work, he was undisciplined, critical of others, and inefficient. He was disorganized, sensitive to criticism, and wasted time attempting to find faults with the "system of work " in order to impress his boss with his great innovative ability. Unfortunately, he had difficulty identifying the "right job" (he has worked in advertising, brokerage firms, real estate, retail sales, and currently, in for wholesale manufacturing) and his successive series of bosses found him arrogant, noncomplying, or unreliable in executing the requested work. What made things worse for him was his constant lying about the reasons for not properly or timely executing the tasks. Most often, either he was fired or he brusquely resigned feeling unappreciated by his supervisor. He liked to brag about his "talents" while invariably making up stories about losing his past jobs. Finally, he hit upon the idea of using the name of small companies that either went out of business or went bankrupt in order to support his phony working record. His frustration about work was exacerbated by his inability to develop a meaningful relationship with a woman. His relationships with women have been superficial, transient, and stormy. Tim's latest problem was an affair with an older woman from whom he borrowed quite a bit of money by claiming he would pay her back after the receipt of a large bonus from the company for which he worked at the time. The whole scheme blew up in his face when the woman contacted his boss to recoup the loan. He justified the conflict by saying it was pure fabrication on her part since she gave him the money on various occasions as gifts. She asked for repayment months later, only after he decided to drop her.

Apparently, Tim will not succeed in fulfilling his dreams with this unrealistic attitude toward work and people, supported by his own rationalizations and prevarications. His lies and manipulations of truth were attempts to maintain a fragile balance between an underlying insecurity and his pseudo-confidence, which he strived to project. His posture contradicted the reality of his inconsistent and scarce achievements. His compensatory lies, when used judiciously, helped him to smooth over, at least partially, the effect of his inadequate ways of handling and coping with social problems until the next crisis, which, in turn, required more lies to deal with it.

Lying as a Life Support for the Borderline Personality

For borderline personalities, lying is heavily interwoven into the individual's fabric of existence, not necessarily to defraud others, but to cope with daily situations as part of their way of dealing with life. These people hold in common certain basic traits of their personality, such as a lack of social direction and focus, impulsive behavior, explosive interpersonal relationships, and a tendency toward self-destructive activity. Lying is interwoven within their approach and their coping with the environment. These people function marginally socially, have no steady work records, and exhibit unexpected mood swings. They attempt to solve their immediate problems of living by inventing stories about themselves and lying about their past history. Many of them recount their childhood or adolescence with stories of having been sexually or physically abused or having experienced unusual emotional trauma. Basically, they reconstruct their past in dramatic colors for the purpose of getting sympathy or help from others. Take the case of Mo, a 38-year-old married woman with a checkered work record, who, in order to enhance her chances of winning a litigation against a mental health provider, described herself to the appointed psychiatrists for the defense and to the judge as a victim of an emotionally traumatic childhood. In a crackling, quivering voice, sometimes wiping tears, she told the court about being sexually abused by her older brother at age 7 and later, at age 14, of being forced to have sex with her brother-in-law while she innocently babysat for her older sister's kids during her working hours. Her odyssey continued with her first husband who after a violent argument in which she threatened to call the police, had allegedly tied her up, put her feet in a basin of fresh cement, and left her there until the cement almost dried. She claimed that her second husband was also cruel and forced her to give her child up for adoption. However, under closer investigation by the defense lawyers and their psychiatrist, her tales did not stick. In their testimony, her brother denied having any sexual involvement with her, her sister declared to have found her in bed passionately making love with her husband, while her first husband stated that her stories about cement or tying her up or beating her were pure fantasies. Interestingly, after separating from her last husband, she approached her first one, who was available at the time, and started an affair. Her second husband claimed that the reason for giving up her daughter for adoption was due to her inability to go to work and take care of her after they decided to split up. While part of her elaborated lies during the trial were told for obvious reasons of financial gain, other lies related to her social functioning of an otherwise fragmented, unfocused, and meaningless lifestyle were simply attempts to make sense of her behavior. She wanted to believe in some of her lies because they justified her erratic behavior to herself and others.[17] Some of the displayed personality features of her are histrionic, as her overdisplay of emotions indicates.

The Web of Lies Embedded in the Histrionic Personality

If people with borderline personality lie in an attempt to survive within a marginal existence, others with another type of personality known as histrionic (hysterical) relish fabricating stories about themselves for the purpose of gaining the admiration of others or for replacing events that they perceive as negative and possibly affecting their social status. Hysterics have a tendency to dramatize events in which real happenings are grossly exaggerated or filled with fictional elements for the sole purpose of impressing an audience or whomever might be listening. This is all part of the need to always be the center of attention. In addition, hysterics tend to display provocative sexual behavior, conveyed by gestures and the way they dress. In close interaction, they may quite often act sexually seductive. Their lies are all part of their social image, which represents an inherent facet of their interaction with others. They complement or substitute for the real traits that they perceive as missing in their personality or attempt to enhance their image in order to produce the desirable outcome. Indeed, many times their public behavior looks like an attempt at calculated theatrical effects, when they act as if the world is their stage. Nevertheless, their web of lies quite often goes beyond the need to impress others as they are directed by the need for financial advantage.

Lyn is an unmarried, 32-year-old, relatively attractive woman who works as an administrative employee for a Wall Street firm. She dresses attractively, talks seductively, openly flirts with executives, and at this time is emotionally and sexually intimate with two men. Lyn is undecided about the best course of action to follow toward organizing her future life. She questions whether she should marry one of the two men she is presently dating or if she should postpone marriage and pursue an MBA degree in order to secure a better job. She is uncertain about which man she loves more and which one will make a better husband. However, at the same time, she is afraid of losing both because of their concerns about her being too temperamental and unpredictable. Her relationship with both has periodically been strained because of her unexpected excessive emotional reactions in situations that otherwise might be trivial. She sometimes loses her temper and makes a public or private scene. Afterward, she tries to make up for it with an overdisplay of affection. In addition, she admits to having a hard time juggling dates with her two lovers because she has to lie to either one. She is ready to drop one of them as soon as she decides which one she should marry. However, there are some sticky problems in her decision to marry either man. She lied to both of them about her family background, claiming to belong to a well-to-do family, when in reality her parents were of modest means. To dramatize the issue, she claimed that both her parents who died sometime ago in a car crash. She told them that the estate left by her parents was squandered by an uncle, acting as trustee, whom she sued but who died before a satisfactory settlement was reached. Obviously, this is all a fabrication, even the source of her present financial assets or about graduating college. At her present job, she said that she graduated from college, but no one in personnel verified her story for its accuracy. In fact, one of her lovers is a mid-level executive within the firm who had supported her in getting a promotion under the assumption that she had graduated college, in addition to helping her cope with various job problems. She is concerned about his negative reaction if she decides to marry the other man, in which case she may be forced to leave her job. However, she has another serious problem with the other lover, namely, he believes, based on her previous statements, that she is four years younger than she is and assumes that she is able to have children. But she cannot have children due to surgical intervention for an ectopic (extra-uterine) pregnancy, which apparently resulted in sterility. When her sterility was confirmed, she sued the surgeon and received a handsome settlement from his insurance, which is the true source of her personal money. Lyn did not tell her lover about it nor the truth about her personal social history, which she embellished on with an exciting background of events. In view of all these complications with her lovers and her job, she is thinking about taking the advice of one of her lovers and possibly pursuing a MBA. Unfortunately, she not only needs to finish college but her ability to study higher math and statistics has always been poor. Interestingly, she is fully aware of her slanting of the truth but she believes that whatever she has done has been justifiable. She thinks that her embellishment of her past life is harmless because it just makes her look good and is closer to what it was supposed to be anyway. All her justifications are based on conditional situations of her past life, which never happened but which now are integrated as possible realities in her life. For instance, she could have theoretically graduated from college; but now because she thinks that she could have, it has magically become a pseudoreality. While she fully understands that her tales are untrue, at the same time she needs to use them to project the image of what she should be, simultaneously enhancing her self-esteem and opportunities for social interaction. Her false memories or deliberate falsifications of childhood events that are recounted in order to give a special meaning and effect to herself should be viewed within the same context. All in all, by our social standards, she can be viewed as a devious histrionic, unreliable, manipulating, and scheming. Yet her lies help her to support her desired but fictitious self-image, which gives meaning to her existence regardless of numerous setbacks.

In the makeup of the histrionic personality, there is a constitutional and familial factor contributing to its formation. The presumed constitutional predisposition contributes to the degree of arousal and the lability of the autonomic nervous system, not to mention the person's grade of suggestibility and susceptibility to conditioning. The familial influences, which certainly are related to the individual's developmental years, involve imitation and assimilation of the behavior of others who acted too emotionally or sometimes hysterically. The combination of these factors promotes a particular style of thinking and coping, which help one to magically change reality by making it more gratifying.[18]

All these hyperbolic stories and misrepresentations that interface with their social interaction make it possible for these people to negotiate their environment more favorably, regardless of how unproductive they might be in the end. They represent modes of coping and solutions to their social needs, which otherwise would frustrate them to the point of inducing a whole gamut of negative emotions, from anxiety and anger to depression. In general, in most cases, lies, distortions, half-truths, or outright deceptions facilitate and lubricate the unfolding of a life that is viewed as overwhelming and frustrating. A puzzling question is the extent to which they believe or not in some of their elaborate memories about their childhood or adolescence, which they reminisce with drama and conviction.

The Remaking of Memories by People

It is important to realize that memory is dynamic, not static and passive as it used to be thought of until recently. Memory does not passively register and store events, but rather modifies and reconstructs their content over years to fit one's concept of himself in order to harmonize past events with his self-cultivated image. The self-image is not only the result of one's factual experiences as they had occurred, but also of their interpretation by the individual who, in the course of his life, tends to subtly reevaluate those experiences, retouching their meaning by adding and subtracting elements.[19] All these mental reconstructions are necessary in order to support one's self-identity, which creates the framework for his interaction within his social surroundings. This reshaping of past memories is selective since it is related to those events (real or sometimes fictitious) that are modified or created only to reinforce desirable traits and to ignore or erase those incongruent with his view of himself. The updating of memories slowly takes place by the addition of new data and the reshaping of other data on a subconscious level. Because of these surreptitious and subtle changes, the individual is not fully aware of any modification, believing that the memories are the original ones. Experiments have been done with students showing their capacity to recall facts in an inaccurate manner when compared to their reports in previous years. The same was noticed about people who had witnessed powerful events and who recalled them later in a modified form in order to suit their revised interpretation of them. For instance, a researcher on memory was able to document the ability to distort memories by planting misinformation after subjects viewed a video of an accident caused by a car going through a yield sign at an intersection. After viewing, it was suggested to subjects in a casual discussion that the sign was most likely a stop sign. Later, when questioned about the type of sign at the traffic intersection, 80 percent claimed to have seen on video a stop sign. The memories of events were contaminated by suggestions that influenced their recollection.[20] In fact, most of the memories of childhood are restructured over a period of time, based on parents' or other adults' recollection. People with personality problems are even more inclined to rely on forged memories to justify their behavior. For instance, self-deceivers surreptitiously integrate into their personality subjectively reinterpreted events that slowly become memories in support of their fabricated self-image. Most types of personalities do the same thing when there are incompatibilities in integrating within the expected view of themselves disruptive experiences of their inordinate lives that are full of unsolved emotional conflicts and unmet expectations. If we talk only about memories that are modified on a subconscious level, then these people with personality problems who report them cannot be considered liars since they are not fully aware of them. However, the trouble is that they complement and reinforce these distorted memories with outright lies. In cases of borderline and hysterical personalities, old memories that are important are represented by a blend of true facts mixed with falsified ones and topped off with conscious fictional additions, which over time themselves become part of their pseudorealities. They become integrated to the point that any meaningful distinction between them and true memories is blurred because they, in time, contribute to the new version of one's past and in a sense represent one's self-created image. All intentional lies, told on and off, are added only out of necessity in order to cope with events beyond their routine ability.

The Compulsive-Habitual Liars

There are people for whom lying is intertwined in their daily activities to the extent to which they have difficulty telling the truth even when the truth does not hurt them. These pathological compulsive liars do not represent a special type of personality, though they are mainly off-shoots of antisocial personality, also found among narcissists, borderline histrionics, and sometimes dependent personalities who have developed a pattern of social interactions with a high reliance on lies. They are doing it compulsively, thinking that it will make the actual circumstances more favorable to themselves. The true habitual liars are unable to relate to others without twisting, distorting, falsifying, or misconstruing facts or events in order to place themselves in a favorable light. They do this either because they realistically illusorily perceive being disadvantaged or in order to create a desired effect. Unfortunately, they do it everyday to the point in which truth and falsehood become so intertwined in their own head that the two are indistinguishable. This style of relating to others helps them cope with everyday life with less pain when failing to meet their social obligations or responsibilities. By remaking reality according to their immediate needs, they receive instant gratification. Joanne is an example. She is a 25-year-old, employed, single woman. Her biggest problem is her continuous tension and conflict with her family, friends, and supervisor at work because of her lying. She was dismissed from a few jobs because of her unreliability in carrying out her duties. During her school years, she always felt less desirable and less accepted than the other girls. To overcome it, she tried to please everyone. To solve this inherent conflict, she lied to her teachers about reasons for not doing her homework, lied to her parents about her failing grades or irregular school attendance, and lied to other girls about herself. In college, whenever confronted by her parents, she lied about passing her exams, when in reality she was failing most courses. She had to repeat many courses and finally, by the end of her third year, she gave up and left school. Joanne always exaggerated her abilities to quickly master subjects. If she failed an exam, she invented excuses to protect her self-image. Over the years, her lying became so bad that she was not telling the truth even about executing routine chores like returning things or paying bills by their due dates. Her relationships with her girlfriends had always been tenuous because of her untrue stories about alleged emotional affairs she had with the most desirable boys in school or false promises made about introducing them to boys whom she did not know. These lies, on top of the previous ones, which she herself often forgot, were eroding her credibility. When caught in her web of lies with no smart way of getting out, she would cry and "admit" to her possible fault because of not recalling well the facts. Lately, her more pressing problem has been her relationship with her boyfriend, whom she believes is insincere and unfaithful to her. In addition, he does not take her expressions of love seriously and questions her credibility. She admits that she lied to him on various occasions but claims she loves him and has difficulty convincing him of her sincerity. This predicament is nerve-wrecking for her. Habitual lying seems partly to be caused by an underlying low self-esteem, which these liars try to uplift by conveying a positive image against evidence to the contrary. The fear of projecting an image of inadequacy due to their behavior "suspected as unreliable" is compensated by lying, which is a fast solution. Yet they like to think of cleverly meeting social demands and hence inviting the much-sought friendship of others. It is an expeditious but inefficient way of social adaptation. Various forms of pathological lying is at the core of distortion of truth perpetrated by other malignant types of liars such as sophisticated con artists, creative sociopaths (antisocial personality disorder), and imposters who breathe and live a life of deception.

Pseudologia Fantastica

There are unusual types of habitual liars who fabricate fantastic, hard-to-believe stories, most often purposeless. Their tales, products of rich imagination, show a total disregard for the truth, as if they live in a dream world. They surreptitiously change the reality into a world of make-believe in which they are the main actors. These people suffer from pseudologia fantastica. A case in point is that of Nick. Nick came to this country years ago as a political refugee from an Eastern European country. According to him, he was a writer who just finished a novel that was too politically sensitive to carry with him, particularly since he unexpectedly left the country. He claimed that his father was imprisoned and died there, while he received a milder sentence because he was young and without a political record. In his country, he asked various organizations for financial help to go to school to learn English and finish his novel, which allegedly was exposing the crimes of the Communist government, based on his inside information. Years later, he claimed to have established himself in business with a partner doing import–exports from Asia. Later, he boasted to have bought two pricey townhouses for investment in New York City. Allegedly, he was a wheeler-dealer constantly busy traveling around the world closing deals of tens of millions dollars, while having a lover in Paris and affairs with models in New York and London. All these fabulous stories, narrated like fragments of a novel, were entertaining but ended with Nick asking his listener-acquaintance for some cash because he did not have time to go to the bank. His pretense collapsed regardless of his convoluted explanations when he desperately called a countryman to get money for a week's rent of a room at the YMCA from where he was supposed to be evicted. Nick, an intelligent man but without a career, unable to adapt to the reality of his limited possibility for making big money here, escaped into a world of fantasy where things magically changed according to his dreams of success and glory. In reality, at one time he thought to write a novel but was unable; at another, he worked for a small import–export office but he could not cope with the paperwork; he also tried to get involved in real estate but that too did not work. Some of these fantasies, after years of repetition, slowly became incorporated in part in his memories as if it might happen in order to support his shaky self-image.

Many reasons have been advanced for this fascinating condition, from cerebral dysfunction to unconscious needs to bolster a weak self-image. Basically, these confabulations play an adaptive role by attempting to maintain a sense of self against surmounting adversities, which overwhelm the person and tend to make him nonfunctional. In finality, these fantastic stories are self-defeating and counterproductive because when verified, they can easily expose the liar.

Masterful Liars: Sociopaths

Many skillful crooks and liars are easily identified as sociopaths. A sociopath is antisocial because his social interaction with others is based on continuous attempts to defraud, cheat, and lie to them. His general psychological profile is that of an intelligent, articulate, charming, and superficially considerate person who is also emotionally detached, cold, and unscrupulous. He cultivates the skill of talking smoothly and lying convincingly while looking straight into the other person's eyes. Confident and alert during conversation, he has a knack of picking up on a possible weakness of his potential victim by skillfully asking the right questions before entrapping the person. In the process of expounding on his elaborate and appealing schemes he does not display any verbal or nonverbal signs of emotional or physical discomfort. It is hypothesized that sociopaths have a less developed capacity than the general population to acquire visible responses of the autonomous nervous system at powerful emotional stimuli. Free of unpleasant physical reactions and guilt, the sociopath does not experience anxiety or fear of being exposed for cheating others. Serene and self-assured, he is ready to sell anything, even the Brooklyn Bridge, to anyone naive or foolish enough to get involved in any of his scams. He likes to deceive people either for fun or, most often, for gain, as his latest needs may dictate. When he succeeds in putting something over on someone for fun, he is delighted to be able to prove his cleverness and superiority. But most often, he lies and cheats people for financial gain. For the sociopath it means a way of making a living in an environment viewed by him as full of suckers.

Sam, a junior-year college student of above-average intelligence, articulate and of pleasant demeanor, academically in good standing, gradually started to display serious antisocial behavioral problems. One of his bizarre acts was to write racially obscene slurs against his own ethnic group on classroom desks. Later, while surrounded by classmates, he would read the insults aloud and would then indignantly complain to the administration. At other times, he would send obscene letters to female students signed with the names of various top students or young faculty members. The resulting uproar, screaming, and complaints of these women were a source of great enjoyment for him and his buddies. When the administration caught him he was temporarily suspended from attending classes and was referred for psychiatric treatment as a condition to remain at college. These prankish activities were regarded by the college psychologist as an attention-seeking device and were dismissed by the officials with a reprimand only after the school received a hefty monetary gift from his rather well-to-do family. However, over time his personal behavior got worse as he started stealing food from supermarkets and clothes from department stores for fun. In fact, a few times he devised very sophisticated schemes when stealing from department stores. On one occasion, he went to a department store, bought a pair of jeans, paid for them, and left. He came back one hour later, put the same jeans on the display table and started trying on other jeans. After he tried on numerous pairs of jeans, he put all of them back on the display table, took his original jeans from the same table, stuffed them furtively into his briefcase, and nonchalantly moved toward the store exit. He knew that his behavior would be noticed by the store detectives who were monitoring the aisles. Indeed, one detective ran after him and stopped him in an attempt to check his briefcase. An argument broke out as to whether he had bought the jeans as he had claimed or he had stolen them. Unaware of his game, the detective thought that he had stolen them and attempted to detain him for interrogation. Sam resisted, and a scuffle followed, at which point he shouted for the police's help while customers started to gather around. He suddenly freed himself from the detective's hold and triumphantly showed the receipt, proving that he had bought the jeans. In front of witnesses, he threatened to sue the store for false arrest and asked to see the management, but not before taking the names of a few witnesses. Later, the store settled the claim and compensated him handsomely. This game worked out very well and thrilled him to no end. It also gained him a high mark with his friends.

Sam continued his petty criminal behavior until he graduated to more sophisticated and crooked deals. After leaving college, he got a job in another state at an investment firm that sold, among other financial products, offshore tax shelters. Sam masterminded a business scheme related to these offshore transactions used by wealthy people for sheltering income. The investment product was considered to be legitimate, but was required to be reported to IRS. As a salesman for the company, he became friendly with some buyers and tried to extract personal and business information from them whenever possible. If he suspected that an investment might represent the hiding of unreported money offshore, he would, according to a prearranged plan, inform his partner in crime, who, posing as a government insider, would attempt to extort money from the investors by claiming to have knowledge of alleged tax irregularities or to accuse them of possible tax evasion. When his confederate was arrested for extortion, Sam denied any cognizance of his alleged acquaintance's criminal activity but admitted to being careless by leaving records of the business transactions on his desk at home, accessible to the other fellow when he occasionally visited him. Sam left town when he was physically threatened by his former partner because of some dispute about money. He moved south, where he started another series of outright swindles, cashing unauthorized pension checks, which temporarily landed him in jail. In order to receive a more lenient sentence, he invoked a plea of emotional distress allegedly related to long-standing psychological problems of having been abused as a child by a nanny. Based on this defense, he received a six-month jail sentence and three years of probation with a requirement for psychiatric treatment. Afterward, his antisocial activities continued because of his low tolerance for frustration, lack of sustained perseverance in any task, and need for immediate gratification combined with a need to prove his cleverness. These negative traits are counterproductive for holding a regular job and adapting socially. Furthermore, Sam lacked respect for the rights of others because he viewed people either as careless in handling their business or using poor judgment. If they are cheated, they do not deserve compassion or concessions because they do not protect their interest. No guilt, no problems of conscience for Sam; he just wants to stay a step ahead of the arm of the law. What makes sociopaths behave as they do?

The psychological explanation for their antisocial behavior is presumably related to two unfavorable factors in their personality makeup, that is, an assumed genetic component that is superimposed on ego-damaging, frustrating environmental experiences. Most people exhibiting antisocial behavior have a history of lying, cheating, stealing, and other deviant behaviors since childhood. It is an early way of coping for some children who have a low tolerance for frustration, a need for immediate gratification and a denial of satisfaction by acceptable means. They gradually learn this deviant behavior that pays off for them, at least for the short term. Interestingly, very few intelligent crooks with sociopathic traits are arrested and fewer, if convicted, get long jail terms for their crimes. Incidentally, some sociopaths are imposters, but not all imposters are sociopaths. In most cases, their behavior might be considered antisocial but their core of personality could be narcissistic with antisocial traits because of their orientation to sensation-seeking, risk-taking and deception.

The Munchausen Syndrome

There are also some imposters who become specialized in assuming the role of patients. They are known as having Munchausen syndrome. They claim to suffer from serious diseases, give dramatic and fantastic histories of their life, and sign themselves into various hospitals under their own or assumed names.[21] They are of interest only because their faked behavior and simulation of diseases represent a poor coping of life events. In order to escape a perceived overwhelming environment, these people with serious coping problems ultimately withdraw into a world of make-believe, where they are the principal actors and the recipients of the yearned attention by others taking care of them. The feigning of illness adds the final touch to the drama of their life, as they obviously force others to listen to their tales and literally nurse them. This was the case of Ellen, a 40-year-old single, unemployed woman, admitted in emergency to a psychiatric ward for attempted suicide. She took an overdose of sleeping pills because she was despondent about her intractable back pain and other emotional problems. Ellen claimed to have developed her pain six years ago during an archaeological expedition to Ecuador and Peru, where she contracted a rare viral condition. After she returned home, the back pain and state of fatigue intensified. She was diagnosed as suffering a rare virus. Medication was of little help. Fortunately, she was able to work from home as an industrial graphic designer. However, the last straw leading to her suicide attempt was the rejection of her boyfriend of four years. The staff was very sympathetic to her tragic life story.

According to her initial story, her mother died when she was 4 years old and she was brought up by a mean aunt who mistreated her. When she was about 15, her cousin raped her and shortly after she ran way. Her adolescence was very dramatic. She held various menial jobs and was sexually exploited until she met an older, rich man who helped her financially to graduate high school and get a diploma in graphic design. She traveled around the world with him and she had a good life for a while. When he suddenly died of heart attack, she was thrown penniless on the street by his heirs. She pulled through by getting a job and reorganizing her life, but after a trip to the Andes, her life became a nightmare.The last straw was the rejection of her boyfriend. Her story was heart-rending. The doctor and the social worker treating her were fretting over finding a solution to improve her miserable life.

However, by chance, it was found that she registered under an assumed name for her visits. She was pressed to tell the truth or otherwise be prosecuted. She recounted a different story: she had been treated for the last four years at various clinics and services of neurology, medicine, and orthopedics under her name and that of a cousin of the same age who died of cancer four years ago. Her stories about a cruel aunt, a dramatic adolescence, and traveling around the world were fabrications. The fact was that her mother died when she was young but her aunt helped her out until her death. Ellen was married for a short time to an engineer who divorced her but retained custody of their baby daughter. She graduated from high school and held various secretarial jobs until she started to take care of her sick cousin. She was unable to get remarried, though she had numerous affairs. She was lonely, had periods of insomnia, and sometimes abused sleeping pills. Ellen's story about viral syndrome was an invention, an attention-seeking device challenging doctors to try to diagnose a rare condition. She switched to psychiatry after exhausting the use of other services. Her overdose consisted of six sleeping pills, which drugged her. Was her revised story truthful? Doubtful. Not all facts were verified.

Apparently, Ellen's loss of her mother, the termination of her short marriage, the loss of her daughter, and her inability to find a man may have contributed to her feeling of rejection and unworthiness. Hospital care compensated for her needs for attention and dependency, although her resorting to feigning illness has damaged her already weak ego to the point of making her hopelessly dependent and socially nonfunctional.

The Factitious Disorder

There are other people who simulate a disease without an inordinate bizarre life story, fabrication of fantastic events, or claim of various unusual diseases. They are more prosaic, clinging to one imaginary disease. Some of them simulate a disease in the hope of gaining a financial or other advantage, such as avoidance of court appearance, collection of insurance benefits, taking time off from work, and so on. These people are known as malingerers.

But there are others who do not have any apparent motive to simulate a disease but they do. They are known to suffer a factitious disorder. Do they make themselves ill? Apparently yes. This was the case of Basil, a 30-year-old draftsman who, a short time after his girlfriend of five years broke off with him, started to feel sick. He complained of episodes of blurred vision, headaches, restlessness, fatigue and poor coordination. He took sick leave and consulted various doctors, took numerious tests, and each one suspected a different cause for his condition. He was not responding to the symptomatic medication received. His parents were extremely upset, his friends concerned, and the doctors puzzled. At a visit, a doctor noticed his large pupils and raised the issue of a possible addiction to some drugs. The urine text came out negative for the suspected drugs. The doctor asked his mother, a nurse, to watch him closely. To her surprise, one day she found an unlabeled bottle of pills in his room. The pills were identified as benztropine mesylate (cogentin) tablets, a medication for the treatment of parkinsonism. When confronted, he admitted taking them irregularly because they made him feel good. He did not relate his condition to them. It is a dangerous drug when taken in nonprescribed quantities, but he wanted to get the sympathy of his ex-girlfriend. In the process, he started to enjoy the attention received from his parents, relatives, and friends. This secondary gain made him continue the game. It was a poor strategy for overcoming an unfavorable situation. In general, it is used by dependent people who tend to ask for sympathy, dramatized by illness, when they do not see better ways of succeeding.

TYPES OF PERSONALITIES MORE VULNERABLE TO DECEPTION

Most people lie whenever it is perceived as necessary, while a distinct category lie as a mode of living. What is intriguing is that many seemingly knowledgeable and otherwise savvy people fall victim to various scams and to the manipulations of others. The reasons are many but are apparently superseded by the overpowering social belief that most people in their routine social and/or business transactions as a rule do not lie, abuse, or cheat others. Yet the uncritical approval of this belief could lead to major financial losses and emotional frustration.

While any person under particular circumstances may be lied to or deceived by a crook, the individual more often vulnerable to their manipulations and deceptions is the dependent personality. Dependent people are easily persuaded because they tend to be naive, uncritical, and believe in man's goodness and honesty. Owing to their lack of confidence, they depend on others who they tend to believe and trust. Because of their own feeling of inadequacy and inferiority they are inclined to overvalue others, to be compliant, obliging, and accommodating, hence susceptible to gullibility. Unsure of their competence and afraid of rejection, they are ready to accept the judgment of others whom they admire and want to please. With these poorly developed social skills of self-protection, they are an easy target for charming con artists and persuading crooks who give them the illusion of acceptance, support, and protection.

By the same token, there are those who are duped because they believe in their own "indisputable" intuitive ability to catch a liar. This presumptuous conviction based on their alleged keen intuition is a self-laid trap, which only helps the liars and the crooks to cast more securely their nets of deception. Most victims of this fallacy are the self-deceivers and narcissists who compensate for their underlying insecurity and pseudoconfidence with presumptions of superiority and competence. Their need for confirmation of their qualities while striving for recognition makes them easy prey to clever flatterers, who support their self-glorifications. The disparity between their fantasies about themselves and their feats is filled with rationalizations that not always succeed to wipe out self-doubt. Then, they need the praise and support of the hypocrites and liars in pursuit of their own hidden agenda. Histrionic personalities fall into the same trap, although for different psychological reasons. In these cases, their need to impress and dazzle others makes the theatrical or appeasing histrionic easy prey to liars and crooks. But greed is another powerful factor that, on one hand, motivates people to lie, cheat, and, on the other, to take foolish risks and fall victim to deceptive schemes. This goes across almost all types of personalities and it is a decisive link that brings together the cheater and his victim for the common goal of easy enrichment.

From a different perspective, these diverse types of liars and victims provide us with an understanding of another facet of the diverse modes of people's ability to cope with social competition or pure survival. Some try to succeed through deceptive or illegitimate methods in order to get a jump start or move faster along the social ladder than others, the ethical ones who play by the rules. Other liars are not competing to win, but to them lying makes the difference between coping with a marginal life and emotionally collapsing. It suggests that at one end of the spectrum of social functioning there are those people who improve their living by using illicit means, such as small-time crooks who feed off of honest citizens while at the other end there are sophisticated crooks—some of them big-time financial, political, and business schemers—who basically do the same thing, but operate within the framework of an ambiguous legitimacy sanctified by their authoritative position. If, and when, they are caught, they are either legally protected by the best lawyers or escape with light sentences.

In general, the gamut of deceptive stratagems used depends on the individual's moral beliefs and intelligence and may vary from case to case according to the needs and opportunity of the liar. It is part of one's adaptive or maladaptive style of social functioning. While all people attempt to use their best available strategies to enhance their living situation, not all are using them appropriately and successfully. The ones who, owing to their biological disposition interfacing with their specific environmental conditions have fostered inadequate or improper behavioral responses, are ill-equipped to operate within the acceptable social framework to meet their goals. Deception, although potentially self-destructive in the long range, offers immediate solutions and gratification. In this context, some of the deceitful methods can enhance some people's ability to adapt to the social milieu, while other extreme and reckless forms of dishonesty may harm those who use them, making them poorly adaptable or unadaptable. The latter are most often either bad liars or pathological ones. Can they function without cheating and lying? Doubtful. The disparity between their expectations of themselves and their realistic means of achieving them is too far apart to be settled by moralistic advice or threats of social coercion. Basically, they are not able to accept a grim marginal existence, which they do not know to escape otherwise.

On the other hand, the victims who are caught in the web of manipulation and deceit of sophisticated deceivers may have to pay a costly price, while showing defective coping skills and blind spots in their adaptive mechanisms.

NOTES

1. B. Siegal, *Love, Medicine & Miracles* (New York: Harper & Row Publishers, 1986), pp. 84–95.

2. M.T. Burton, "A Prostate Researcher Tested Firm's Product and Sat on Its Board," *Wall Street Journal*, March 19, 1998, p. 1.

3. *Feminist News*, May 28, 1997. Internet. http://www.feminist.org/news.

4. A. Abelson, "Comedy of Errors." *Barron*, December 18, 1995, p. 3.

5. N. Weiss, "Premenstrual Syndrome (PMS) and the Law in Critical Issues," in *American Psychiatry and the Law*, edited by R. Rosner (New York: Plenum Press, 1985), pp. 270–73.

6. "Wachtler Plans to Seek Reinstatement as Lawyer," *New York Times*, June 27, 1998, p. B6.

7. B.L. Schlesinger, "The Catathymic Process in Exploration." In *Criminal Psychpathology*, edited by C. Schlesinger (Springfield, IL: Charles C. Thomas, 1996), pp. 121–141.

8. G. Serban, "Multiple Personality: An Issue for Forensic Psychiatry." *American Journal of Psychotherapy* (1992), p. 269.

9. M. Navarro, "Huge Money Laundering Scheme Revealed in Florida," *New York Times*, May 8, 1998, p. A10.

10. A. Lucchetti, "Sec Alleges Penny-Stock Firms Defrauded Investors," *Wall Street Journal*, September 25, 1998, p. C1.

11. C. Mackay, *Extraordinary Popular Delusions and the Madness of the Crowds, the Tulipomania* (New York: L.C. Page, 1956), pp. 89–97.

12. T. Millon, with D.R. Davis, *Disorders of Personality DSM-IV and Beyond* (New York: John Wiley & Sons, 1996), pp. 9–74.

13. N. Polmar, & B.T. Allen, *The Encyclopedia of Espionage* (New York: Gramercy Books, 1997), p. 3.

14. K. Crowley, "Scammer a One-Man Film-Flam Clan," *New York Post*, October 23, 1997, p. 3.

15. R. Crichton, *The Rascal and the Road* (New York: Random House, 1961).

16. M. H. Stone, *Abnormalities of Personality* (New York: W. W. Norton, 1993), pp. 14–19, 75–93.

17. G. Serban, "Multiple Personality Disorder and Crime," in *Criminal Psychopathology*, edited by C. Schlesinger (Springfield, IL: Charles C. Thomas, 1996), pp. 255–271.

18. G. Serban, *The Tyranny of Magical Thinking* (New York: E.P. Dutton, 1982), pp. 123–140.

19. E. Loftus, "Maleability of Memory," *Psychiatric News*, December 2, 1995, p. 21.

20. E.F. Loftus, & G.R. Loftus, "On the Permanence of Stored Information in the Human Brain," *American Psychologist* 35 (1980), pp. 409–420.

21. V. Ford, *Lies, Lies, Lies* (Washington, DC: American Press, 1995), pp. 160.

Chapter 6

Trust versus Envy

Ingratitude, thou marble hearted fiend!
Shakespeare, *King Lear* 1.4.283

BETRAYAL OF TRUST

"I know that people lie and cheat others but I never thought Sam would do this to me. I trusted him without reservations. We were friends and knew each other's families well. As my business partner he always seemed straightforward and honest with me until I found out that he had been cheating me for the past years out of hundreds of thousands dollars. He, being in charge of production, contracted an additional manufacturer to the regular one who gave him a big discount on the price of certain lines of goods and in complicity with him wrote up phony invoices for higher prices and then they shared the booty together. At that time I, in charge of the creative end, could not figure out the high returns of clothes from stores and the loss of business until a customer brought to my attention that a particular line of dresses that came from an unknown factory to me were of inferior quality as compared with another lot produced at the regular place. That story did not make sense to me. Sam's explanations of using different factories to meet orders' deadlines were dubious at best. To make a long story short, I brought in an investigating team and the truth came out. It did not cross my mind before that Sam was in his heart a plain crook. You see, there was no reason for Sam to steal since we were making good money. I guess it was plain greed. Worse, he denied any wrongdoing in spite of overwhelming evidence."

Another case in point: David has had a couple of bad years in business and was being harassed by creditors; unless he got a loan fast, he would have been forced to close his store. As his credit rating was poor, his only possibility for obtaining a loan was either paying exorbitant interest or getting one from his family. He decided to appeal to his sister Rachel, a teacher who, far from being rich, has lived frugally and saved a bit of money for her retirement. Since they have had a fairly good relationship, she agreed on the condition to be paid back with in one year with minimum interest. In case of losing the business and with it her money, he would sell his apartment to satisfy his debt to her. Inasmuch as Rachel trusted him, she did not ask for a lien on his apartment. David took the money, put it in his business, and gradually his fortune changed. He started making a good profit but decided to pay her only the interest on the principal. Suddenly he asked her to defer altogether any payment for a year. The alleged reasons were the obligation to pay back other creditors and the need to expand his business by taking advantage of the favorable economy, which would require every dime he made. In exchange, he promised to pay her later at a higher interest rate. David argued that the extension of the debt would not affect her, as she did not need the money, which had been put to good use by him. However, she adamantly demanded repayment since she was afraid of another downturn in the business. In addition, she felt that the risk taken was far greater than the interest paid since she was not a partner in his business. Rachel became angry because she could not understand his unfair attitude. She was torn between the idea of taking him to court, which would mean the end of her relationship with him, or of waiting and hoping for the best. Meanwhile, her trust in him and in other people had been shattered for good.

But what about lawyers or trustees appointed by the probate court, who quite often abuse the fiduciary trust to shamelessly and methodically steal from the entrusted estates of widows and children or clients who relied on them? In many cases, there are underlying irrational assumptions supporting the trust—a belief that shapes the judgment of the victims and often contributing to the abuse of the fiduciary trust by the lawyers or appointed trustees.

Let us take for example the case of an intelligent, divorced, professional woman, Diana, who used the services of a lawyer, Nick, for some administrative transactions. She became impressed with his ability to expeditiously deal with the bureaucrats and solve her problems, particularly when her previous lawyer whom she fired had procrastinated and complicated the execution of legal papers. In the process of working together, she and Nick got friendly to the point of discussing personal matters of their lives, going out for lunches together and even expressing mutual admiration for each other. However, during their nonbusiness meetings Nick casually brought up some personal problems that were troubling him. He unexpectedly needed money for running his new office and was deeply upset about it. Though he knew Diana was quite rich, he did not ask her for money outright; he just continued to interject his financial difficulties into their conversations. Graciously, she offered to loan him a substantial sum without any contractual agreement. He eagerly took the money, promising to repay it when a large payment came from the settlement of a suit. Unfortunately, after a couple of months, he found out he had serious tax problems with the IRS, and since the decision for the court settlement was delayed, he was financially broke. Now, Nick asked for her financial help. According to her, because she totally trusted him, she lent him another substantial amount of money, still without any contractual agreement. He was grateful and promised to repay both loans. After waiting a while she sent him a letter asking to discuss the repayment of the loans. They talked and he claimed he was unable to repay her unless he secured a new loan in order to maintain his practice, since he had incurred some new debts from splitting from his old partners. At this point her story gets hazy, since inexplicably Diana decided to make yet another loan to him, still on the basis of a simple verbal agreement. She claimed she had continued to talk or meet with him only to be able to get back her money because he claimed he would otherwise have to close the office. But even at this stage, she made a final loan to him. After waiting a year, she lost her patience, realized his insincerity, and took him to court. His defense was that the money was given to him as a gift, although he was ready to settle the last portion of the alleged debt. He also claimed the gifts were given to him on the basis of their close friendship, developed after their short professional relationship had ended. Nick also maintained that her demand to return the money was based on her "vindictiveness" for apparently not receiving enough of his attention. Both denied any outright romantic involvement. Diana contended that she only admired his intelligence, knowledge, manners, and charming personality. She trusted him without reservations. However, none of these reasons could have justified a series of undocumented and unsecured large loans. One may suspect that there might have been, at least on her part, certain ulterior motives, if not expressed outright, at least hidden at the fantasy level. For an intelligent, experienced, highly educated, and socially successful woman, who had dealt in the past with lawyers in numerous business transactions, to make even the initial mistake of offering an unwritten loan would be unlikely, let alone an unsecured one, a situation repeated by her two more times in the course of one year. The key to all her justification was that she trusted him, though it was hard to account for such a blind trust. At best, her wishful thinking in making him a "loyal friend" who would advise and "protect" her might have been a contributory factor. Nick realized it and as a smooth operator cultivated this illusion of a commonality of feelings and exploited it under whatever circumstances favored him in order to extract money from her. Diana paid to keep her hopes alive, propelled more likely by her belief in his loyalty to her.

We so often hear about retracted promises solemnly made by leaders, swindles by business partners, breaches of confidence by close friends, devastating political or military betrayals by loyal associates, and acts of treason against the country, not to mention the violation of the sacred trust between parents and children. All these dramatic reversals are examples of the complex, fragile, and unpredictable pattern of human relationships resulting from broken trust.

A hidden mental agenda based on personal beliefs, preconceptions, impulsive drives, and emotions acting as ulterior motives tend to influence if not determine human actions and behavior. Hence, the outcome is certain to be a derailment of logical decision making by which a person might otherwise be able to resolve a conflict or problematic situation. Only rarely, in the clash between emotional needs, reinforced by hidden beliefs, and rational thought does the latter triumph. In fact, logic is often twisted by rationalizations to support the beliefs. Worse, most people are either unaware or have difficulty in accepting the extent to which their decisions are influenced by their "hidden mental agenda." Blaise Pascal, a French mathematician and philosopher, noted a long time ago that "the heart has its reason which reason knows not."[1]

As a matter of fact, we would like to believe that any transaction negotiated between people who know each other well is decided in good faith. This refers to intended transactions between people belonging to the same close community of interests, such as associates in business, politics, and/or siblings who believe in the other's probity from past experiences. Whatever doubts they might harbor in some recesses of their brains tend to be dispelled in the negotiating process when each party attempts to impress on the other his irreproachable responsibility and trustworthiness. Yet one party may lie or be dishonest, while the other may end up the victim. But until this happens, each party implicitly trusts the other. The closer they are as business associates or family members, the more they tend to trust each other.

The paradox is that this trust, which is at the root of human relationships, is violated every day. Unfortunately, no society can function without some basic degree of trust fostered by its members. Most activities are inconceivable without a fair assumption of honesty of intentions, by either participating party, whether stated or not while involved in those endeavors. It is that "confidence reposed in one or entrusting someone with something," (Oxford Dictionary), as included in any definition of trust, which is an implicit and explicit part of human interaction. A simple statement like "I will see you tomorrow at such a time and in such a place" assumes a mutual obligation and responsibility to respect the specified conditions determined for that meeting. In fact, it is a verbal contract, expected to be fulfilled by both parties, unless modified by mutual consent. Any failure to comply with the agreement without informing the other party in advance is considered a sign of unreliability. Broken promises also affect trust by the plain assumption of irresponsibility on the part of the party who made them. That person, if he repeatedly goes back on his word, is viewed as unreliable in any attempted future dealings by the people who know him. Yet many people tend to change their mind after committing themselves verbally to doing something without fear of reprisals. Hence, verbal agreements are no longer enough for most people; now they need to be supplemented, particularly in business, by written contracts. Certainly, these measures are acts of protection against potential deception, suggesting a mutual lack of trust. In business, extensive contracts are drawn that increase dramatically the cost of doing business and sometimes still lead to even costlier litigations, since they are unable to cover all contingencies arising from the actual transactions.

Unfortunately, not every transaction can be supported by written contracts. Some are based on the elusive reliance on someone's alleged loyalty to the person who entrusted him/her with their sensitive vital knowledge. Sometimes this information can seriously damage the other person's future. Why would anyone be so foolish as to place his well-being, much less his career if not his life, into the hands of another person, regardless of how close that human being may be? There are many compelling reasons, all of which ultimately converge on the human need for closeness, acceptance, support, and love. However, one's close business partner, loyal political associate and confidant, previously worshipped lover, long trusted friend, or a beloved family member with whom one has shared the most intimate secrets may turn around and betray him in an attempt to destroy his life or career. It happens all the time. Are people so gullible as to fall into this abysmal trap, unable to learn from the mistakes of others, or are there overwhelming needs overriding any prudence? Does this mean that any sharing of confidence with someone closely associated to us is a mistake, an open invitation to betrayal? Is it possible to trust anyone? And, if so, under what terms and conditions? On one hand, there are compelling emotional and social factors directing people to act in a trusting manner toward each other, while on the other, there are powerful forces tending to weaken or destroy that very trust.

TRUST AS AN OUTCOME OF HUMAN BONDING

The forces favoring trust, originating with various human biological and social bonds developed through evolution and cultural history, have helped individuals survive in a harsh and unfriendly environment. For example, the need for trusting one's intimate partner, as in pair-man-woman-bonding, is deeply ingrained in most people, arising from the oldest and most powerful human bond, that between a mother and her child. Furthermore, the mother–child bond stimulates other types of social bonds, acting as a springboard for the various degrees of trust conferred later in any communal human interaction. The biological maternal bond is at the matrix of not only the child's social development, but his very existence which initially had been so dependent on his mother. This maternal bond is biologically programmed and triggered at birth as an intrinsic part of the child's survival. No wonder we are shocked today to hear about the physical or mental abuse or abandonment of a child by its mother. Instinctively, we question the mother's mental state. We cannot believe that a normal, healthy mother would turn against her child unless she was under the influence of drugs like heroin, crack, or alcohol, or in an otherwise psychotic state. We think so, because we know that in the whole animal range, including man, this bond is in its broadest terms, at the basis of the learning process of helping offspring begin to integrate and function socially.[2] The outcome for children deprived of normal bonding could vary from that of an inability to express emotions to a chronic state of depression or disturbed social relationships. They lack the ability to reach emotional maturity by being "affectless" and incapable of loving or caring for others.[3] At the same time, they show a low degree of confidence and interest in exploring their surroundings, another reason for their adult maladjustment. However, regardless of the intensity of social disapproval and legal punishment of the mother of any intentional deprivation of her bond with the child, this still happens from time to time for a variety of social reasons not even related to serious mental illness. These include the mothers' own deprivation of a healthy bonding with their mothers in infancy or their poor social adjustment to a hostile environment, triggering a brutish egotism in dealing with others. In other cases, the death of the mother during the child's infancy may be the problem. Sometimes impulsive judgments, precipitated by the desire to gratify immediate needs combined with a lack of elementary scruples, have weakened or distorted this innate maternal drive to the point where the mother commits infanticide. By the same token, an overprotective mother could interfere with the child's process of socialization by her oversolicitous and protective attitude. As such, she reinforces the continuation of a bond that with the growing of the child would otherwise fade and be gradually replaced by a different sort of emotional bond, that between the child and his peers. The result is bad for the youngster since he would not be able to make strong social bonds with his peers—potential friends—or later, to give allegiance to social groups of mutual interest. The final outcome is improperly learning to relate to others. Under these circumstances, it is fair to assume that social trust can be weakened, distorted, and ruined by the simple impairment of the maternal bond. This means that innate trust can be subject to the vagaries of the individual's upbringing, experiences in the family and the social forces shaping his personality. Let us see how these innate forces can shape the social expression of trust.

The burgeoning social bonds of the child, acquired in the process of socialization, gradually lead to the formation, particularly among men, of a higher degree of bonding based on a spirit of cooperation. At one time, this bond enhanced stability and increased the community's chances for survival against enemies. Going back in time, the male-to-male bond played a very important role for primitive hunting groups by increasing their chances for hunting more game and helping them to protect large territories required for the kill. This bonding, while attempting to better control the individual aggression among tribesmen, also acknowledged the hierarchical competition within the group. If initially it was required for younger members to show feats of courage and guile to move higher up within the group, progressively, cunning became the prized characteristic, combined or replaced with elements of deception because of increased competition. In the evolutionary transformation of society, the goal of social bonding has also changed, but its essence has remained almost the same. For instance, the above-mentioned gender bonding of man-to-man, so crucial in hunting societies, has gradually evolved into the bond among soldiers belonging to the same platoon who fight and/or die together in war. There is not much difference between the bond of tribesmen expressing their allegiance to each other in various rituals and ceremonies before hunting or fighting the enemies and the modern soldiers at war relying on the emotional support of their buddy before a coming attack. They confide in each other about dear ones left at home, while mutually promising in case of one's survival to tell in person how he died to the other's family. In this respect, a ritual of the Crow Indians before raiding the enemy, reported by two anthropologists, Lionel Tiger and Robin Fox, is very revealing about the power of the male bond.[4] Before any attack on the enemy, the male Crow, among other rituals, go through a lengthy process of confessing in front of the group their previous sexual indiscretions, which might have created hidden resentments among other members. Each one has to confess the names of all the women with whom he has lately copulated, even if they were the wives, lovers, or daughters of other present members. All members listen in silence regardless of how painful the revelations might be. This act of confession automatically gives absolution to the transgressors, and together, they reaffirm their mutual support in fighting and defeating the enemy. Thus, the need for cooperation in war based on restored trust increases their chances for survival. At the same time, we find out that for these Indians, there is a scale of priority in which male solidarity overrides the male–female mating bond.

A more diluted and symbolic form of this bond has been developed by college fraternities where the interaction of young males is mostly based on boasting and bravado behavior or the pursuit of daring and macho activities, associated in the past with ceremonies of induction of new members. The purpose of these bull sessions and rituals is to enforce loyalty and secrecy among members. Closely related to fraternities are the more structured all-male social organizations like the Elks or Rotary Clubs, whose members distinguish themselves by dressing up in fancy costumes for parades, and use complex rituals for induction, but basically promote a spirit of camaraderie and mutual help. A more limited and elitist remnant of the male bond still persists today in the previously all-male clubs now integrated with women by court order. The male-to-male bond has been progressively weakened by the changing role of women in society; it still tends to reappear in any situation, like hunting, sports, or the military.

The dilution of this bond has serious implications for men's social conscience and interaction with other men. The absence of the previous sense of camaraderie has led to a dilution of moral responsibility toward others, making men feel socially freer to act selfishly. The net result is a higher pursuit of egotistic activity with less concern about the feelings of others and a higher tendency to take advantage or exploit them. Naturally, the more self-involved a person becomes in the gratification of his egotistic needs at the expense of others, the more prone he is to create conflicts with others. The resolution of a conflict provoked by the abuser will lead, as we know, to further attempts at deception, treachery, and duplicity, in order to support his false claims. This attitude runs counter to any honest participation in a social bond based on trust.

As previously discussed, there are social factors that may contribute to the weakening of of social bonds. An important one is a surge in individualism, which antagonizes community orientation and participation. This may further contribute to the process of weakening and deterioration of the social trust. In the last decades, the tendency toward increasing individualism combined with the erosion of the Protestant work ethic has started to affect the moral conduct of people in business. This is bad for business since, according to some economists, business trust and ethics have strongly contributed to the growth of this country as the number-one industrial power.[5] Indeed, trust plays an extremely important role in business transactions, in many cases reinforcing if not superseding legal contracts. While legal contracts may deal with the components of the transaction and offer legal protection in case of dispute or fraud, the details of their execution largely depend on trust. The New York business community still remembers the legal dispute between the buyers and the seller after the sale of a discount chain of electronic stores called "Crazy Eddy." The buyers accused the seller of delivering false inventories, defrauding them of tens of millions of dollars. The losses in inventories were so massive that the buyers were forced to close the chain stores. Certainly, they trusted the seller and did not verify thoroughly the huge bogus inventories. The discount chain owner fled to Israel and was later extradited to the United States where he was brought to trial and convicted.

All business transactions presuppose a minimum of trust, a degree of certitude that other people are reliable, will keep their word, and deliver the promised goods. We tend to take for granted that most of our daily transactions are based on trust. Anyone who buys, for example, vitamins wants to believe that the pills contain the specified ingredients written on the label. The consumer would be outraged if the vitamins were proven false. Yet the vitamin industry is poorly regulated by the FDA, and basically people rely on the honesty of the manufacturers. Recently, it was discovered after lab testing that a vitamin manufacturer's herbal product contained less than a quarter of the effective ingredients indicated on the label, which the company denied. Yet, this suspicion forced the buyer, a chain of stores, to verify most of their products.[6] The same implied element of trust applies to all routine interactions from paying bills to bidding at an auction. Social trust is maintained as long as all people have the same expectations of honesty and truthfulness and believe in the same moral values. This is not always the case since even in matters of social decency, people may hesitate to tell the truth out of fear of inducing resentment and/or reprisals. A sign of the lack of trust in our contemporary society is the increase in the frequency of litigations to resolve real or alleged differences. For example, take the simple matter of a business reference: if at one time an employee trusted his former employer to write a recommendation when he changed jobs, now both parties are suspicious of each other. Employers do not want to write honest recommendations for fear of being sued, which has happened, while employees are suspicious of what their bosses really think of them.

We are facing a rise in individualism that has promoted self-sufficiency, a competitive spirit, and the pursuit, often successfully, of entrepreneurship has inadvertently reinforced a previously condemned trait of personality—that of boasting and flaunting one's success to others. It has become socially acceptable for an individual to boast either about his achievements or even about his intention to achieve. Furthermore, people tend to take credit for a successful activity even when their contribution was only partial or minimal.[7] The braggarts who make extravagant claims of their successes seem not to care that by doing so they may actually increase their chances of inducing resentment in others who may think they are the main contributors to the proclaimed success. Other people may just dislike this crude display of immodesty and may retaliate at an opportune moment. This is exactly what happened to a CEO of a corporation who touted himself as being able to turn companies around and make them profitable by laying off thousands of workers, which gained him the nickname of the "chain saw executive," until it was discovered that in his new job his alleged success was mainly supported by doctored financial statements. While he denied any knowledge of the fraudulent statements on the balance sheet by the accounting service, he was unceremoniously fired by the board.[8]

ENVY, THE LETHAL ENEMY OF TRUST

This brings us to the evaluation of the most powerful enemy of trust: a basic human emotion called envy, which is vented within the normal range of relationships. Its effects, when it strikes, are devastating to what might have been previously thought to be a very close and trustful interaction. Envy is a basic human emotion that greatly affects man's social functioning. To paraphrase La Rochefoucauld, it is "more implacable than hatred."[9] The word *envy* has many connotations, which can be summed up in two general meanings. One implies a feeling of displeasure with someone else's success, happiness or good fortune, and the other assumes an element of spite and hostility against the other person's life advantages or superiority. Envy is quite often confused with jealousy, which is a passionate desire to guard closely something precious and rightfully belonging to one. In both these emotional states, the individual could become hostile, but in jealousy the hostility is aroused by a feeling of provocation by a rival who challenges his possession, while in envy the hostility is incited by the better life of the other person as compared with his own. Envy may be triggered by the better qualities of personality or social advantages which another person may have. The person is resented for the simple fact of achieving a higher social status. Indeed, the envious individual mostly resents others who somehow are superior to him, while the jealous person defends his turf, which he fancies to be or factually is under attack from another party, whether equal to him or not. Another chief distinction between the two is the fact that while the jealous person calms down as soon as his rival disappears from the scene of competition, the envious one always begrudges others' successes, enjoys their misfortune, and actively seeks, whenever he can, their downfall. Yet, these emotional states are not mutually exclusive. Sometimes they are interchangeable. Superficially, when envy is not suppressed, its expression is justified by the envious person as being triggered by the unfair deprivation caused by a disappointing job or other social frustrations, if not even blamed on class warfare. From the social point of view, envy is a spiteful and destructive emotion that can affect all types of human relationships in which one feels at a disadvantage. What is even worse, the party against whom these negative feelings are directed is most often totally unaware of the hidden resentment and malice harbored by the other party. In fact, he may unknowingly consider the envious person his trusted confidant, a friend, and close associate. Paradoxically, malevolence is fos-

tered by familiarity between people in which one of them perceived the relationship as not truly equal. While the one in better circumstances extends
his goodwill to the other person in a spirit of acceptance and unity, the envious one at first gladly accepts the other's overture, but sooner or later his
feelings may change to resentment. He is overwhelmed by the other's real
or imagined advantages, be it wealth, success, or personal qualities that he
himself aspires to possess, and as a result, he gradually starts to wish ill for
the other person. The successful one, by demonstrating his goodness and
going so far as to make the envious one financially and socially comfortable, only creates an artificial equality that will be resented by the benefi-
ciary of his generosity as a proven sign of his own inferiority. It will
produce a forced indebtedness that by itself induces a sense of obligation
toward the benefactor. The inescapable conclusion is that many men seem
unable to shake off their displeasure toward other people close to them
who they perceive to be somehow better off.

This basic human tendency was recognized a long time ago by primitive
societies, which attempted to reduce the feeling of envy among their members through a variety of methods, from diverse rituals and customs to
magic incantations. They realized that envy was an obstacle to social cooperation between tribesmen, affecting the well-being of the entire community. As a matter of fact, societies from time immemorial have fought hard
to suppress the resentment among their members who felt excluded from
sharing the same privileges of hierarchical status and class created by their
social organizations and justified by divine sanctions. But the stratification
of prestige in the community is only one potential source of envy, among
numerous others. To compensate for this, all societies have created opportunities for people to compete in certain activities that are highly valued in
that social system, thereby spreading the opportunity to gain prestige
among their members. Yet, it does not prevent the spread of envy among
those members who were unable to succeed. For example, Navaho Indians,
in order to control envy, encouraged their financially better-off members to
attempt to appease the poor ones by offering them help and hospitality. The
reason is very simple: in their culture, there is the assumption that anyone
getting rich did so at the expense of the others. In the case that the rich refuse to help the others of lesser financial means, they would arouse envy
and might become the target of black magic and suffer its consequences.[10]
While the Navaho of North America have nothing culturally in common
with the inhabitants of some Polynesian islands 5,000 miles away, they do
share the same fears about the effects of envy. If a team of Polynesians went
fishing and only one or two of them caught fish while the others did not, the
ones who did used to offer their catch to the others in order to prevent any
envious feelings. Behind this generosity was the fear that the unsuccessful
fishermen would otherwise claim that the others used magic to succeed or
would invoke magic themselves, calling on "the evil spirits" to adversely

affect the others' future catches.[11] Black magic has often been used by people to bring down the person who became the target of their envy. No wonder other tribes like the Hopi or Zuni Indians, in an effort to reduce or control envy, considered it wrong for someone to boast about his possessions or successes, as this might create negative feelings like resentment among others.[12] Such reservations against bragging were reinforced by the fear of possible tribal reprisal against the boastful rich, who were perceived as uncaring and devious. This was based on the tribe's traditional belief that anyone's wealth or success was the result of his secretly practicing witchcraft, which represented a danger to the community. By the same token, the threat of practicing black magic by an envious person also could have turned against him by making other people aware of the witchcraft power that he was capable of wielding against them. As such, quite often the alleged sorcerer or practitioner of black magic was either ostracized or killed. Recently, in various Indonesian villages on the island of Java, over 100 people have been murdered because they were thought to be sorcerers using black magic to gain power.[13]

There is no need to refer to primitive societies to document the power of envy in the shaping of social relationships when the Bible gives us ample evidence of this fact. To control envy among the people, the Ten Commandments promulgated as a divine law the necessity at maintaining neighborly good relationships by stating "not to covet your neighbor's house or his wife nor man servant nor his maid servant . . . nor anything that is your neighbor's." The New Testament, while in its parables chides the envious men for displeasing God, tacitly accepts the inequities of this world with the promise of retribution at the Final Judgment. This vision of equality seems a step above the philosophy of the ancient Greeks, who explained the inequalities of this world as a result of the blind game of fate that implacably controls all human endeavor. Ironically, to extrapolate to a more scientific interpretation one may assume that the differences among people are created by their genes, which to a great extent determine their destiny.

CAN AMBITIOUS PEOPLE CONTROL THEIR ENVY?

People have been unable to accept the inequalities among themselves, much less the institutionalized differences between social classes or social statuses, with the result that they continuously act out their envious feelings. In Western societies, some religious ethics regarding the need to control envy led to the aberrant teachings of self-denial, which advocate the suppression of any display of pleasure over one's personal achievements. Furthermore, it is widely believed that any feeling of envy induced by someone else's achievement is one's own fault and that person should feel ashamed and guilty about it. This ascetic morality was an overreaction to the fear of being responsible for triggering envy. However, it was emotionally as unsustainable as it was socially unenforceable. From this religious point of view, eliminating envy would require either a monastically organized community or an imaginary egalitarian one. An attempt to eliminate any form of inequity has been represented by the idealistic or perverse attempts to create a utopian egalitarian society. Yet even here, natural biological and intellectual differences between individuals will lead to a stratification of social positions, automatically creating envy with its disastrous consequences. The still unanswered question is to what extent all social reformists advancing an undiluted egalitarianism are not opportunists manipulating the envious disadvantaged class or minority groups. Are they cashing in on those people's envy in order to fulfill their personal ambitions? As we already know, the new rulers act in the same manner toward the people below them as their previous alleged or real oppressors. The envy is now felt by those left out of the sharing power equation, with its fringe benefits.

The real problem faced by society is in finding ways to control the conflict between the people's emotional striving for social recognition-status and the inherent envy induced in those unable to attain their goals. The intellectual, emotional, and physical differences between individuals within the same group have always made unequal their personal contributions to the welfare of the community and hence conferring on some people higher rank than on others. This has become the basis for the stratification of society, resulting in unequal rights for its members. If in a primitive society the inequalities were minimal, related mainly to the keeping of a bigger share of meat from hunting or of greater access to women's sexual favors by the skilled hunter, gradually, with the growth of societies and the institutionalizing of power within a ruling class, the individual's need for social recognition obtained by acceptance into the privileged circle became a strong source of social tension. People's manipulations, machinations, and intrigues in the quest for higher and higher rank were directly or indirectly weakening the rulers' grip on power, if not knocking it down completely. The only viable solution for the rulers was to offer at least a modicum of power and relative social recognition not only to their loyal and ambitious subordinates, but also to selected categories of supporting subjects. The cooperation of a larger base of citizens was needed for maintaining power and stabilizing the state. At the same time, this helped to reduce the tension and frustration among those who felt entitled to be part of the power machine, and goaded by their envy could have acted as catalysts for radical change, using whatever devious or confrontational means were available to them. The lower classes left out of the power equation resented the oppressive rulers and hence had the moral incentive to topple them without pity. Yet after any realignment of power by forceful or peaceful means, the competition for status continued unabatedly, since others were dissatisfied and unwilling to accept their lower role to which they had been relegated by the new order.

Modern society has tried to do something about the unquenchable need of people to attain a social rank equal or higher than that of their peers and to participate in the governing process. One social development has been the creation of various types of organizations that support the social and economic interests of particular groups and help to vent their political frustrations. For some people, it helped to advance their need for leadership. Yet for the status seekers who have higher ambitions, this was not enough. They moved ahead politically, beyond their organization, by embracing social causes for which they fought with the support of interested groups, cleverly using them as ideal vehicles for reaching their goal of leadership. They cynically discarded those bold social ideals after their aims were achieved and the new politics of governing conflicted with them. This happened with many union and sometimes minority leaders.

Ultimately, the acceptance of the social status of individuals depends to a large extent on public opinion, which decides whether or not to honor it. When the battle for social status takes the nasty form of violence and the betrayal of a friendship, then the offender meets with social rejection. Take the incident preceding the 1996 Winter Olympics, when Nancy Kerrigan, an ice skater favored for the gold medal, was brutally hit on the legs with a metal object by a male friend of the husband of another close competitor, Tonya Harding, in order to eliminate Kerrigan from Olympic competition. Though Harding apparently denied any direct involvement, her attitude was considered reprehensible by the public. She later was found guilty by a court.[14] Her social status plummeted, regardless of her impressive skating skills. Others who attempt to achieve social status by devious means may be more successful. This was the case of the now-famous Monica Lewinsky, a 24-year-old former intern at the White House, who by her own statements, recorded on tape by a friend, described her 18-month affair with President Bill Clinton. She was known to the White House intern staff as following the president in order to reach any degree of closeness to him. She succeeded beyond her expectation. The only problem has been her mishandling of the trust bestowed on a casual friend, Linda Tripp, who taped the conversations and gave them to the appointed public prosecutor. This is an interesting case of double betrayal, both based on poor judgment: Monica Lewinsky versus Clinton and Tripp versus Lewinsky, with unpleasant consequences for the ones betrayed.

The fact remains that throughout history regardless how much people, particularly those in power, have recognized the role of envy as an uncontrollable emotion that can disrupt the lives, they were unable to overpower it. They have attempted in vain to develop various ways of protecting themselves against it. The methods have changed from culture to culture and from time to time, yet envy has continuously remained a factor to consider in any relationship. The trouble with any garden variety approach for controlling envy, ranging from that of ignoring its existence to that of appeasing it by supporting the illusion of the final divine retribution, is that it does not work. People are faced with situations in their daily lives that either provoke envy in them or, because of their own actions, in others. Then the desire to bring down and harm the successful person may consume the envious one emotionally to the point of attempting to use whatever unscrupulous means are available to him. Lying, maligning, fabricating stories, cheating, or ultimately even killing are all results of this insatiable and unappeasable envy. There is no area of social or private relationships, even those built on what may apparently be regarded as an indestructible trust, that is not subjected to the deleterious consequences of envy. History is littered with vile and unbelievable tragic stories of the effect of a relentless envy triggered by people's drive for power or greed for accumulation of material possessions. The explosion of these hidden and uncontrollable ambitions has ultimately abused the imparted trust. After all, according to the New Testament, Jesus was betrayed and sold for 30 silvers to the Romans by Judas Iscariote, one of his 12 disciples. Apart from the religious importance of this event, viewed from the perspective of human psychology, it was just another instance of betrayal in the never-ending drama of plots against trust conferred to unscrupulous characters. The intrigues and betrayals among aristocrats at the European courts where relatives were fighting each other for power or among the heirs of the king at the royal courts of France, Italy, Russia, or England who were episodically conspiring for the throne, are quite familiar to any reader of history and do not need further elaboration. Too many heads had literarily fallen owing to betrayals of close confidants during those treacherous times of Lucrezia Borgia, the Medicis, or during the royal confrontation between Queens Mary Stuart I, Elizabeth I or Henry II of England. The case of Henry II versus Thomas Becket is an unusual and intriguing one that only reinforces the reality of perils faced by anyone who becomes more popular than the king.

Regardless of how astute people think they might be, rarely have they tried to gain a historical understanding of human psychology, particularly about the craving for self-enhancement and power, which overrides any preexistent feelings of friendship or closeness. Such a need is evidenced by modern history, which shows that things have not changed too much. The history of Germany under Hitler or of Russia under Stalin give us ample confirmation of betrayals and executions among members of the inner circles fighting for power. Neither has the United States, with its liberal government, been spared from betrayals. Though to a much lesser degree, the same kinds of political conspiracies here have involved trusted associates of former leaders who wanted them to be thrown out of office, indicted, or liquidated. Was this not the case with John Dean and of "Deep Throat," whose betrayals in the name of high principles contributed to the resignation of former President Richard Nixon? What other reasons might there have been for "Deep Throat" to double-cross Nixon than that of resenting him for whatever personal slight? No wonder popular wisdom came to the conclusion that envy and jealousy kill the strongest man.

THE ABUSE OF TRUST IN BUSINESS

What is more interesting about our twisted morality is that there are special businesses that rely solely on the trust conferred on someone by the very institution that he betrays. Most acts of successful spying are based on one's betrayal of his country. How was Aldrich Ames, the chief of the Soviet Desk at the CIA, able to spy for nine years for the Russians unless he had access to the most sensitive classified documents of the agency, based on the absolute trust awarded him by his superiors? Yet the damage he has done to this country during the last decade of the cold war is incalculable, not to mention his responsibility for identifying 25 CIA "human assets" to the Soviets. In addition, he knowingly sent to their death at least 10 top Russian agents working for the United States in exchange for receiving over $1 million from the KGB. The obvious reason for this was greed, a desire for a good life beyond his means, but on a deeper inquiry we also discern by his own admissions in an interview with a reporter a strong element of envy of other colleagues who were more successful and better paid at their jobs.[15] It seems a more pragmatic approach than the alleged ideological idealism of Fuchs, Rosenberg, and others who had stolen atomic secrets for the Russians during the war, and were more likely driven by a sublimated envy against society that emotionally frustrated them.

Without the same political motivations as claimed by national traitors, there is industrial spying, where stealing industrial patents has become a big and highly profitable business. The latest famous case is that of Ignacio Lopez de Arriorta, a corporate executive at General Motors, head of purchasing for the company who resigned and illegally took the business plans of an automated car plant in Spain, among other sensitive corporate information, which he gave to the Volkswagen company in exchange of higher position with a higher pay. After repeated denials against overwhelming evidence, he was convicted by a German court and the case was settled by Volkswagen. He still faces U.S. prosecution.[16] Industrial spying has become an international business replacing military spying in the new economic battle between companies and countries for improving their position in the marketplace by creating the most technologically advanced products. The FBI recently reported that between 1995 and 1996 alone there were 800 cases of industrial spying on record.[17] Apparently, one of the major offenders is Japan, where large companies have trained their own technical spies who, with the full knowledge of their government, collect information about the latest research at American companies. According to a recent report in a magazine quoting the General Accounting Office and our counterintelligence services, Israel is the major offender involved in stealing industrial secrets to advance their economy or sell them for cash to other nations; it is followed by France, where technological companies, in order to survive, resort to industrial spying. In fact, according to the same report, French telecommunications are monitored by their secret service for international business phone calls and fax messages by using signal intelligence (SIGINT). This permits them to get information on bidding contracts, which they pass on to their respective companies for underbidding. If our friends are cheating us, it is only normal to expect Chinese or Russians to do the same thing. For instance, Russians are maintaining a telecommunication spying station in Cuba at a cost of $200 million a year, in order to intercept military or business satellite communications from the United States. Russia, with a long tradition of stealing military and economic secrets from the West, is embarked on large-scale industrial spying for the purpose of reviving their outdated industry. Since the price of research and development to produce new technologies is exorbitant, stealing has become a shortcut to gain access to the secret plans of another company or nation. In addition to satellite or telecommunications monitoring, used also by the U.S. to spy on other nations (Echelon) the method of choice remains the old way of either infiltrating the targeted company with one's own trained spies in that field who collect information there, or even easier, buying the trust of someone from that company who has access to the desired information. This was the case with a design engineer at Wright Industries, who was indicted for attempting to peddle trade secrets of a new razor design to other rival businesses in exchange for a better job.[18] But most of these treacheries would not be possible if it were not for exploiting the trust given by the company to the traitor. These instances of cheating are part of the abuse of an objective trust, taking place in the detached atmosphere of business interaction where the harm is not immediately and personally felt. However, other assaults on trust that are more emotionally devastating are because they are less expected, owing to the intimate nature of the relationships between the protagonists in the unfolding drama. One of the shocking effects related to the dissolution of trust may take place in a legal feud between previously close members of the same family.

THE FAMILY DRAMA DUE TO ENVY

An unusual example of the family intrastruggle was the recent bitter battle for power and money among the members of the Gucci family, owners of an international company of luxury goods. The result was the conviction of the father, who had greatly contributed to the building of the business empire, to a jail term for tax evasion, at the disclosure of one of his disgruntled sons. Almost the same drama took place in the American multimillion-aire Haft family, where the charges and countercharges between father and son, supported by a former wife, ended up in court. One parent against an-other parent and their son, all marching with batteries of lawyers to court, to wrestle money and power from each other. Although all these conflicts are about power and money they are also triggered by envy due to the real or imaginary perception that some siblings are more favored than others by the father. The envy and the hate among siblings may become directed to-ward the parent considered responsible for the injustice. Any logical expla-nation is refuted, any emotional appeal to past parental care or closeness is discredited, while confidences known from the previous trust are used to advance the disgruntled family member's cause. In these cases it is not un-heard of for intimate or illegal business secrets, known only to close family members, to be used as a blackmail tool to extract financial advantages. The reality is that trust is dissolved because of the hate and envy of the alleged injured member who perceives himself at a disadvantage within the fam-ily. If cases of conflict between parents and children leading to betrayal of trust are infrequent, the fight between siblings for inheritance money is not unusual. There, lying and deception become the main weapons in the fight to succeed. Childhood and adolescent rivalries among siblings can take an ugly turn when the children mature. A case in point is the bitter feud within the wealthy Koch family of Kansas. For 12 years, the court battle went on between two brothers against another two who claim to have been cheated out of billions of dollars at the settlement of their inheritance. They did not talk to each other for a decade, although three of them had attended MIT, where they shared the same quarters and were friendly toward each other. According to a press report, one of the plaintiff brothers was jealous of his twin brother and the older one because they were more athletic and popu-lar than he was.[19] This situation is somewhat comparable to a medieval drama when different members of the same royal family fought for the throne, each one raising an army (in this case an army of lawyers) against the other. After all, no one should be surprised, since we know from the Bi-ble that Cain killed his brother Abel out of envy. But what about the biblical story of Joseph, son of Jacob and Rachel, who was sold into slavery by his brothers? These stories are repeated in thousands of modern versions if one just looks at the court records of claims and counterclaims made by siblings accusing each other of stealing assets from estates left by parents or from their own business partnership. These conflicts are more often provoked by the narcissistic or paranoid-prone personality types of the contestants, which easily facilitate distrust and negative interactions. For instance, Phil, a writer, always had a tenuous relationship with his mother, who appar-ently liked and paid more attention to her younger son, Greg. She preferred Greg's sedate personality and felt closer to him than to Phil. In her will, she designated Greg, who happened to be a lawyer, as the executor of the estate. After her death, Phil felt that as executor Greg took advantage of his personal and legal relationship with their mother by not only convincing her to make the will in his favor but also by empowering him to discretionarily appraise and distribute the estate's assets. The outcome was a nasty court battle, settled out of court but resulting in even higher profits for Greg, whose law firm charged fees for the defense of the estate in court.

BETRAYAL OF TRUST AS A MARITAL WEAPON OF CONTROL

The most common vulnerability of trust is in the adult love interaction and marital relationship. This possible conflict between love and trust, evolved during the lovers' interaction, represents a serious dilemma for them. Love is supposedly based on an exchange of the most intimate feelings and confidential knowledge about each other's personalities and past behavior, including possible violations of the law, thereby solidifying the bond between the lovers. However, the full disclosure of each other's lives and of their true selves could become a liability in case of a serious crisis in their interaction or a threat of breakup by one of them. The seeds of discontent may be sown during the process of courtship when each party, following more or less a social script of courtship, presents one's self to the prospective partner in the most favorable light, intertwining facts and lies and intentional omissions of faults. Frustration arises when the superlative promises about their future potential of happiness, while both partners are fully aware that their comments will be highly appreciated by the other, fall short of their possibilities. While these promises may simply represent desirable goals, in reality they are bait to enhance the chance for sexual acceptance. However, by insinuating as remote as may be those hyperbolic goals, both inadvertently help to build unrealistic expectations of each other, leading to future recriminations and resentment. Male behavior during courtship directed toward obtaining sex may compel him to take liberties with the truth about his degree of emotional involvement in the relationship, while the female, looking for a husband, tends to play up to the prospective lover's touched-up image and to hide her own shortcomings. If they do not tone down their exaggerated claims and do not evaluate more critically each other's statements until they can fully trust each other, they may be in for unpleasant surprises. It becomes each one's responsibility to spot any attempt at deception, regardless of the ulterior motive. The question is to what extent is this hypocrisy and deception carried over from dating into the marital love relationship. Could it be true what the French mathematician Pierre Laplace allegedly thought on his death bed, that all things are trifles since the only true thing that counts is love; or what the German philosopher Arthur Schopenhauer mused about love in one of his essays, rating it as a natural insanity or a temporary delusion suffered for the sake of reproduction?[20]

Theories about what love is have abounded over the centuries. Love has been extolled by the romantics as the most desirable ecstatic state to be achieved, while it has been viewed by psychologists as a neurotic response to a subjective, distorted perception of another person based on self-deception. Social scientists have reduced it to a self-induced illusion in the service of the biological drive for reproduction, while moralists have attempted to separate love from sex, by likening sex with carnal passion and love with a spiritual state of elated intimacy. Skeptics think of love as a transient sentimental and irrational state, a harbinger of social and emotional misery. The opinions are as diverse as the subjective experience of lovers. Yet all tend to agree that the initial exaggerations and lies of the courtship become magnified and embellished to unrealistic proportions in love as a result of the distortion of reality by the lovers. The difference between these two situations is relative: in courtship, all lies are part of a calculated game of conquest but not necessarily an expression of love, while in love, most deceptions are based on false perceptions of each other, related to the lovers' specific state of mind. Lovers create a subjective world of their own in which they idealize each other with little attention paid to reality. However, in the process of interaction, intentional lies may abound, induced by the partners' unrealistic need to please each other. The fear of rejection causes lovers to lie when either one is faced with a partner's unreasonable demands, which cannot be satisfied.

John, a successful, young, commercial real estate broker, deeply loves Mona, a pretty office employee in another firm, with whom he has been having a passionate affair. However, recently, he was torn at the prospect of helping her get a specific job in his firm because of her limited skill and experience. Her potential failure might unfavorably affect his standing with the company, so after some soul searching he decided not to recommend her for the job, even though she coveted it very much. Out of fear of upsetting her, John preferred to lie to her about it, claiming the chief of that section had already filled the job with an insider. This is what he calls a "constructive" lie, beneficial to the relationship because telling the truth would have jeopardized their harmony, and doing what she had requested might have threatened his job. As a part of the test of their deep commitment to each other, they faced another sticky situation: John thought he had a high degree of knowledge about the stock market and wanted to play the game of options but needed more capital in order "to make a killing." He knew Mona had inherited some money and he wanted to use part of it for trading options. Although they professed undying love for each other, Mona hesitated to loan him the money, as she thought the investment was too risky and was afraid to lose her only assets. So to avoid an argument she lied to him, saying she had already loaned most of her money to her sister.

John was not convinced but since he could not disprove it at the time, he decided to drop the whole matter. However, he justified her refusal as a sign of her insecurity. While all these lies might have been constructive because they supported their love by avoiding immediate conflicts, they nonetheless have established a deceptive pattern of interaction that would turn out to be detrimental to their future relationship.

Already, other forms of deceptions have developed between them. For instance, John thinks that their sex life has been bliss. According to him, at the beginning, Mona was not always sexually responsive but later she regularly had orgasms. Actually, she has faked orgasms because she did not want to hurt his feelings, and hoped that her sexual response would improve with time. They have had other areas of simmering conflicts, hidden tensions, and potential trouble, which, if not squarely faced, will sap their otherwise proclaimed everlasting love. John, at a moment of boasting after drinking too much, told Mona he is smart because he handles a job that requires an MBA and everybody believes that he has one. He forgot that during courtship he had lied to her about having master's degree. She did not confront him but reserved the right to do so, if necessary. If their passionate love fades in a cloud of misunderstandings, accusations, and mutual incrimination, as it may happen, he will have to pay for his boasting. But, assuming they would not be able to solve satisfactorily their differences and do not get married, the problem remains that of their ability to handle the confidences that they imparted and not use them as weapons of revenge after the termination of love.

The history of love relationships is full of dramas of betrayal initiated by the jilted party or by the one who just terminated the relationship with the idea of making some financial or political gains at the expense of the other. The most recent famous cases of discreet blackmail are those of Profumo in England and Willy Brandt in Germany, both related to spying. The Flowers–Clinton affair can be entered in a different category of love affairs used as bargaining chips for personal advantages, after amiable termination. The sourly ended affairs on corporate suits most often end in court either as blackmail or sexual-harassment cases.

The nagging problem is why so many marriages born out of love end in bitter divorces, with the most horrendous accusations being thrown at each other in the pursuit of revenge. In our society, where the spouses operate under the assumption of total marital equality between the sexes, justified by their separate financial contributions to the upkeep of the household, their interaction does not necessarily reflect their basic emotional needs and personality orientation. The departure from the old biological paradigm of marital division of labor compounds their problems in dealing with household responsibilities, negotiating personal wants, and making significant decisions vital for the functioning of the family. To cope with the interminable difficulties of meeting the demands of marriage, while maintaining an illusion of cooperation and harmony, usually either one accepts the demands of the other or they both resort to lies and deceptions. When the feelings of passion and the craving for blissful intimacy fade, marriage is maintained on the basis of an unstable equilibrium of limited satisfaction. This requires that each spouse carefully develop strategies of communication and persuasion where the truth may be cautiously combined with its omission so as to reduce any undesirable impact on the partner. One's inability to cope with the marital interaction by skillfully negotiating it in his/her favor, whenever necessary, will result in frustrating situations. The resentment built up against the other spouse will generate a need for revenge, which demolishes the previous trust created by love and intimacy. With love changed to hate, the unhappy spouse ruminates schemes for destroying his/her former love by taking advantage of the former mate's business or personality weakness acquired through the previous trust. And here begins the conflict between lost love and selfish betrayal. This is exactly what happened to the marriage of Mat and Lora.

Lora, an attractive technician in her early 20s and Mat, a successful professional man 10 years her senior, met at a party. After a few dates they fell in love with each other and ended having a romantic wedding in a small chapel in Venice. Their marriage was considered a success. His career was growing nicely and with it their standard of living. Yet, gradually Lora became dissatisfied with her life as a well-off housewife living in suburbia and taking care of their two children. It was boring, nonchallenging, and too dependent on the attention of her husband for emotional and intellectual satisfaction. After the children started to attend school and she could afford to have a nanny taking care of them after school hours, she decided to get a college degree. During her five years of college, Mat accepted the situation, although their social and sexual life started to suffer. To compensate for her unavailability, he spent more time in the office with his customers, making even more money. As a gift for her college graduation, he bought a bigger house, in a better location. Their life together still seemed pleasant, though the first warning of an oncoming storm was slowly gathering. Lora started to accuse Mat of using her socially for enhancing his business and status. To free herself from this subservience, she decided to go back to school and get a master's degree to become an independent professional. Grudgingly, Mat accepted her new aspirations, though he realized there would be future constraints on their marriage, which in fact was slowly crumbling. Their sex life became infrequent and mechanical, while their communication was reduced to her accusations of alleged undesirable changes in his personality triggered by envy of her new independent self. She felt the main obstacle to their relationship was his inability to accept her as an equal partner. Unfortunately, at that time, Mat, in order to support her expensive lifestyle, became involved in some shady business deals that ended up in a court action against him and led to his being suspended from doing business in his field for five years. Indignant, Lora claimed to be socially embarrassed by his reckless and illicit activities and asked for a divorce, but threatened to report him to the IRS unless she received in cash half of a substantial amount of money illegally gained and placed offshore, in addition to 50 percent of their commonly held assets. Mat was shocked and crushed. Faced with emotional and financial collapse with his business closed and limited prospects for starting a new career, Mat settled for a modest life. Lora, suddenly wealthy and independent, started a carefree life of social and sexual gratification. From their new perspectives on life, both looked back on their forgotten years of loving each other with disbelief: he wondered about his foolishness to create in his mind a fantasy woman, tailored to meet his emotional needs and to worship and adore her, oblivious to the reality indicating the contrary, while Lora pondered at her folly to dream of a man who would accept her own fantasy of a glamorous life full of excitement, yet free of the daily marital obligations. She wanted marital security and also social independence. Mat lied and committed illegal acts in the pursuit of his illusions, while Lora cheated on him, lied to him, and neglected her children in the pursuit of her fantasy of an independent and exciting life.

Since love seems to be an emotional state that is actively sought by most people, regardless of its transitory nature or effects, the point of interest for potential players in the drama should be the consequences, in case they are unable to meld their personalities, needs, and styles of thinking and life. Then can they realistically afford to blindly trust each other, while they may learn about the other's unflattering behavioral patterns, thereby increasing the risk, over a period of time, for disappointments and abuses if not for blackmail and betrayal. Unfortunately, lovers suspend any sensible judgment under the assumption that the loved one can do no harm or be potentially fiendish, which makes any protection, including a prenuptial agreement, unwarranted. Ironically, the one who has a more rational orientation is considered cold, selfish, and unloving.

Accepting that human beings have conflicting emotional needs varying from the need for status to that of uncontrollable envy or from that of love to that of hate when rejected, all affecting the balance between trust and disloyalty, the gnawing question remains the extent to which people have the ability to properly handle these emotions, without prejudice to themselves. It varies according to their personality type and philosophy of life. While achieving status increases the chances of bringing out envy in others, trusting a close partner does not necessarily presuppose betrayal if that person is able to avoid any accidental misstep in managing the relationship that otherwise may be disastrous, if not fatal. The ability to handle relationships requires an awareness of the possible shifting of emotional allegiance in the opposite direction, in the pursuit of what is perceived as self-interest. Anyone seeking status and recognition needs to seriously pay attention to the written and unwritten rules of the game of power as accepted and practiced by the pros in that field; otherwise, he may have to pay a high penalty. For instance, in academia, if an honest researcher does not play by the rules of his department by offering to the chief of his service unearned scientific credits in either a submission of a research grant or publication in a better journal, he will have hard time advancing his career. Without appeasing the "little gods," the career of a young researcher will drift. A case in point is Kim, a bright, young researcher working in a hospital, who wanted to do a social study of an important issue but in order to do it he needed to use the facilities of a big hospital. To write the grant he required the approval of the director for the use of patients who acceded on the condition that he be named as principal investigator of the project for the first year. Kim realized he did not stand a chance to pursue his research without the director's approval so he accepted and the grant was approved. But after Kim started the project, the director took a sabbatical and left town. At the regular inspection by the government concerning the progress of the grant, Kim covered for the director by claiming to be regularly in touch with him by mail and phone. The grant entered in its final phase and Kim published a paper with the director named as principal author. At a subsequent professional meeting where Kim wished to present the new results, he met with the resistance of the director, who wanted to present the data prepared by Kim himself. Kim acceded, but, at the last minute the director requested the cancellation of the meeting, which for technical reasons could not be done and Kim triumphantly made the presentation. Unfortunately for Kim, the director thought his request had been denied by Kim's maneuvers. At the time of the renewal of the grant, Kim named himself as principal investigator, with the director as coprincipal investigator, as initially agreed with the director. The director reneged on the initial deal and requested Kim's removal from the project. Kim retaliated by telling the officials that the director, the principal investigator, while on sabbatical leave for one year, did not make any contribution to the project as proven by the project's research team, and worse, he cashed in on his salary for a year for no show–no work. After some investigation and political maneuvering, the grant was not renewed. Three months later, Kim was demoted to a lower position, allegedly due to the restructuring of the service, and a year later his contract was terminated for good.

Kim, who successfully completed a project, lost because he did not understand the real ethics of academia. He naively trusted the director and believed that hard work and good results override the politics of power and deception. On the contrary, the director, relying on arbitrary academic ethics, felt that his actions were legitimate because he was giving a chance to a young unknown doctor to use his facilities in order to build a career. In his view, Kim was ungrateful and "betrayed" him. Once again, this shows the relativity of moral principles, which are admissible or rejected, depending on which side one stands.

This brings us back to the problem of the relativity of trust. Why should trust be considered sacred when nothing in human relationships is entitled to this status? Nobody denies that the need for confiding in someone close, particularly when there is a relationship of dependence, is a natural tendency in most people, with the exception of suspicious people or paranoid personalities. Yet, when it is granted without restrictions and vital exclusions to protect one's security, it reflects an error of judgment rather than an excessive need for intimacy. Nobody can anticipate the possible change of heart of a close associate, relative, or friend who resents the relationship and may use the confidential information about the other party for revenge or personal advancement. By the same token, withdrawal of trust from relationships with close associates or family members can severely restrict if not make any social interaction almost impossible and meaningless.

There is a precarious emotional balance in any human relationship whose preservation requires an understanding of the limitation of any intimacy. Yet, people cannot relate to each other believing that others are conspiring against them, until proven otherwise, and they do not think presumptively that people intentionally seek to betray them, unless they suspect ulterior motives at play. Ironically, mistrustful or overly suspicious people have difficulty functioning socially, precisely because they are handicapped by doubting the motives of others, always suspecting ulterior reasons behind any expressed interest or attempt of befriending them. They always assume that "the others" allegedly want to take advantage of them somehow. It is for good reason that society considers them socially poorly adapted. Why this social stigmatization when anyone might have experienced himself at one time or another the abuse or betrayal of his trust by a close partner? While society is fully aware of the pitfalls of people confiding in others, at the same time, it assumes that any mature individual uses caution and critical judgment before openly exposing his highly personal life activities to another. The people who fail to do so appear to show a lack of understanding of human unpredictability and its implications for social interaction. The gullible who put the accent on "natural" trust and by overconfiding in the need for mutual support are the ones whose trust is abused, while the suspicious, who tend to underscore envy with its corollary of deceptive manipulations and intrigues, are the ones who may be inclined to overreact to another person. Yet, both the gullible and the suspicious may be missing the mark, since they view human nature in absolute terms of either–or. The reality is that the same people capable of devotion and loyalty to one cause or person could change under the influence of a strong conversion of convictions or new emotional needs and turn against the person previously held in high esteem, or against a religious or political organization with which the person fully identified before.

Converted to another ideology or dogma, that person is now ready to topple his/her former partners without any compunction. This was apparently the case with St. Paul, who, after officially persecuting Christians for years, suddenly had a revelation on the road to Damascus, which turned his beliefs 180 degrees around, causing him to become one of the most ardent advocates of Christianity. These changes of mind, called conversions, could occur not only among religious followers but also even more frequently among politicians. There is a blurred line of distinction between conversion and betrayal, particularly since there is an overlap of complex psychological motives that may range from frustrations with the old beliefs or with the people associated with them to a burning desire for revenge against those who, realistically or not, did not treat them right. In fact, in any social context of human interaction, one person may switch his allegiance without any hesitation and serenely justify his/her behavior in response to unfulfilled expectations. In all these situations, that person will use whatever real or fabricated facts he has at his disposal to further the newly embraced cause and directly or indirectly inflict pains on if not destroy the newly acquired adversary. All these happenings take place in the process of routine human interaction controlled by its contradictory needs, which want gratification most often at the expense of others. It is up to the individual to overcome any obstacle raised by rivals, to avoid any hidden trap surreptitiously waiting for him, to ignore any clever words of flattery or advice that attempt to misdirect or distract him from his course of action. To steer and maneuver through all these potentially dangerous situations and to reduce his exposure to unnecessary risks, the individual wanting to reach his goals needs to use his best judgment, free of any biases, untested assumptions, or emotional needs incompatible with his goals. Is it possible to do so, when most people are prejudiced, driven by their emotional wants and unable to objectively evaluate confronting situations? Obviously, the answer is yes; otherwise there would not be successful people, capable of achieving their goals. Then, within what ethical frame of reference were they able to achieve their success? Any careful inquiry into their methods of social operation reveals a clever manipulation of events and people within more or less acceptable legal boundaries, but without confiding in others incriminating matters. Bluntly said, their success, to a large extent, is based not only on avoiding whenever necessary all the self-imposed moral trappings and reservations of regular guys, but on the contrary using them to their advantage. In this high moral relativism, it is up to the individual to decide on whom he should depend on or whom he should trust, keeping in mind that ultimately he will dearly have to pay for his wrong decisions and choices.

NOTES

1. B. Pascal, *Pensee and the Provincial Letters* (New York: Modern Library Books, 1941), p. 95.

2. J. Bowlby, "Some Pathological Processes Set in Train by Early Mother–Child Separation," *Journal of Mental Science* 99 (1953): 265–272.

3. J. Bowlby, "Separation Anxiety: A Critical Review of the Literature," *Journal of Child Psychological Psychiatry* (1961b): 251–269.

4. R. Lionel, & F. Tiger, *The Imperial Animal* (New York: Holt, Reinhart, Winston, 1971), pp. 56–57.

5. F. Fukuyama, *Trust* (New York: Free Press, 1995), pp. 26, 150–159.

6. B. Alpert, "Off No More," *Barron*, September, 14, 1998, p. 23.

7. A. Brayant, "America's Latest Fad," *New York Times*, February 9, 1997, p. 3.

8. J.R. Laing, "Now It's Ron's Turn," *Barron*, October 12, 1998, p. 31.

9. F. La Rochefoucauld, *Maxims of La Rochefoucauld* (New York: Modern Library, 1959).

10. C. Kluckholm, *Navaho Witchcraft—Papers of the Peabody Museum of America Archeology and Ethnology*, Vol. 22 No. 2. (Cambridge, MA: Cambridge University Press, 1944), pp. 68–111.

11. F. Firth, *Primitive Polynesian Economy* (London: Routledge, 1939), p. 282.

12. C. Kluckholm, *Navaho* (Cambridge, MA: Cambridge University Press, 1946).

13. S. Thoenes, "Indonesia Jolted by Killing," *Financial Times*, November 7–8, 1998, p. 4.

14. J. Tung, "Harding's Hankering for a Second Chance," *New York Post*, October 28, 1999, p. 34.

15. P. Early, "Treason?" *U.S. News & World Report*, February 17, 1997, pp. 29–35.

16. CNBC News, "DOJ Charges Former GM Executive of Passing Secrets to Volkswagen," May 5, 2000, www.cnbc.com.

17. J. M. Waller, "These Spies Steal American Jobs," *Reader's Digest*, February 1998, p. 165.

18. M. Maremont, & J. Pereira, "Engineer, Indicted on Charges of Stolen Trade Secrets," *Wall Street Journal*, September 26, 1997, p. B2.

19. L. Wayne, "Brother versus Brother," *New York Times*, April 28, 1998, p. D1.

20. A. Schopenhauer, *The Will to Live* (Garden City, NY: Anchor-Doubleday, 1962), pp. 69–102.

Chapter 7

How to Catch a Liar

I am determined to prove a villain.
Shakespeare, *Richard III*, 1. 24

LIARS VERSUS VICTIMS

It is frightening to assume that people whom you have entrusted with important secrets of your life may cheat or betray you; it is disquieting to contemplate that your trusted business or political associates who have ridden on the coattails of your successful career will turn against you and sell you to your competitors or political adversaries; it is financially hurting to believe the sales pitch of an apparently credible investment salesperson and lose your money in a well-designed scam; it is downright embarrassing and irritating to find out you have been socially manipulated by someone whom you had previously respected, not to mention how humiliating it is to act or take a stand and look like a fool because of someone else's fabrications and concoctions you believed. The possibilities of being directly or indirectly deceived by others are unlimited. Then, how can someone protect himself from liars, enchanters, cheaters, imposters or traitors while still being able to confide in friends, relative(s), family members, or relate to coworkers and do business with others? In other words, how can someone reach a satisfactory balance between trusting people within his/her sphere of social interaction and avoid being exploited or cheated?

THE BATTLE OF WITS BETWEEN LIARS AND THEIR POTENTIAL VICTIMS

People are faced almost daily with making hard decisions about accepting statements, contentions, or declarations made by others in their business or private life, which ultimately may turn out to be lies harmful to them. There is a battle of wits going on between liars and their potential victims, and the winners depend on a set of complex psychosocial factors underlying the game. These factors range from the authoritative status of the party making the false assertions to the discriminative abilities of the targeted listener(s). The qualifications of the person telling a lie, his social or personal credentials, such as social standing in the community, authority figure role, real or perceived expertise, degree of closeness as an associate, family member, or lover will grant him the needed credibility to the targeted listener. In addition, the liar's intelligence and ability to communicate—to discuss things in a believable manner—represent significant pluses in persuading the other party. On the other hand, there are psychological and emotional factors leading to the acceptance of the lie by the potential victim. The psychological ones can be reduced to two basic traits, those of ignorance and credulity. The underlying emotional reasons for the receiver's need to believe the liar may vary from lack of critical judgment, often related to one's tendency to self-deceive, to that of outright greed, to mention just a couple. The outcome is the same, a disregard for any critical evaluation of the statements of the liar.

Against this general background of their personalities and drives the liar and the potential victim as antagonists start their intellectual and emotional duel. The disadvantage for the potential victim begins from this point on, because chances are, he is unaware of the dishonest and fraudulent intentions of the liar. The targeted listener fails to see the whole interaction as a calculated game of deception played by the liar for his own benefit. In fact, the liar evaluates his chances for success at deception, beforehand or in the course of their discussion, by estimating the emotional and psychological weak spots of the listener. By the same token, the listener does not realize that he is under scrutiny and any mistake or incompetence on his part will be used against him. Zeroing in on his prey is an art. The successful liar has to use careful and subtle means to manipulate the victim's shortcomings to his own advantage. However, not all liars, seekers of gaining illegitimate advantages, are good liars. Fortunately, the potential victim may get a break in this alleged duel of wits when the liar is a bad one.

GOOD VERSUS BAD LIARS

In this context, liars can be divided like people in any other social activity, into good and bad liars. The bad liars are basically unconvincing for two main sets of reasons: one is associated with their emotional and moral makeup and the other with their poor imagination and creativity, making them unable to produce persuasive arguments capable of disguising their false statements. A bad liar tends to have an ambivalent attitude about morality and lying, stemming mainly from his indecision about identifying acceptable and unacceptable lies. This makes him feel self-conscious about lying in certain situations. He might even feel guilty about lying in situations when his loose code of ethics might consider it unnecessary or unjustifiable. In those situations when he doubts his ability to tell a lie with a straight face, he may become quite flustered. He is afraid that the inflection of his voice, facial expression, or other observable physical discomfort or noticeable psychophysiological reactions will betray him. By then, he may appear anxious because, in addition, he is unsure of the believable impact of his lie. On an intellectual level he may doubt his ability to come up with a good, credible lie. A case in point is Jill, a 42-year-old single woman with a boyfriend of many years, Gideon, who constantly found new reasons to postpone any firm commitment to her. Since he was undecided about getting married, she decided to date other men. However, she was afraid of losing him if she was not available for their meetings, particularly on weekends. So, in order to date other men, she invoked family obligations whenever they interfered with weekends. But after a few weekends of separation, Gideon became increasingly upset and, in order to appease him, Jill decided to tell him she has been assigned to a big project, requiring her to travel frequently over weekends. Once, when he asked of the name of her hotel and the telephone number where she stayed, she became flustered, uncomfortable, and promised to let him know. Afterward, she claimed to have tried to call him but was evasive about the hour and did not leave any message because she thought they could talk during the week anyway. She lied badly and he knew it. Moreover, he had been home during the evening, the time of her alleged call. He became suspicious and installed a caller ID telephone device without her knowledge. Indeed, during the next weekend when she said she had to leave town to visit a sick aunt, she called and left a message from her alleged hotel room. In reality, the call came from a man's apartment in the same city. Confronted with her deception, she denied it at the beginning, but after the ID evidence she became hysterical and accused him of controlling her life and spying on her. To her intense chagrin, he decided to terminate the relationship.

In fact, extensive scientific work has been done on the verbal and nonverbal processes accompanying the communication of a lie, which suggest the emotional difficulties that might be experienced by some people intending to lie or while lying. The liar, particularly if he is a bad liar, may show unwarranted emotional reactions like a sweaty forehead or palms, flushed cheeks, or uneasy posturing of the trunk, which may convey his emotional discomfort. These physiological reactions are thought to betray an inner conflict related to the discrepancies between what he utters and what he really thinks or knows about the presented story. But no one should rely only on these signs to catch a liar, because these verbal and non-verbal communication signs are not by themselves necessarily indicators of lying. Even people who are not timid or insecure if placed in situations viewed by them as unpleasant or threatening may exhibit signs of anxiety and uneasiness in their conversations with others that might easily be confused with lying. One encounters this quite often when such persons are questioned about an infraction committed by someone else but are afraid of being suspected anyway. In most of these cases, the assumption that a person is a liar may be even greater if during the communication or interrogation he does not make eye contact. This assumption is not always supported by the facts. Such behavior may be induced not because the person is afraid of being discovered lying but because he habitually just does not look at the other party when he talks. As a result, that person may be wrongly accused of lying, particularly without any corroborating evidence. The circumstantial proof of lying allegedly related to avoiding eye contact or exhibiting clumsy gestures and postural changes are meaningful only in the context of evaluating the truthfulness of his statements by factual methods. Otherwise, anyone guided by such alleged body language and signs may judge in a biased manner and wrongly identify the innocent person as a liar. In fact, the best liars are either able to control the potential betrayal of their verbal or nonverbal reactions in their communication with others, or they naturally do not exhibit them in any perceptible degree. It is well known that sociopaths and other pathological liars do not show signs of anxiety while lying "straight in your face." They do not mind lying and they don't feel guilty about it because of their lack of sensitivity to social morality.

SOCIETAL BIASES MAY PLACE THE POTENTIAL VICTIM AT RISK

Finally, strong religious beliefs may create a tremendous disadvantage for the potential victim if his religious morality taught him to promote love and trust people while ignoring lies and cheating as punishable sins eschewed by "nice persons." Acting on this faith, the potential victim tends to believe that most people are "nice" and are ashamed to lie because of social disapproval and fear of divine retribution. In practical terms, someone's inability to protect himself from the lying and deception of others may incur emotional and/or financial losses. However, many people are inclined to rely on the potential protection of the secular justice as a deterrent to lying and deception. Indeed, they tend to believe that liars and cheaters may be discouraged by this justice that with all its imperfections, at least tries to punish, some of those whose scheming has engendered financial losses for their victims. The victim may derive some moral satisfaction for having punished the cheater whenever he is fortunate enough to obtain a conviction. The point is that neither the remote threat of celestial punishment nor the immediate fear of earthly justice can stop people from lying and cheating or committing even worse criminal offenses. This situation can place any decent individual in a terrible quandary, for if he trusts people easily he may be viewed and treated as gullible, but if he distrusts them indiscriminately he might be considered to show paranoid tendencies. Either way, he may have serious difficulty relating to others and functioning socially. Worse, he might be judged as poorly adapted socially because he has failed to understand the nature of human interaction with all the underlying egotistic needs that direct and quite often determine its course. In reality, most people, being fully aware of the human disregard for the societal norms regarding the control of deceit, are neither so naive as to uncritically believe anyone nor so oversuspicious in their daily association with others as to treat everyone as a potential liar or crook. There is a delicate balance between these two extremes, and sometimes people fall into one or another trap, more often into that of being tricked and gypped.

Yet, strange as it may sound, in most cases of deceit, part of the fault lies with the victim. Although most people are selectively lying while trying to benefit from any circumstances perceived as important for enhancing their status and fortune at the expense of others, at the same time they expect others to be truthful and trusting of them. Ultimately, their blind faith in securing the truth from others is supported by a magical reasoning that others would not dare to cheat them or to lie to them because of the respect they command. This is further bolstered by another belief that they can easily spot anyone who may try to lie to them. No wonder they are surprised if not shocked when they find out that people have taken advantage of them with impunity. The reality is that people should be aware of the possibility of the others' interjection of elements of untruthfulness in any dealings to supplement or twist objective and factual situations. But, though important, it is not enough to be aware of the possible insincerity of others; as undesirable as it may be, it is also beneficial for someone to be able to identify a lie on the spot or at least the intent of deceit. One's belief of possessing instinctive skills to recognize a lie or a scam can place him in an unwarranted state of complacency, hence an easy prey to deceivers. While it is true that bad, transparent, and inconsistent lies or exaggerated fabrications are easily detectable, this does not hold true for sophisticated and calculated lies or for well-devised schemes by expert crooks. The bad liars are, at worst, a nuisance; hence they are basically harmless. The good liars are dangerous. To detect them requires more than just a hunch, one needs special knowledge.

THE PSYCHOLOGICAL DYNAMICS OF A BELIEVABLE LIE

Before someone considers trying to catch a good liar, he must first understand lying is a process of persuasion based on at least three cardinal principles that are guiding the liar. First the lie has to have a logical content similar to any regular exchange or transaction in which one person has the intent of persuading the other to a point of view different than previously held by him. In the case of the lie, the exception is that the persuasion is directed toward the acceptance of fraudulent statements as facts. A process of persuasion does not necessarily represent an intent to lie. A persuader may be an honest person who is trying to convince another person—the listener—by the power of his argument and validity of his data, which speak for themselves. In this case, the logical argument is convincing because the facts are irrefutable and the conclusions are sensible. However, this is not always the case, because the persuader's argument may not be supported by hard facts, although he still wants to prevail upon the listener in order to satisfy his ulterior motives. In this case, the persuader has to slant, twist, or selectively ignore facts in order to give the illusion of factual data and logical argument. To do so, he surreptitiously tries to bend the laws of logic by using unqualified generalizations, misuse of definitions, equivocations or irrelevant propositions that only appear to be related to conclusions in order to obtain the desired agreement. What is important to note is that a good, convincing lie has a logical structure that imitates formal thinking, but in which the validity of the logical propositions behind the argument are twisted by the introduction of various forms of fallacies—those of formal logic combined with those of nonformal logic.

The fallacies of formal logic are divided into fallacies of deduction and induction. These intentional errors of communication are created by manipulating the laws of syllogistic reasoning. They may range from the fallacy of undistributed middle term (the middle term must be present in at least one premise of the argument, otherwise it invalidates the deductions) to drawing particular conclusions from universal premises.

For instance, in case of the loose use of the middle term, a successful salesman-liar may argue that the new product X is the best on the market since it is made by the reputable company Y, well known for its excellent product Z, which in turn means that product X must also be very good, even though there is no evidence to support this assertion.

Dishonest persuaders also use fallacies of the nonformal logic from emotive ones such as "ad hominem" arguments (personal attacks unrelated to the disputed facts; e.g, candidate X is not fit for the office of presidency because he engaged in wild behavior when he was young).

Other fallacies are: "ad populum" arguments (appealing to peoples' common emotions; e.g., the argument used by some members of Congress during the debate for welfare's reform, claiming that the reform will result in the starvation of children), or people arguing from ignorance (equating accusations with guilt; e.g., the English royalty conspired with their secret service to kill Princess Diana because she was going to marry Dodi Al Fayed, a wealthy Egyptian).

Most often used is the fallacy of ambiguity related to incorrectly defining the evidence, for example, O.J. Simpson could not have killed his ex-wife since the evidence of DNA are not foolproof to identify him or were possibly contaminated at collection.

In politics, quite often a candidate is attacked on issues based on circumstantial evidence (referring to special considerations of unrelated past inconsistencies on the part of the opponent; e.g., Clarence Thomas cannot be appointed to the Supreme Court because he allegedly harassed a female attorney subordinate, though without any evidence). These statements are also combined with unqualified, hasty generalizations (generalizations that are universal; e.g., all lawyers are crooks, all women are good mothers, etc.),

Another frequently used fallacy is using sentences that have a double meaning, generally interjected to favor one's own argument by confusing the issue (known in logic as amphiboly; e.g., George Bush lost reelection because of his tax problems; Clinton refused to resign because of Monica Lewinsky).

All of these are used for the purpose of persuading the other party to a particular point of view or for reaching an intended conclusion. The method of debate approximates the rhetorical argument but with one big difference: the desired conclusion is substantiated by manipulating syllogistic reasoning with the help of probable inferences, projection of probabilities, and all other types of fallacies embraced mostly by opportunistic politicians, trial lawyers and social activists. Incidently, this style of persuasion, often combined with "ad populum" argument, which arouses popular passions, had been extensively used by the fascist and Communist propaganda machine to maintain control over the minds of the people and justify their actions, often contradicting their dubious ideologies. Their cynical attitude toward truth has led them to use deft argumentative techniques for manipulation and interpretation of facts in order to attain their desired goals.

Certainly, as we have seen, there are other gross distortions and manipulations of facts and information in the process of persuasion, from the partial omissions of data or subtle changes of their content to the inclusion of nonexistent findings in support of the pursued slanted conclusions. The most brazen defensive method used for devious persuasion is total denial of real facts by replacing them with pure fabrications, cleverly devised to create a semblance of truth.

A second principle of lying, hence the way of catching a good persuader-liar, is to have an understanding of the ulterior motives that drive him to resolutely push fraudulently convincing conclusions. If the outcome of persuasion is emotionally or financially beneficial to the persuader, regardless of the apparent plausibility of his conclusions, then the listener has to take a closer look at the validity of the arguments presented. The greater the benefit for the persuader, the better are the chances that his argument is flawed and biased in his favor. This smooth persuasive approach is used by clever politicians, subtle religious activists, smart social reformers, and astute media people in their quest for power, recognition, and money. Shrewd salespeople, in order to win their commissions, routinely use persuasion based on false logic in order to sell their products. How does the process of this artful persuasion practically work?

For instance, Joe, an aggressive real estate broker, is pressed but generously rewarded by his company to find and sell to investors timeshare ownership in a converted large inn in an undeveloped and third-rate resort area. Because the company's advertising in the press did not help sales, Joe decided to pay off the desk clerks at some motels in the area to get the names and addresses of last years' visitors. He sent a brochure to them describing the unique opportunity to buy cheap shares in a "luxurious property," permitting them to either enjoy a vacation at a low cost or to rent the apartment and make money. They were invited to visit the place as soon as possible because already "more than 50 percent of the units were either under contract or on deposit." Since the sales campaign took place out of season, they were given the opportunity to sleep overnight at the inn for a reduced charge, and in case a deal was made, the company rebated $100 per person for travel expenses. The offer seemed promising and enticing. David and Laura, a young couple of moderate means who had spent a one-week vacation during the previous year there, decided to take advantage of the opportunity. They visited Joe who after giving them a warm welcome and a tour of the facility showed them charts delineating the future economic growth of the area, to which he added the fact that it was still undiscovered by the big resort business and as such it maintained its unspoiled charm. According to him the price per square foot was much lower by comparison with the cost of buying a house in the same area. David and Laura were still undecided. Then after asking them the reasons for their reservations, Joe questioned them about their ability to pay while stressing the need to have their own recreational place, which would have the added value of a solid investment for the future. He demonstrated to them that the investment paid for itself if they were to rent out of season, while vacationing for free in season. No headaches with maintenance either, since as part of the deal a small monthly charge was paid to the management for taking care of it. But the couple was still not ready to give Joe a nonrefundable deposit.

Then he suggested that they should buy a smaller unit, even though, as he confessed, it would be harder to rent. In order to try to close the deal, Joe threw in as a "bonus" a low-rate mortgage, specially offered by the company to young, socially upward couples. He also mentioned that the price might change pending special circumstances that he could not divulge. At the insistence of the couple and after some faked hesitation, he shared the "secret" with them because he trusted their confidentiality, that is, the imminent approval of a bill by the state assembly to permit gambling in that area, which would increase the value of the property tremendously. After some further deliberations about the details of the deal, David and Laura signed the agreement and left the deposit. They took possession of the place within two months. A closer look at this negotiation shows that Joe was far from being candid, as he claimed. First, the ability to rent out of season was nonexistent; second, the price was all right, except that there was no market for resale and they had to pay a fee for the management of the place. The owner reserved the right to sell the whole place if not enough shares had been sold. The idea that the value of the property would grow was as baseless as was the fantasy of the casino, a local rumor circulated by real estate agents for years. No bill was debated by the state assembly. The net result for the couple was to sell the shares back to the company three years later for a fraction of the initial price because of an inability to rent in and out of season. The loss was even higher if one added the money spent on the mortgage and maintenance. David and Laura's mistake was their cavalier approach to the negotiation and impulsive buying without a careful investigation of the data presented by Joe. They lost because they proved to be inexperienced and gullible.

This method of twisted persuasion with even more distortion of facts is also used by other people who socially operate at the edge of truthfulness. In fact, it may be used by anyone who wants to win an advantage in a negotiation of a situation materially or emotionally important to them. An example is Gail, an aspiring actress, and her a boyfriend, a businessman who was not ready to marry her, though he basically took care of her financially. After a while, she considered dropping him, but before terminating the relationship, she thought it might be a smart idea to get some money out of him. Her scheme was a simple one, namely to claim to be pregnant, which she knew would upset her boyfriend. Enthusiastically, she broke the news of her pregnancy over the phone, and said she did not want an abortion for reasons of moral convictions. He was stunned because according to their understanding she was supposed to always use protection. She claimed that she did, but that somehow she had become pregnant and wanted to keep the baby. He would either support the child or marry her. He professed not to be ready for marriage and tried to convince her to get an abortion, but she refused. After a few fruitless discussions, he threatened to finish their relationship but she reminded him that she had taped the phone conversations regarding her pregnancy in which he had admitted paternity. She was ready to hire a lawyer and if necessary to go to court. However, since he had behaved in such an irresponsible manner, destroying their wonderful relationship and causing a great deal of emotional damage, she was ready to settle for $45,000. After some negotiating, she accepted $35,000 for the sake of their "past love." Later, she claimed to have had a miscarriage and allegedly lost the baby. Her well-planned deception was based on a variety of emotive claims but was successful because of his failure to ask for the indisputable evidence, a pregnancy test.

In general, an analysis of the evidence presented by any sophisticated but dishonest persuader will show us that the whole dialogue between him and the listener is approached by him as a form of negotiation in which the projected result is advanced by a process of clever manipulations of facts. The model used in the negotiation is that of a persuasive dialogue-deliberation, which is modified according to circumstances. It has the main aim of inducing new beliefs and values in another person by influencing one's reasoning and behavior through an emotional, half-truthful, and distorted or unrelated factual demonstration. It is important to note that the persuader in this negotiation is highly psychologically attuned to respond to and manipulate the needs of the listener.

This leads us to the third cardinal principle involved in a twisted persuasion, that is, the use by the devious persuader of strong or subtle emotional messages to facilitate the interaction by attempting to create a comfortable and pleasant rapport with his listener(s) before making his pitch. He not only tries to put his listener at ease but he also conveys to him that the subject of their discussion will have a pleasant and beneficial result. At the same time, the persuader has to exhibit an air of confidence and a feeling of credibility about the rightfulness of his position. To achieve it, he will strengthen his position of expertise, authority, or know-how, as required by the situation, by either emphasizing his knowledge or embellishing his credentials. The sought-after rapport is further facilitated by knowing in advance how much the listener is interested in the matter under consideration, as Joe the salesman did. The experienced persuader, after the initial perfunctory introductory exchange, will tactfully explore the listener's degree of knowledge, previous involvement, and interest in that specific area in order to use them as a basis for the proper strategy in making "his pitch." To further enhance his chances of success, the skillful persuader will casually chat from time to time with the listener(s), as Joe did, about social issues of concern to the other party by making a point to agree with his opinions and values. Under no circumstances will he pursue any political or religious issue, which by their very nature are sensitive subjects and might irritate or antagonize the other party. In this regard, he will cautiously take his cues from the listener's comments. This initial approach may vary from one prospective victim to another, and the rules are modified for any group persuasion, but they always have the same goal, that of creating a receptive state in the mind of the listener(s).

Assuming a good rapport has been established, the persuader-liar will slowly advance his argument-solicitation by alternating, according to the situation, between two types of messages, one that is a mixture of half-truths and selected facts pursued on a pretense of logical reasoning (like Joe's documentation with statistics and charts, etc.) and another appealing to the emotional needs of the listener (Joe's emphasis on their need to have their own place as a socially upward couple, etc.). Each of these approaches plays its role in the persuader's attempt to convince the listener to follow different beliefs or convictions than those of his own and/or to alter his values. The degree of distortion, lies, and misrepresentations in the process of persuasion depends on the need of the dishonest persuader to win that coveted transaction. Let us go back for a moment and take a closer look at Joe's ultimate method of persuasion. Joe, in order to convince his listeners—David and Laura—to "buy" his ideas (product), associated his sale pitch with two alternating basic emotional states, which he attempted to arouse in the couple: one, a state of pleasure induced by the vision of possessing a piece of that "paradise" and the other, a subtle evocation of fear related to alleged unpleasant financial losses in case of ignoring his buying advice, particularly after sharing with them his "secret" of the casino. This cascade of well-interjected lies in the negotiation had only one purpose: to create the impression in the mind of the couple of having stumbled onto a fantastic bargain that cannot be passed up.

THE ATTITUDE OF THE LISTENER-POTENTIAL VICTIM TOWARD THE PERSUASION PROCESS

Here is one of the most difficult tasks for the listener, that of separating an honest persuader, who is correct in his argumentation and indeed believes in his intellectually or spiritually expounded position, from a liar who uses the same process of persuasion but in which his alleged beliefs are part lies supported by the exploitation of emotions for maximum effect. The distinction between honest and dishonest deliberation becomes harder and more confusing if we consider that a great percentage of human transactions in which people attempt to influence others blend various shades of truths with personal beliefs and lies in order to win the argument.

In the decision-making process, people may argue about the best approach to be taken in reaching the appropriate conclusion and certainly they will try without the intention of cheating to sway the opinions of others to their own, which they consider more desirable to be followed. But then, there is the possibility that in daily interactive communication, certain people surreptitiously implant lies, totally unbeknownst to the other person(s) for making their arguments more palatable. Basically, the dishonest persuader will do two things to change or create a new opinion in the mind of the listener(s): he or she will question and doubt the views of the listener in order to shake that person's logical coherence and the validity of held convictions, while at the same time introducing his own opinion as the new, acceptable, factual reality. This sneaky approach may go unnoticed since most people have been taught to argue their case by honest, persuasive debate and, as such, they would expect the exchange to take place within the framework of truthfulness. They are unaware and unprepared when the other party has suddenly decided to change the rules of discourse by distorting facts, introducing false statements, and manipulating the truth in their favor. The first guiding rule for the listener—the prospective victim—is to evaluate the weight of the evidence and stick to the verification of the assertions and documentation offered by the persuader as the only valid defense.

The second one is to admit his ignorance when he is not familiar with the issue under consideration. If the listener is not fully knowledgeable about the discussed matter and if he does not grasp the subtle fallacies used by the other person in support of his position, he has to recognize his ignorance in that area and not feign any competence. On the contrary, the persuader would try to discuss it with him as if the listener has enough knowledge to understand the transaction since this favors him. The more the ignorant listener pretends proficiency on the intended transaction, the easier it will be for him to succumb to the persuader's argument and accept falsehoods as truth. Disregard for these rules places honest people at a disadvantage because they implicitly assume a frank communication while they encounter the smooth arguments of convincing liars and crooks.

A good liar, like a good persuader, almost intuitively understands how to combine an apparent logical documentation with enticing emotional projections in order to obtain the maximum convincing effects. It is the duty of the listener to stay cool in order to be able to separate fact from fiction in the liar's statements and to finally elicit the truth. This brings us to the third rule desirable to be followed by a listener who wants to avoid being cheated, that is, to remain emotionally detached in the process of negotiating the transaction. His emotions will interfere if not control his reasoning, which will make him unable to see the subtle introduction by the deceiver of pure emotional arguments in line with his wishes, but not truly meaningful for the basic debated issues. Let us see how a simple negotiation between a seller and a buyer is carried out in which the buyer placed himself at disadvantage. For example, John wanted to sell his 5-year-old car to a prospective buyer, Dean, who was relatively inexperienced in checking the mechanical condition of the car. The car, with over 65,000 miles, looked clean and properly maintained, though it appeared to have minor problems related to aging. After some small talk about their area of work and each one's need for a car, John took Dean for a ride, and the car seemed to run properly. John, a smart seller, tried from the beginning to give the semblance of truth to his sale pitch, by analyzing and debating the positive and negative values of his product. However, on a closer look, his presentation heavily tilted the balance toward the positive attributes of his "sale," which far surpassed its shortcomings. John mentioned to Dean that the tires were somewhat old and that the motor might require a tune-up. Since he did not have time to do it, he has included it in his reasonable price. What John left out of the presentation was the fact that the car overheated in the summer, used an excessive amount of oil, and had some undetected electrical wiring defects that affected its proper functioning. The deal was clinched by John's introduction in the negotiation of another element of persuasion known as product comparison. John compared the selling price of his car with other similar cars listed at a much higher price in the automobile "blue book." He closed the sale with an emotional argument that he has to undersell his car since he needed the money for a surgical operation for his mother, which was untrue. Instead of getting excited about buying the car cheap, Dean should have admitted to himself his limited knowledge about cars and should have taken the car for inspection and evaluation by a mechanic and he would have avoided getting stuck with a lemon.

What is important to note is that even in a small, more or less common transaction, both parties routinely use the rules of negotiation based on persuasion with the assumption to be mutually acceptable. The reverse of this assumption—its negative counterpart—would be when both parties are crooks and each attempts to cheat the other, as in an old anecdote about the making of a deal at a horse market. According to this story, an older man went with his nephew to a horse market to buy a horse where he started to negotiate with a horse dealer for a horse that was less expensive because it had passed its prime. They argued for a while about the merits of the horse versus the right price and finally they struck a deal. The old man bought the horse and left, accompanied by his nephew. While walking down the road holding the rein of the horse, the nephew, surprised by his uncle's decision to buy this old horse, asked him whether he had noticed that the horse was painted. The uncle smilingly remarked that for that reason he had paid the horse dealer with counterfeit money. But in real life this kind of deal is an exception and not the rule. Most often only one party attempts to get the better of another person who is victimized.

THE DYNAMICS OF POLITICAL LYING

The art of unscrupulous persuasion gets more sophisticated in more complex negotiations related to certain political or investment deals. Here, the arguments of persuasion introduce subtle forms of sophistic reasoning, which means using the whole gamut of formal and nonformal fallacies. Let us take for example a political candidate who wants to convince the constituents that he is the only candidate who can understand and solve their pressing problems. The first thing he wants to impress on the voters is his integrity and credibility. He quotes or advertises the statements of other known politicians who vouch for his past civic probity and eminent political performance. He even offers a highly selective political and social biography carefully edited by special image makers. To avoid too close a scrutiny from the press, he courts and accommodates reporters as much as possible. He does everything in his power to suppress publications of unfavorable articles about past unsavory business or political deals. In case of being unable to do so, he presents a different version of them, in which the facts are reinterpreted, if not sanitized. If necessary, he hires his own public relations firm, which attempts to create a positive image of him. After remaking his image, confident of having gained the public's trust, he feels free to sell to the voter in hyperbolic slogans his program for "rejuvenating," moving forward the country.

Here starts the art of sophistry for a good politician; to paint the truth in broad strokes (in logical terms, a fallacy of hasty generalizations) and be evasive about concrete facts and details (an ambiguity of facts) unless they are highly favorable to him. The incumbent did not do enough to solve the pressing problems of the community, state, or nation. The candidate promises to offer bold solutions to solve these major issues, from education, children's health, social security, and medicare for elderly to protection of citizens. These are unbeatable issues to use for an attack on the incumbent, since people love to hear about them. At first glance, their rhetoric about their alleged ability to solve these issues sounds powerful and believable to the naive public, but at a closer look their proposed solutions are conditional and hence meaningless because they depend on too many unforeseeable economic and social conditions.

In addition, the upsetting candidate has to project a vision of economic and social decline if the incumbent will be (re)elected, contrasted to a state of heightened satisfaction and economic blossoming if *he* is elected. These critical predictions about the adversary and all the promises of solutions to all social ills offered by him are more than simple slogans and declaratory statements; they are presented as facts cleverly supported by fragmented statistics and/or selected data taken out of context. Most of the facts presented are assumptive, inferred, bolstered by, or extrapolated from the general policies of the party he represents (ambiguous fallacies: thousands of children are dying because of lack of medical treatment, or illegal aliens are left without medical care, and so on). To appeal to the naive voters, the candidate presents the incumbent as insensitive to certain groups of constituents. In turn, the incumbent counterattacks, accusing the opponent of inexperience, hollowness, biased judgment, and selfish ambitions with the underlying assumption of being unfit or unprepared for the high responsibility of the coveted office.

Most of the imputations against each other's political faults are presented by the contestants in well-crafted newspaper and TV ads. By subtle implications, associations with negative events, or direct attacks, each one of the candidates attempts to downgrade the political qualifications or even smear the image of the other. The press plays its role in influencing the public to support its candidates while claiming to be neutral in the contest. To add to the confusion, the candidates debate the issues on TV, which changes the political-ideological contest in a unique form of theatrical performance with the scripts and accompanied choreography carefully rehearsed.

Couched by experts in communication, they try to debate their records of positive and negative performance but with subtle modifications, omissions, and interpretations in their favor. However, the attempt to compare the record contrast between the opponents is irrelevant since there is little to compare to the extent to which they have held different jobs. Indeed, it is not so hard to see how the game of devious persuasion is played by opponent candidates for any political office where the whole argument is based on the projection of intangible expectations that they claim to be able to fulfill. They try hard to identify with the needs of the voters regardless of how unattainable their goals might be, and to appeal to their beliefs and values in order to win their heart. The decision of the voters for choosing the right candidate is influenced by too many variables unrelated to the true qualification of the contestants. Most often, only when the public is either dissatisfied with the incumbent's inconsistent support of political issues important to them or if he was convicted by a jury for corruption while in office, then they may reject him. Sometimes a newly elected politician may succeed if he is charismatic and a more convincing communicator of the learned script, basically a better actor. He moves into the seat of power and continues the same type of manipulation of truth but for different constituents and with a different supporting lobby.

Shameless misrepresentations and lies are found again and again in the life of almost all politicians at every level of elected office and yet they continue to be chosen to govern the nation with impunity. Why? The answer is simple: They are supported by a vast army of opportunists, politically committed, who have wagered their careers and future on the chosen candidate. They are in a manner of speaking political co-conspirators of the politician's hyperbolic programs by mutually supporting each other with the tacit understanding of access and the opportunity of sharing power for mutual benefit. They have more than an inkling about the half-truthfulness and misrepresentations of their endorsed politicians, but this does not disturb them; on the contrary, they know that it makes the candidates more amenable for cutting lucrative deals. But how about the ordinary citizens, the outsiders of the political machine? They either have their own little social and ideological beliefs, which they hope will be fulfilled by their endorsed candidates, or are mesmerized by the politicians' skills of persuasion.

An open question is the reasons for people's acceptance of the psychological game of misrepresentation of facts and false promises played by all candidates for public office, assuming that they understand it. They can, at least, surmise for sure that under the candidate's administration, if elected, his financial and party supporters will do well, but not necessarily the other taxpayers. Ordinary citizens will fare well only if services do not deteriorate or the governing team does not abuse the system with excessive favoritism and corruption. Under these circumstances, ordinary citizens are often confused about their ability to make the right choice and rely either on their herd instinct by depending more and more on the political polls or on their political convictions, which have little to do with the competence of the chosen party candidate. The benefit for the citizens comes out more often from the political clashes among politicans, triggered by envy, greed, and suspicion of each other for attempting to usurp their power, or ultimately, fear of being thrown out of office by the voters. A case in point is offered by the recent cooperation in Congress for the balanced budget. Most members for reelection of both parties in the House voted in favor of the bill, regardless of their ideological affiliation, afraid to face the wrath of their constituents at election.

In general, people vote for these kinds of candidates for two obvious reasons: first, since the difference between candidates is more of form than substance, the one who better articulates his program message appears to have higher credibility and second, the one who succeeds to better capture the electorate's hopes for a better life. Yet, the main thrust of his campaign is his appeal for the acceptance of his program as an article of faith, which, if uncritically accepted, might temporarily reduce any previous elements of anxiety that were induced by him regarding his opponent, who would allegedly do a terrible job if elected. Trusting him blindly assures the prosperity and peace of mind of the voters!

After all, what do certain dubious political and legislative manipulation of Congress or hyperbolic pitches of candidates for state or local office have to do with our issue of learning how to protect oneself from lying and deception? It tells us quite a lot about citizens' ability to detect or not the degree of political lying and also of their attitude toward lying. People who have elected and reelected these officials either do not care about their deviousness and tacitly approve of their behavior, or they are just unable to see the politician's demagoguery regardless of the evidence to the contrary. By extension, this is exactly the reason why people let themselves be cheated by allegedly respectable salespeople peddling any other types of goods.

In all fairness, there is not much difference between "buying" the program of a politician, elected on the public's faith that he would keep his word to follow the policies he advocated as a candidate, and that of a salesperson, making unproven extravagant claims about a product, for example, an investment plan. The thought process is the same, with slight modifications to the emphasis placed on one rule of persuasion over another, according to the type of that financial investment. The public buys the financial plan either because they believe the advertisement made about it or because they trust the salesperson. People feel cheated when the product they bought or the political candidate they voted for does not deliver the promised goods. In both cases, the misrepresentation shattered a belief in the public, their expectation of honesty. The success achieved by the clever and persuasive argument of a politician or a salesperson only abused the voters' or buyers' trust. To do so, ultimately they appeal to the people's emotions, which overrule any noticeable serious inconsistency and in addition, reinforce unsubstantiated promises in line with their hidden needs. In fact, these subtle emotional strategies are the motivating factor in swaying the decision of voters by weighing more on balance than on any logical argument.

WHY THE MASSES BELIEVE "BIG" SOCIAL LIES OF THE LEADERS

The most serious problem faced by people is in dealing with the big lies of the alleged political and social reformers who have periodically taken over countries in the name of justice and equality for the masses. Throughout history, big social and political lies, promoted by military and rebel leaders or social reformers, have governed societies for the benefit of a minority group who seized power, professing a new social order superior to the previous oppressive one. The more appealing and generous their social or political platforms had been, the more opportunistic and demagogic the leaders were. The same demagogic process filtered down to all levels of societal organization, negatively affecting the daily existence of common people. Unfortunately, naive people who had hoped for a better life have always been betrayed by their trusted "saviors."

People, beyond their routine activities, live on the expectation and hope of fulfilling their most intimate desires and ambitions. The need of the masses to have their illusions reinforced by a rescuer who will miraculously solve their problems and take care of their needs is as old as mankind. It has been exploited thousands of times throughout history, by political demagogues, magicians of social change, phony spiritual leaders, or lately, by financial investment crooks. Regardless of how esoteric their message might appear in the perspective of our time, they won as long as their promises fitted the longing and hopes of the masses. In politics or religion, as the claims for the purported schemes of change that will bring the desperately sought happiness become more grandiose, the more inspiring the created vision of the future will be, the more enthusiastic the masses will become, and unreservedly they will support and follow the new leader. Common people, because of their limited social horizon and endless frustrations, always have had difficulty in distinguishing between what is real and possible and what is desirable but only remotely believable.

The charismatic political or religious leaders of the 20th century who promised a new era of prosperity and happiness and who delivered their messages with an electrifying power of persuasion happened to be demagogues with strong narcissistic and sometimes psychopathic traits, enamored with power and with themselves. During their campaigns for power, dictators such as Hitler, Mussolini, or Lenin were able to sell to the masses an illusion of glorious, flourishing times to come, combined with a skillful attack on the living social conditions that indeed were woeful either due to corruption, war, and/or the ineptitude of the ruling class. Under these circumstances, these clever, unscrupulous political reformers and masters of deceit, convinced of their mastery of people and infatuated with their political cleverness, were able to mobilize people and to lead them to rebellion or revolution. Their talent was in manipulating people's thinking with skillful but fallacious arguments and in responding to their frustrations in life with tempting but fictitious solutions. With big ideological lies and magical promises for a better future, these fascist and Communist leaders took over power from a weak and corrupt ruling class after their countries had been ravaged by the first world war.

The unhappy, impoverished rank-and-file, ready for a change, embraced the new leaders without any understanding of the meaning of the newly espoused political doctrine and its consequences for its implementation. Since any change was better than the disastrous status quo, people supported their becoming leaders, believing in them as the agents of the aspired change. Later, when they realized the true despotic nature of the political system and the intellectual farce played on them by its ideology, they were hopelessly faced with the brutal reality of its terrible effects on their lives. But by then, it was too late for the exploited and enslaved masses to rebel against their alleged saviors. Their masterful demagogues had been responsible for committing the most evil crimes against mankind, orchestrating the most vicious accusations against millions of innocent people in order to send them to death in the name of a new social order and morality. While it is true that our historical repertory is full of enslavement, persecution, and torture of citizens or minorities by other more powerful nations or by unscrupulous demagogues who seized power, none of this domination had been as systematically planned and on such a vast scale against alleged internal enemies as those of these totalitarian regimes. This tells us quite a lot about the degree to which the masses can be manipulated, deceived, and lied to by unscrupulous politicians and reformers.

This also implies that people are either politically naive or indifferent, hence uncritical of big lies cleverly presented. Naively, they either believe that they have nothing to lose or at best it will be a change for the better. Accordingly, they favorably respond to verbal techniques that create illusions of meeting their dreams for a better life and are conducive to suspending their critical judgment. In fact, the ability to create the illusion of meeting one's expectations by clever arguments based on deception play a very important role in human interaction by allowing the sharp ones to win points or the whole game over the naive ones.

CAN PEOPLE PROTECT THEMSELVES FROM LIARS AND CROOKS?

The puzzling perennial problem is why people fail to protect themselves from the powerful suggestions of dynamic, unscrupulous persuaders. After all, the ability to protect oneself from the injurious acts of others is part of our adaptive system to life. A simplistic and obviously absurd conclusion would be to assume that a great number of people are socially poorly adapted since they apparently do not respond properly to protect their interests. However, this is not necessarily the case. At a closer look, it seems that the two previously mentioned sets of factors, built into human psychology, are continuously affecting people's interactions. Working separately or together, they are responsible for this otherwise puzzling situation.

The first set of factors, as we know, belongs to the domain of cognition and rational thinking. People evaluate the statements of others based on their experience, knowledge, and quality of reasoning. If they do not know the presented facts or they do not understand them, they are at a disadvantage in any attempt to reach a meaningful conclusion. Common sense tells us that the normal course of action for anyone should be that of obtaining a maximum amount of information on a subject, seeking advice, if necessary, before making any decision. Yet sometimes it may be difficult to secure valid data or objective opinions on predictions about future conditions in order to pass meaningful judgment. Consider, for example, an individual approached by a financial adviser who wants to sell him an investment fund for his retirement account. He is told that in addition to the advantage of deferred taxes, this fund will bring the investor a high amount of profit according to some statistics indicating its high performance for the last three years. Assuming that all the data are correct, the conclusion to invest could be erroneous. The stock market could go down, the manager of the fund could leave it, or even worse, by the time of his retirement, the tax structure could negatively change, thereby affecting his profits. Was the financial consultant totally dishonest? Not really. From a strictly business point of view, he has acted within his rights, though someone might think that the disclosure was incomplete and prejudicial for the client. He left out some negative aspects of this particular investment, such as back loading fees, an imposed penalty if the fund is liquidated before a certain time, or a high percentage of risky derivatives in the fund's portfolio. In addition, as a financial advisor, he should have told the prospective investor that he might not need this type of risky investment for his retirement account and that there were other, more beneficial financial products for his plan, but in that case he would not get a commission.

This mixture of half-truths and assumptions make it hard for an investor to detect the weak points in the persuasion process, unless he is armed with solid knowledge that could help him interpret data and ignore unwarranted predictions. However, if the client is well informed, he does not need a financial advisor. In our case, since the prospective investor was little informed about the investment instruments, he might rely on his financial advisor on two conditions: first, the investor has strong references about the integrity and credibility of this advisor and second, he understands the nature of the risk that he is undertaking. Under these circumstances, a consultant's hyperbolic projections are immaterial because they are factored into the accepted risk. Otherwise, the investor can be considered negligent or gullible. For sure, an investor has to be gullible or greedy for letting a broker churn his investment account under the illusion of making a "killing in the market." In fact, by accepting the broker's self-serving advice for dubious investments, the investor showed uncritical and poor judgment. But also his decision reflects another set of factors that belongs to the domain of his emotions. This is the second powerful factor influencing a decision. Quite often people who may appear at first sight to be credulous have less problems in the area of critical evaluation of facts and more problems in controlling their emotional needs. This is a major problem for most people, with the result of exposing themselves to unwarranted risks and deceit. Their overwhelming hidden needs, projected in an important transaction, get the best of them. This explains why any clever persuader addresses most of his arguments to the known or assumed emotional needs of the listener(s). In order to win them over, a good persuader, whether honest or devious, tells the listeners exactly what he thinks they like to hear, and promises them what they want, arousing their emotions in the direction of his intended goal. The reality is that people are ready to make allowances for disparities in the persuader's point of view or for inconsistencies in his statements, as long as the persuader offers them the hope of getting what they want.

In this respect, an individual, before accepting someone else's statement in any transaction, should have in mind two possible personal shortcomings: one related to his inflated ego, which may lead to a miscalculation of his assumed ability to spot the other person's deceit or to contain its negative effects; and the second, his irrational conviction about the persuader's ultimate intention to deliver the promises. This ultimately amounts to a blind trust on the part of the listener-potential victim, unsupported by any reasonable evidence. The first inference evolves from the person's high opinion of himself, which assumes he is able to outsmart his counterpart in negotiation. Examples of these situations are abundant even among seasoned businesspeople. The negative results can be costly. Take, for instance, a group of businessmen on the East Coast who recently bought a factory and showroom inventory from a manufacturer for what they thought to be a fair price, partly decided by the owner's wish to retire because of an alleged serious illness. They found out after closing the deal that the inventory they purchased was millions of dollars below the declared value. The seller was confronted with the evidence of the falsified inventory data, but he denied any wrongdoing, claiming that the errors were the pure fabrications of the buyers. As a result, the buyers sued the seller and each party accused the other one in court of wrongdoing and misrepresentation. The mystifying question is how an intelligent and experienced group of businessmen, supported by accountants and lawyers, could have been cheated by another businessman who was able to smartly alter and hide his fraudulent data. The only reasonable explanation is that either they trusted the "old man" based on their "gut feelings" or that their supposed experts did a sloppy job in verifying the details of the deal before it was finalized. Certainly, there is another explanation that fringes on business naïveté, namely, the deal looked financially good enough to them as to ignore other areas for potential concern for deceit. Blindly trusting others, even with reasonable past credentials, could lead to financial disaster.

Most business deals go sour not because people are gullible or ignorant, but because some businesspeople overestimate their ability to detect any intention of fraud based on their assumed expertise in the field, which results in their underestimating the shrewdness of their opponents. Their miscalculation is reinforced by another belief, that their counterpart in any negotiation will work within the same framework of relative honesty as they do. They may expect the seller to attempt to exaggerate the qualities and value of his product in order to justify the requested price, but they would not suspect an outright swindle. By the same token, the seller would be enraged if the buyer of his company gave him a bouncing check for payment. Yet these assumptions are often violated by one party, just because of their disregard for the law. They believe that they will be able to manipulate justice and win. It is baffling how many people, in negotiating transactions for either a product or an important social obligation, fail to be sufficiently cautious and probing about the validity of the assertions made by the other person. They end up being duped.

Another important element not to be ignored by people is facing their own blinding greed, which significantly increases their chances of being abused or duped because it suspends their critical judgment and hence eliminates a powerful protective safeguard. Someone acting on these assumptions and beliefs is not very different from the absurd situation of a person loaning a thousand dollars to a vague acquaintance for a supposed emergency with only a verbal promise that is not secured by at least a notarized letter. Another example would be buying an alleged expensive diamond ring for a cheap price on the street that turns out to be a worthless piece of glass. Anyone who gets involved in these kinds of deals will be considered foolish. Yet, these foolish transactions are taking place every-day among ordinary people who are either too trustful of others or are looking for a great "bargain." Strangely, this cavalier way of "doing busi-ness" may differ only in a manner of degree from that of buying a product on an Internet auction from an alleged legitimate but deceitful seller or act-ing on the suggestion of a treacherous person who may have apparently credible credentials. The error will be the same, that of nonverification of the validity of the presented argument or the comparable value of the pur-chased merchandise. To put it bluntly, people are most often cheated be-cause of their own fault for letting their own emotional shortcomings cloud their judgment, hence failing to objectively relate to the situation. Further-more, they tend to ignore the fact that there are enough respectable-looking people that are really con artists acting like wolves in sheep's clothing who are ready to cheat and make a "financial killing" when they realize they have met credulous or greedy persons.

If the "buyer-recipient" is fully aware that the "seller-persuader" ped-dles an idea or a product that is favorable and profitable to him, then it would be normal to assume that the seller might have twisted a few facts to facilitate the deal. The issue for the "buyer" is to question the validity of the statements of the seller, his vested interests which may be the reason for us-ing false arguments to enable the sale. Practically, the issue for the buyer-listener is to discover the fissures in his contentions, to identify the discrepancies in the reasoning of the persuader-seller's presentation, which may help him to separate truth from fiction. This should be facili-tated by the buyer's wariness of the declared motives and vested interests for the purported transaction by the other party. It sounds elementary and yet it has been ignored again and again because many people are not realis-tic or attuned to the idea of people's negotiating in bad faith due to their selfish pursuits, most often at the expense of others. The uncritical assump-tion of the goodness of man is a dangerous and harmful supposition, con-tradicting reality but unjustifiably supported by certain religious and moral beliefs. But by acting so, they show an indiscriminate trust in the per-suader-liar, while placing themselves at a grave disadvantage.

It seems to be easy to catch a liar or a con artist if one keeps in mind three crucial principles: first, many people may try to cheat you if they can derive a meaningful benefit out of the situation, hence question their motives; sec-ond, any persuasive solicitation requires careful evaluation of the offered documentation, hence verify the validity of their arguments; and third, no one should be blinded by greed and try to outsmart someone who offers a deal that is "too good to be true," hence one should ask himself about his own hidden motives for concluding the transaction. It sounds simple, yet there are situations when trying to establish the truth about an issue could meet serious obstacles that are related to the nature of the facts under consideration.

DIFFICULTIES IN DEALING WITH THE RELATIVE TRUTH

It is hard to validate truth when the truth itself is not factual but is either inferential or circumstantial. It is easy to determine if someone has lied about some factual data for which there are records independent of him that attest to whether his statements are true or false. Certain facts such as demographic data, working credentials, or claims of personal success may be falsified or embellished, but in the end they can be verified. One's acceptance of these "factual" lies shows only a sign of his complacency and negligence and any negative consequence is his own doing. A good example of the misrepresentation of one's factual data is that of an actress/scriptwriter who, in order to promote her career in Hollywood, posed as a prodigy teenager, home-schooled, single, and familiar with adolescent problems and the drama of their social interaction. This self-promotion earned her a three-year contract with Walt Disney. She was also featured as a guest actress in one episode of her show. In reality, she is a 32-year-old divorced actress, who graduated from high school and was previously unsuccessfully peddling her scripts. As a ruse to sell her writing talents with the right age credentials, she changed her age and background history, taking advantage of her youthful looks. Her lie was discovered only because someone close to her blew her cover.[1]

However, sometimes the factual truth is intertwined with the relative truth, making it hard to separate hard facts from self-serving interpretations. A case in point is of a rogue stockbroker in Texas who churned the financial account of a living trust made by an old couple with the trust department of a regional brokerage firm. By using presigned stock authorizations that the couple gave the broker in the past to buy and sell stocks, he manipulated the accounts for his own benefit, making over $100,000. Meanwhile, the couple had become senile and died in a nursing home. Investigated by the state prosecutor for the losses at the request of the heirs, the broker claimed that he had received authorization for each deal and he, as a friend of the defunct client, informed the party about each transaction on the telephone. The catch was that the client had Alzheimer's disease at the time and allegedly had been in a state of confusion, confined to a psychiatric hospital. Yet, the broker had gone to visit his client at the psychiatric hospital, and obtained a power of attorney to handle his investments. However, with aplomb, the broker stated that whenever they talked, the client appeared alert, discussed the issues, and approved the transactions. There were no records of the telephone conversations, though the physician and nurses' notes indicated that at the time the (client) patient had serious cognitive damage. What is more interesting was not the fact that the broker was a fraud, but that his prestigious brokerage firm supported him all the way by withholding the financial records from the official investigation and attempted to negotiate a deal with the client's heirs, which favored the broker. The case was settled out of court due to the lack of action on the part of the Justice Department.[2] There is another moral to the story, that is, powerful interests may lie and/or deceive with impunity.

While these types of lies, bordering on fraud, are used quite often in human interaction for immediate gains, they may be pure distortions of factual truth but are difficult to verify. For example, someone may doubt the degree of the client's confusion, denied by his broker, when he visited him in the hospital but disputed by the nurse's record. Was the broker an outright liar or was he a bad broker who did not try to protect the interest of his client? The answers are not absolute.

However, there are nonfactual lies based on the presentation of subjective, relative truths that deal with general social and political data that cannot be confirmed at the time of the statement. For example, John, a pleasant and quiet man, married for five years, is accused of marital rape by his wife. In this example of relative truth, the task to verify the honesty of the statements can be a difficult one, even insurmountable, as the accusation of marital rape depends, to a large extent, on each one's perception of the event and of their view on sex. If the wife is against her husband and wants to divorce him, then she may lie, but if she is an avowed feminist who would consider any alleged forceful approach to sex a case of marital rape, then she is right. However, her husband may have a different opinion about their sexual relationship. Furthermore, the search for truth becomes even more complex in certain cases involving politicized social issues. In these situations, there is quite a difference. The social reformist (activist) tends to seek the truth that emerges from the social reality of the situation, while the social-traditionalist (rationalist) sees it strictly based on the inquiry of the facts themselves. The reformist sees truth as a continuous, unfolding reality that depends on the particular circumstances of the moment; it is socially constructed. In this context, a crime committed by an underprivileged person has a different meaning for the reformist-activist than a similar crime committed by another from a better economic class. For the rationalist, who is purely scientifically oriented, the respective crimes are the same because they were committed by individuals knowledgeable of what is accepted as right and wrong by society. This clash between different interpretations of the social facts by these concepts of truth has become the battleground for the opposing views of what might constitute right and wrong in morality and legality. It has lead to a distortion of justice, as proven by various recent judicial decisions. Unfortunately, the neoreformist relying on acceptance of the subjective nature of reality as a guideline for establishing truth may lead to outlandish accusations, self-serving explanations, and/or invocations of special privileges. In this context, how can someone prove or disprove a date-rape charge made by a woman who has previously dated her partner or a claim of sexual harassment made by a nonpromoted subordinate who is unable to corroborate her story with hard evidence? The simple awareness of the possibility that it might happen under some circumstances is not enough to protect or prosecute someone, particularly when dealing with a potential revengeful person who does not mind abusing a liberal interpretation of the facts.

Another set of relative truths is related to intangible, projected data, which mistakenly are treated as statements of facts. While it is easy, for instance, to notice the discrepancies between the statements made by a surgeon about the low mortality or minimal complications resulting from his operations and his prior poor record, it is not as easy to catch the unverifiable hypothetical economic forecast for the next five years on which the balancing of the national budget is based, or, as a matter of fact, of any sophisticated financial investment. Are they liars? It depends on the mode of presenting their forecast. In the case of a balanced budget, if they present these projections about economy as facts, on which promises about national policies are made (e.g., reduction of national debt, salvage of social security, extended coverage for medicare, etc.), they lie. But if they present them as desirable goals to attain, they do not lie. A more compelling argument is offered by the recent collapse of a most admired hedge fund run by Wall Street wizards and Nobel Prize winners. The reliability of the persons involved in the economic and market forecasts is the hardest thing to verify since their projected conclusions have been inferred from generalizations and predictions based on selected existing data, which in any case could not have anticipated unforeseeable events. Yet major banks, by ignoring the inherent risk of these optimistic predictions, lost hundreds of millions of dollars by investing in these hedge funds with the hope of making money.

The trouble is that we are not dealing with factual truth versus falsity here, but with theoretical assumptions that either may be partially true or are total speculation. At best, we are confronted with a projection of a hypothetical truth, based on a disputable premise derived from an educated guess. If one can reach a valid conclusion from the fact that since all men are mortal, John is mortal, not the same is true in stating that since the growth of world population results in the depletion of earth's natural resources, at some point in time, mankind will starve. The first statement about the mortality of John is an absolute truth, while the second one is a conditional and inferential truth, basically a relative truth. The difference between them is dramatic. The acceptance of the absolute truth automatically includes its consequences, in this case, the fact that John is mortal, while the endorsement of the relative truth presupposes the recognition of a degree of uncertainty-risk, commensurate with the probability of the actualization of the projected assumption (e.g. the depletion of some natural resources would not be substituted by high technology). What makes things worse in dealing with any assumption of the relative truth is the fact that any addition of half-truths dramatically increases the risk for coming to false conclusions. However, since most people do not make a clear distinction between these two types of truths, nor appraise them differently, they get burned. Unfortunately, most human transactions are based on assumptions, predictions, or probabilities.

A case in point is a criminal lawyer telling his client that by entering a plea bargain with the prosecution he will get a lighter sentence than if he goes to trial. Is the lawyer dishonest? On the one hand, to a certain degree he is dishonest. He has already received a lump-sum payment from the client for the purpose of defending him in a court trial against the charges brought against him by the prosecution and plaintiff. By entering into a plea bargain, he not only deprives his client of the best defense before a judge at the trial, but he has also pockets the extra money meant for trial. An honest lawyer could have studied the records and after reaching a conclusion to seek a plea bargain he could have later asked for the appropriate fee. Even assuming that he did not have all the facts available from the beginning, he still could have informed the client of his probable chances of winning with either approach. After the client accepted the possible course of action, he could have provided for the return of a part of the fee in the case of not going to trial. Can the client coolly evaluate his options under the extreme stress of the impending arrest and negotiation for bail? Obviously not. He had no other choice than to trust his lawyer, hoping that the lawyer would use his best judgment to defend his interests, which is not always the case. This is exactly what happened to Don, who, after being arrested for criminally assaulting his ex-wife under the influence of a certain medication, hired a criminal lawyer, a former prosecutor, for a handsome fee. The lawyer, who was supposed to defend him in court, told him that he had a strong chance of winning it on the grounds of acting under the influence of drugs. But before the trial, the lawyer changed his mind, claiming that the prosecution had overwhelming evidence to prove that the act was intentional. As a result, he suggested that Don's best chance was to enter a plea bargain; otherwise, he might get double the time in jail. Afraid of increasing his risk of jail time, Don accepted the terms, and was sentenced to three years in prison. While in jail, he found out by hiring another lawyer that his initial lawyer had not properly defended his interests and that the sentence agreed upon by the plea bargain was out of line with his crime. In retrospect, it is a moot question whether his initial lawyer was unskilled, complacent, or outright dishonest. Could Don, under the pressure of those circumstances, have made a better judgment to avoid the possibility of being misled? A possibility would have been for him to get a better-qualified lawyer by asking the American Bar Association or some prestigious litigation law firm for the name of a lawyer who could meet his financial means. Could this approach have guaranteed a better result? Possibly, but it is hard to predict, since we are dealing here with a relative truth. Another more practical approach would have been for Don to consult with another lawyer about his retained lawyer's advice and recommendations to enter into a plea bargain and then afterward to decide the course of action. And this brings us full circle to the main issue of attempting to reduce the chances of being fooled by continuously verifying the statements and actions of the person with whom one intends to have a transaction.

This is exactly why in medicine it is recommended to have a second opinion before undergoing a major operation. For example, should a patient with terminal cancer accept a physician's unproven, unconventional, "self-discovered" curative treatment based on certain herbal or mineral substances without consulting a good oncologist? The physician may extoll his "new breakthrough treatment" based on his own experience, but not supported by independent findings. Can the patient accept uncritically the doctor's account and believe in the efficacy of the treatment without any outside verification? What if the doctor has an overblown ego, which ignores any scientific reasoning? He might be a greedy, dishonest person taking advantage of the patient's desperation. These are the questions to be answered by the prospective patient who has to decide whether or not to entrust the remainder of his life to the physician's alleged expertise. But can the patient, already disappointed with the results of conventional treatment and feeling that his life is slipping away from him, make an educated and objective judgment? While he may doubt the curative value of the treatment, by the same token he feels that he has nothing to lose and at best, can gain some survival time. Certainly, this type of thinking fringes on defeatism. In this case, the terminal patient excluded himself from the possibility of receiving experimental treatment from an approved program. The doctor, regardless of his justifications, acted in bad faith.

This tells us that society does not have firm rules for validating truth in all types of human activity. There is a lot a leeway for the interpretation of factual data related to human activities where people have professed justifiable intentions. It explains why attempting to establish the truth requires an objective, critical reasoning to be able to separate hard facts from ambiguous, subjective information. However, there are "experts" claiming that by using special techniques of communications or interrogation someone will be able to extract the truth from another person. These advices range from reaching the topic on a nonaccusatory manner or indirectly to that of soliciting other's help in establishing the truth. It may work, depending on the naïveté of the other party or on his lack of fear of the consequences for lying. However, it might not work, if one invokes the classical defense "I don't recall," famously used by the White House.[3]

In conclusion, we have to accept as a fact of life that people distort, obfuscate, and manipulate facts, selectively or not and for a variety of reasons, as part of the social process of interaction. Only naive people would assume on moral grounds or alleged fear of social castigation that others are customarily honest. The reality is that until honesty is confirmed by hard proof, anyone may be suspected of lying whenever he perceives that lies are beneficial to him. He may consider his lies innocuous or self-protecting, but that is for the recipient, the potential victim, to decide.

Ultimately, the only sure method to protect oneself from liars is to always be aware of the possibility to be misled by others in any intended social or economic transaction, particularly when their arguments are shaky or their motivation is questionable. Then, one has to pay close attention to their persuasive statements, looking for solid proof to validate them. At the same time, he has to be aware of his emotional needs in that transaction, which may interfere with his ability to reach the correct decision. After weighing all these facts, if he still has doubts but wants to conclude the transaction, then he has to evaluate the amount of risk that he is able to accept.

NOTES

1. K. Pope, "Hollywood Falls for Teen Scribe's Tall Story," *Wall Street Journal*, October 16, 1998, p. B1.

2. R. Karp, "Nest Egg Cracked," *Barron*, July 6, 1998, p. 19.

3. D.L. Sharp, "The 'I Don't Recall' Defense," *Wall Street Journal*, February 1, 1966, p. A18.

Selected Bibliography

Andrew, S. *The Plural Psyche*. London: Routledge, Kegan Paul, 1993.

Appleman, P. (ed.). *Darwin: A Norton Critical Edition*. New York: W.W. Norton, 1970.

Ardrey, R. *The Social Contract*. New York: Atheneum, 1970.

Badikian, B. *The Media Monopoly*. Boston: Beacon Press, 1992.

Bok, S. *Lying: Moral Choice in Public and Private Life*. New York: Vintage Books, 1979.

Bolick, S. *Affirmative Action Fraud*. Washington, DC: Cato Institute, 1996.

Camus, A. *The Myth of Sisyphus*. New York: Vintage Books, 1961.

Crichton, R. *The Rascal and the Road*. New York: Random House, 1961.

Eliade, M. *Shamanism*. Princeton, NJ: Princeton University Press, 1974.

Frank, J. *Courts on Trial*. New York: Atheneum, 1970.

Fukuyama, F. *Trust*. New York: Free Press, Simon & Schuster, 1995.

Galbraith, J.K. *The Good Society*. Boston: Houghton Mifflin, 1996.

Lash, C. *The Culture of Narcissism*. New York: Warner Books, 1979.

Levi-Strauss, C. *Structural Anthropology*. New York: Doubleday, Anhcor Books, 1967.

Levy-Bruhl, L. *The Notebooks on Primitive Mentality*. Oxford, England: Basil Blackwell, 1975.

Machiavelli, N. *The Prince and the Discourse*. New York: The Modern Library, 1950.

Mackay, C. *Extraordinary Popular Delusions and the Madness of the Crowds*. New York: L.C. Page, 1956.

Millon, T., with Davis, D.R. *Disorders of Personality DSM-IV and Beyond*. New York: Wiley & Sons, 1966.

Montaigne, M. *Essays*. New York: Penguin Books, 1981.

Nietzche, F. *On the Genealogy of Morals—Ecce Homo*. New York: Vintage, 1969.

Packard, V. *Pyramid Climbers*. New York: McGraw Hill, 1963.

Petras, R. & Petras, K. *The Stupidest Things Ever Said by Politicians*. New York: Pocket Books, 1999.

Piaget, J. *The Moral Judgment of the Child*. New York: Collier Books, 1962.

Reinisch, M., Rosenblum, L., & Sanders, S. *Masculinity/Femininity*. The Kinsey Insitute Series. New York: Oxford University Press, 1987.

Rothwax, H. *Guilty: The Collapse of Criminal Justice*. New York: Warner Books, 1997.

Russell, B. *A History of Western Philosophy*. New York: Simon & Schuster, 1965.

Sartre, J.P. *Essays in Existentialism*. New York: The Citadel Press, 1967.

Schlesinger, B.L. (ed.). *Criminal Psychopathology*. Springfield, IL: Charles C. Thomas, 1996.

Serban, G. *The Tyranny of Magical Thinking*. New York: E.P. Dutton, 1982.

Serban, G. (ed.). *Cognitive Defects in the Development of Mental Illness*. New York: Brunner-Mazel, 1978.

Twain, M. *Following the Equator*. New York: Dover Publications, 1989.

Unamuno, M. *Tragic Sense of Life*. New York: Dover Publications, 1954.

Whyte, H.W., Jr. *The Organization Man*. New York: Doubleday, Anchor Books, 1956.

Wright, R. *The Moral Animal*. New York: Vintage Press, 1994.

Index

About the Author

GEORGE SERBAN is Clinical Associate Professor of Psychiatry at New York University School of Medicine and is certified by the American Board of Psychiatry and Neurology. Dr. Serban is the author of numerous books and articles, including *The Tyranny of Magical Thinking*. He has appeared on many radio and television programs. He also is in private practice and is a consultant to business corporations.